**The United States, Great Britain, and the Cold War
1944–1947**

The United States, Great Britain, and the Cold War 1944-1947

Terry H. Anderson

University of Missouri Press
Columbia & London
1981

Copyright © 1981 by The Curators of the University of Missouri
University of Missouri Press, Columbia, Missouri 65211
Library of Congress Catalog Card Number 80-25838
Printed and bound in the United States of America

Library of Congress Cataloging in Publication Data

Anderson, Terry H.   1946–
    The United States, Great Britain, and the Cold
War, 1944–1947.

        Bibliography: p. 236
        Includes index.
        1.   United States—Foreign relations—1945–1953.
    2.   United States—Foreign relations—1933–1945.
    3.   Great Britain—Foreign relations—1945–
    4.   Great Britain—Foreign relations—1936–1945.
    5.   United States—Foreign relations—Great Britain.
    6.   Great Britain—Foreign relations—United States.
    7.   World politics—1945–1955.   I.   Title.
E813.A78   327.73   80-25838   ISBN 0-8262-0328-0

To Howard and Emily Anderson,
In appreciation
for those warm years
growing up in Minnesota

Preface

America's policy toward the Soviet Union between 1944 and 1947 evolved from cooperation to confrontation. Hope for collaboration was shattered by postwar problems that arose from differing ideologies and irreconcilable aims. What emerged became known as the cold war.

Historians have investigated the cold war since the late 1940s and have offered a number of interpretations. Throughout the 1950s the "traditionalists" examined the different political and diplomatic aims of the United States and the Soviet Union. In general, these historians accepted the premise that Russia was the aggressor, attempting to spread communism and to dominate Europe, Asia, and perhaps the world. The American government reacted to this threat by adopting a policy to contain Soviet expansion. To the traditionalists, Soviet Russia was responsible for the postwar conflict.[1]

During the 1960s a number of scholars challenged this interpretation. These "revisionists" extended the scope of inquiry, reexamining political and diplomatic topics and investigating economic and atomic issues. Although many revisionists recognized that some Russian behavior was provocative and that some Soviet policies were uncompromising, they emphasized the aggressive nature of American diplomacy. They contended that American officials initiated an open-door policy of economic penetration into areas controlled by the Soviet Union, especially Eastern Europe, and that the administration of Harry S. Truman used the new atomic bomb in an attempt to intimidate Kremlin leaders into accepting a capitalistic postwar solution. The revisionists thus place the onus for the cold war on the United States.[2]

In the 1970s historians again analyzed postwar diplomacy; their efforts resulted in "postrevisionism." Aided by the opening of almost all official American documents, these scholars probed even deeper into political, diplomatic, economic, and atomic issues. They found evidence that supports and refutes some contentions of both traditionalists and revisionists, and they offered an interpretation that placed responsibility for the postwar struggle on both the United States and the Soviet Union.[3]

In the examination of the cold war, however, most historians have promoted what could be called the superpower thesis. They have scrutinized Soviet-American relations but have tended to neglect the third member of the wartime Grand Alliance—Great Britain—because British power declined suddenly after 1947, allowing Washington and Moscow to become the main protagonists in a bipolar world. Also, and more basic to historical research, during the late 1960s and early 1970s only the American documentary record was open for scholarly inspection.

The superpower thesis is an oversimplification of a complicated and dynamic era, the mid-1940s. Many historians have either forgotten or neglected that during the war and until the Truman Doctrine of 1947 there were not just two nations fighting for control and influence in the postwar world, but three, and that until the second half of 1946, Britain—not the United States—was Russia's primary adversary.

More recently, after the opening of war and postwar British cabinet and foreign-office documents in the mid- and late 1970s, historians have begun to investigate Anglo-American relations. Articles have appeared concerning the British Foreign Office, the policy of Foreign Secretary Anthony Eden toward the Truman administration, and British and American policies toward Greece. A book has been published describing Anglo-American policies toward British colonies, and another scholar has written a general survey of military, diplomatic, imperial, political, and economic issues between London and Washington.[4]

I have a different aim. In investigating Anglo-American policies toward Europe in war and peace, my book is concerned with British efforts to influence the Roosevelt and Truman administrations. It discusses Britain's attempts to keep America involved in Continental affairs after the war and eventually to assume the burden of Greece. Above all, this study deals with an issue that is fundamental in understanding the origins of the cold war: the evolution of Anglo-American relations toward the Soviet Union from wartime cooperation to the Truman Doctrine.

Among the three interpretations mentioned earlier, my thesis is most similar to postrevisionism. As we will see, American and recently opened British documents both support and reject some contentions of the traditionalists and the revisionists.

Franklin D. Roosevelt's wartime policy was to mediate between the European allies and as far as possible to cooperate with the Russian leader, Joseph Stalin. During the last year of the war the British attempted to persuade Roosevelt to abandon this cooperation and to join them in blocking Soviet ambitions on the Continent. Suspicious of Prime Minister Winston S. Churchill's motives, the Americans rejected such suggestions until the tripartite negotiations in March 1945 over the postwar government of Poland. Roosevelt then reevaluated Soviet behavior and accepted the British plan. His successor, Harry S. Truman, continued this Anglo-American strategy until mid-May. Then the new president reinstituted the wartime policy of mediation and cooperation, an approach continued by Secretary of State James F. Byrnes at the 1945 meetings in London and Moscow. But by early 1946 Soviet behavior had reinforced the tactful warnings and proposals of British diplomacy and convinced the Truman administration to confront the U.S.S.R. An Anglo-American partnership was a reality by autumn, and during the winter of 1946–1947, Foreign Secretary Ernest Bevin sought to shift the responsibility for defending Greece—and all Western civilization—to the United States. America's response of March 1947—the Truman Doctrine—marked the beginning of the cold war.

How much responsibility—whether credit or blame— should the British bear for this change in American policy? Until now the answer to that question has largely depended on the writer's nationality. By neglecting that issue American historians have implied that Great Britain was unimportant in redirecting Washington's approach toward the Kremlin. Britons have usually given their countrymen too much credit, while criticizing the "shortsighted" policy of the United States. Because documents have finally been opened in both democracies, the issue can now be addressed. The answer lies somewhere between the British and American interpretations.

ACKNOWLEDGMENTS

I have acquired many debts while writing this study. Diplomats on both sides of the Atlantic have been very helpful. I spent several memorable afternoons in London with Lord Sherfield, Sir Berkeley E. F. Gage, and Lord Brimelow discussing British policy and personalities. Lord Gore-Booth and Sir Frank K. Roberts were interviewed twice, read all or parts of the manuscript, and did their best to keep me on track concerning Britain's relations with both wartime allies. In Washington, former American diplomats Samuel Berger and Theodore Achilles expressed their views on Anglo-American relations, and George F. Kennan offered encouragement while the study was in a preliminary stage. Special thanks must be given to the minister and occasional chargé d'affaires of the U.S. embassy in London, Waldemar J. Gallman, who allowed me to read his unpublished manuscript concerning his years in Britain, gave many hours of his time being interviewed and answering letters, and then read the manuscript, providing most helpful comments and suggestions.

I am also indebted to a number of historians who have read and criticized the manuscript. Thomas Etzold at the Naval War College, Eugene Trani of the University of Nebraska, Richard Bradford at West Virginia Institute of Technology, Paul Dukes of the University of Aberdeen, and Arnold Offner of Boston University all analyzed chapters and offered encouragement. Two other scholars—Robert M. Hathaway, Jr., of Wilson College and Calvin Davis of Duke University—read the entire manuscript and commented on almost every page.

At Indiana University three men aided me at every stage of the project. Richard S. Kirkendall shared his knowledge of the Truman era, prompting me to consider carefully my ideas about the man from Missouri and his foreign policy. He read and reread the manuscript, and so did David M. Pletcher, whose keen analysis challenged and provoked, stimulating revisions of substance and style. Robert H. Ferrell taught an eager student to use his own language, to become an author. During the last few years he read this work a half-dozen times, and if asked again, he would pick it up tomorrow. He is a professional who truly deserves his title: distinguished professor. These men have been my mentors, and my friends.

Finally, I would like to thank my parents, to whom this book is dedicated, and Rose Eder, for being my companion and many other things . . .

T. A.
College Station, Texas
8 December 1980

Contents

Abbreviations

Cab—Cabinet records, Public Record Office, London

FDR Library—Franklin D. Roosevelt Papers, Franklin D. Roosevelt Library, Hyde Park, New York

FO records—Foreign Office Records, series 371, Public Record Office, London

FR—Department of State, *Foreign Relations of the United States,* annual and conference volumes, 1944–1947

HST Library—Harry S. Truman Papers, Harry S. Truman Library, Independence, Missouri

Military records—Modern military records, National Archives, Washington, D.C.

OF—Official File, either in Roosevelt or Truman Papers

PREM—Premier's Papers (Churchill), Public Record Office, London

PSF—President's Secretary's File, either in Roosevelt or Truman Papers

SD records—State Department records, record groups 45 and 59, National Archives, Washington, D.C.

Wartime Correspondence—Francis L. Loewenheim, Harold D. Langley, and Manfred Jonas, eds., *Roosevelt and Churchill: Their Secret Wartime Correspondence* (New York, 1975).

Chapter 1

Britain and the "Great Unwieldy Barge"
The Deterioration of Anglo-American Relations, 1944

In June 1944, on the eve of the Allied invasion of France, the British and American political advisers for the Supreme Allied Headquarters, Harold Macmillan and Robert D. Murphy, discussed future relations between the two great democracies. Both men agreed—the "honeymoon stage between the President and the Prime Minister is over and the normal difficulties and divergences, inseparable from staid married life, are beginning to develop."[1]

This indeed was the case. Although British-American relations had been close during the first few years of the war, by 1944, when postwar planning became necessary, differences emerged. Most important, London and Washington disagreed on policy toward the Soviet Union, and this disagreement in turn contributed to conflicts over military strategy and diplomacy toward liberated nations. The British, lacking the strength to confront the Kremlin alone, sought American support in opposing Russian aggrandizement on the Continent. When the Roosevelt administration refused, British leaders initiated their own plans in the Balkans, Italy, and Greece. These actions irritated the Americans, and during the closing months of 1944 a series of minor arguments threatened to expand into a major quarrel. By the beginning of 1945, the eve of the Big Three conference in the Crimea, Anglo-American relations had deteriorated to their wartime nadir.

I

The term often used to describe the connections between the United States and Great Britain—"special relationship"—

1

was particularly appropriate during the first few years of the Second World War. Similarities in language, culture, and heritage molded the two democracies into a natural alliance against Nazi Germany. The remarkably close association between Churchill and Roosevelt personified this fraternity. From 1939 to 1945, they corresponded some 1,700 times, and after the United States entered the war, they had nine meetings comprising about 120 days of personal contact. Their regard for each other was illustrated in late November 1944 when Roosevelt sent a present for Churchill's seventieth birthday and enclosed a card with the inscription, "For Winston on his birthday—I would even go to Teheran to be with him again." Touched, Churchill responded, "I cannot tell you how much I value your friendship or how much I hope upon it for the future of the world, should we both be spared."[2]

Close collaboration had been institutionalized shortly after America entered the war. The two allies quickly established the Combined Chiefs of Staff, Combined Food Board, Combined Production and Resources Board, Combined Raw Materials Board, Combined Shipping Adjustment Board, and later the Manhattan Project to develop nuclear weapons.[3] Before the invasion of Europe in 1944, the Supreme Allied Commander, Gen. Dwight D. Eisenhower, received a military commission from both countries, and during that year fraternal feelings were demonstrated after the death of the director of the British military mission in Washington, Field Marshal Sir John Dill. Posthumously Dill was given a special citation from Congress and a state funeral at Arlington National Cemetery, both of which were unusual honors for a foreigner.

During the war years the closest cooperation existed between the Foreign Office and the State Department. Waldemar J. Gallman, minister and occasional chargé d'affaires of the U.S. embassy in London, remembered Whitehall officials as very free in sharing information. When he asked their views, they often would ask him to sit down at a table in the Foreign Office, with pad and pencil, and then open their files and say, "Go ahead, whatever you want. Take it out of there."

Another State Department official who worked closely with the British, H. Freeman Matthews, was later asked if Washington had a special relationship with London. "Yes," he answered, "I would have thought so. I *did* think so. I don't know that I can be specific about it, but we did have this close relationship . . . it certainly *was* very useful and very logical." Britons held similar thoughts. A member of the Foreign Office's North American Department, J. C. Donnelly, could write that even occasional outbursts of American "hatred" for Britain amounted to family squabbles. In a crisis, he continued, Anglophobia usually gave way to the soothing qualities of underlying kinship.[4]

But the special relationship was much more complex than a working arrangement between government officials. Because both countries had strong popular presses, it also included the sentiments of both peoples. In this context, Anglo-American relations during the war could be difficult and even strained.

Anglophobia had been customary in the United States throughout its history, and many Americans still harbored the traditional suspicions of Britain, the mother country. Some Americans could not forget Britain's mercantile policies toward the colonies, the Revolutionary War, the burning of Washington, D.C., the border disputes over Maine and Oregon, London's flirting with the Confederacy, the *Alabama* claims, the Sackville-West episode, and Britain's inability to pay its debts after World War I. Catchwords such as empire, imperialism, colonialism, monarchy, and old-world balance-of-power diplomacy expressed American feelings toward England. A favorite tactic of many American politicians had been needling Britain, "twisting the lion's tail," to win votes, especially in Irish districts. As late as 1927 William Hale Thompson ran for mayor of Chicago on a flagrantly anti-British platform.[5] Somewhat of a showman, Thompson ran a campaign attacking the local superintendent of schools for using "pro-British" history textbooks. "Big Bill" also declared that, if King George V tried to visit the Windy City, he would punch His Royal Highness right in the snoot!

Such sentiments continued to appear after the United

States entered the war. In autumn 1941 Rep. Fred Bradley of Michigan and some of his colleagues met the British ambassador to Washington, Lord Halifax. Bradley labeled the British extremely selfish, noting that they would use others to achieve their goals and then would "dump them overboard." He feared that British statesmen had too much experience in power politics for American negotiators and that the English wanted the Roosevelt administration to help police the globe—London would establish the policies and the United States would pay the bills. The congressman also complained that Great Britain had no intentions of repaying any past, present, or future war debts. Just ten months after the United States entered the war, the editors of *Life* magazine published an open letter to the English people: Americans were "*not* fighting . . . to hold the British Empire together. We don't like to put the matter so bluntly, but we don't want you to have any illusions." In his world tour in 1942, the Republican presidential candidate of 1940, Wendell Willkie, proclaimed that the war meant an end to empires and called for a timetable for colonial independence. President Roosevelt also held such beliefs and at the Cairo conference of 1943 told Churchill without a trace of diplomacy, "You have 400 years of acquisitive instinct in your blood and you just don't understand how a country might not want to acquire land somewhere if they can get it." Roosevelt charged that Great Britain would grab land anywhere, even a rock or a sandbar. According to an opinion poll in June 1942, almost six out of ten Americans regarded the British as oppressors who took advantage of their imperial possessions. About 15 percent of this group characterized Britons as grabbing, selfish, and exploitative imperialists because they still had colonies.

Since 1776 Americans had usually professed the feeling that having colonies was morally wrong and that all peoples had a right to self-determination. Roosevelt stated this view before America entered the war, declaring that there had never been a race of people on the earth fit to be masters over other men, that every nationality had the right to nationhood. In this spirit FDR had helped to draw up the Atlantic Charter, of which point three declared that the United States and Britain respected the right of all peoples to choose their form of government. At that time Roosevelt had remarked to Churchill: "I can't believe that we can fight a war against fascist slavery, and at the same time not work to free people all over the world from a backward colonial policy." An opinion poll in April 1943—when India was under dire threat from Japan—revealed that only one in five Americans opposed immediate independence for India.[6]

The State Department paid careful attention to opinion polls and to editorials in Anglophobic newspapers such as the Hearst chain, the *New York Daily News* syndicate, and that champion of midwestern isolationism, the *Chicago Tribune*. Officials were well aware of anti-British sentiment; the head of the department's Office of European Affairs, John D. Hickerson, wrote to Undersecretary of State Dean Acheson: "As you know, there is a tendency in this country to blame the British in some way for everything that happens that we don't like."[7]

On their side, the British were apprehensive about America, and officials were especially concerned about Franklin D. Roosevelt. The president's diatribes about backward colonial policies hurt British pride and increased animosity. Macmillan later wrote that despite Roosevelt's apparent sincerity and charm there was "behind the outward show of friendship a feeling of hostility—perhaps even jealousy—of the great Imperial story of the Old Country. The British Empire was a bugbear to him. Without any precise knowledge he would lay down the law about Indian and colonial affairs; and the liquidation of the British Empire was, whether consciously or unconsciously, one of his aims." Foreign Secretary Anthony Eden was aghast when Roosevelt suggested that Great Britain give independence to Hong Kong as a gesture of goodwill to the peoples of Asia; Eden privately complained that FDR had never offered to grant independence to Hawaii or to any other American imperial possession.[8]

Naturally, the British were sensitive about attacks on their colonies. When the topic of mandates came up at the Yalta conference, Churchill abruptly ended the discussion by informing Roosevelt and Stalin that "while there is life in my body no transfer of British sovereignty will be permitted."[9] According to Churchill, Roosevelt had misinterpreted the Atlantic Charter. It was a vague document, not a law but a star, and point three applied to Germany's satellites, not to British colonies.

Other British officials were weary of Roosevelt. Undersecretary of State Sir Oliver Harvey confessed in his diary that power corrupts—adding, "How true of F. D. R. who becomes more and more arbitrary and unaccountable in his acts." Suspicious diplomats at Whitehall wondered what Roosevelt hoped to gain from the empire's dismemberment. Eden put it bluntly: Roosevelt hoped that former colonial territories, "once free of their masters, would become politically and economically dependent upon the United States."[10]

In many ways the British resented the United States. To receive aid from Washington, Britain had been forced to agree to abandon its system of imperial preference—in the postwar era efficient American factories would trade throughout the empire on an equal basis with bombed-out British industry. Britons felt that fighting Germany alone for two years and protecting the Western Hemisphere ought to be ample payment for military assistance. After the United States entered the war, many Britons grumbled with Harvey that "we don't like inexperienced American generals taking command of British troops over the heads of Alexanders and Montgomerys." Some Britons complained that the United States took all the credit for the Allies' military successes. Eden wrote Halifax that "Americans have a much exaggerated conception of the military contribution they are making in this war. They lie freely about this, e.g. figures of percentages of forces for Overlord [the invasion of France] and their share of sunken U boats, and we are too polite to put them right." Members of the Foreign Office disliked being taken for granted or pushed around by their more powerful ally. They realized that Washington's relations with Moscow were of primary importance but lamented that the Americans were "much more polite to the Russians than they are to us."[11]

Moreover, the British were painfully aware of their changing status in international affairs. After a century at the pinnacle of world power, they were being supplanted by their transatlantic offspring. By 1944, the most important global decisions were being made in Washington, not in London. All this must have been humiliating to the once-proud "honest broker" of Europe, and the natural outlet for Britain's frustration was resentment toward its successor, the United States.

Anglophobia and mutual resentment, then, lay just beneath the surface of the special relationship. For the most part, these sentiments remained submerged during the first years of the war, subordinate to the overriding aim of crushing Germany. But when postwar decisions had to be made, these feelings often formed a tenuous background to discussions and complicated Anglo-American relations.

II

Britain and the United States had to settle several very intricate issues. Americans continually suggested tightening pressure on such right-wing nations as Spain, Portugal, and Argentina. With important economic interests in those countries, the British were more cautious and at times even conciliatory. Churchill worked closely with the self-chosen leader of the Free French, Gen. Charles de Gaulle, while Roosevelt virtually refused to deal with the "prima donna" until after the liberation of Paris. Major differences existed over the future of British colonies, postwar trade and economic relations, and the repayment of lend-lease. There were almost endless squabbles over military strategy and policy toward the liberated nations of Europe.

All these issues were important, and all of them sequestered the Western allies. But by 1944 the most important and most pervasive difference concerned one question: how should the democracies deal with the Soviet Union?

Before examining that issue it should be stated that Britain and the United States had similar long-range aims in Europe. After crushing Nazi Germany, they wanted to establish nations with governments and economies that were similar to their own. In other words, they desired to establish capitalistic democracies throughout Europe. They wanted open access to trade and investment in those nations, including the areas occupied by the Red Army. These basic Anglo-American aims on the Continent seem quite natural. After all, one would not expect two democracies heavily dependent on trading to try to establish anything else in postwar Europe but capitalistic democracies. Nor, for that matter, would one expect the Soviet Union to accept Western aims.

The democracies usually did not discuss these long-term aims because they were taken for granted. Instead, they concentrated on short-range tactics or policies, especially those toward their Communist ally. They both realized that only the Soviet Union could prevent them from obtaining their goals on the Continent.

President Roosevelt dealt with the Soviet Union by attempting to create a spirit of cooperation. Throughout the first few years of the war he chose to express America's aims in generalities, fearing that arguments over specific issues would delay victory by creating dissension among the Allies. When diplomatic questions could no longer be avoided, he felt that the best approach was to build a reservoir of trust with Stalin. FDR incessantly attempted to dispel Russian suspicion by advocating a western front as early as 1942, by imposing virtually no conditions on the Russians for lend-lease, and by rejecting suggestions that the Kremlin be forced to adopt Western postwar designs by the old diplomatic method of the carrot and the stick. He worked hard to convince Stalin that there was no sinister capitalistic plot to prevent the U.S.S.R. from emerging as one of the world's most powerful nations after Germany's defeat. As FDR apparently said at one point, "I think that if I give him everything I possibly can and ask nothing from him in return, *noblesse oblige,* he won't try to annex anything and will work with me for a world of democracy and peace."[12]

To create this relationship with the Russians, the president and most of his advisers felt that they should deal independently with the Kremlin. Roosevelt refused to "gang up" on the U.S.S.R. by combining America's diplomatic representations with Britain's. As he informed Churchill in March 1942, "I know you will not mind my being brutally frank when I tell you that I think that I can personally handle Stalin better than either your Foreign Office or my State Department. Stalin hates the guts of all your top people. He thinks he likes me better, and I hope he will continue to do so."[13] On this hunch, Roosevelt initiated an independent approach toward the Soviet Union, attempting to build a friendship that would produce an acceptable postwar settlement.

Most American officials supported the idea of cooperating with the Russians, but not just for altruistic reasons. Roosevelt's chief of staff, Adm. William D. Leahy, informed the president in May 1944 that any future world conflict would find Britain and Russia in opposite camps. Conflict would result if either ally attempted to take too much of Europe. In case of war, Leahy continued, Britain would ask for support and the United States would give it; Anglo-American forces could defend the British Isles but could not defeat Russia. Therefore, the administration must "exert its utmost efforts and utilize all its influence to prevent such a situation arising and to promote a spirit of mutual cooperation between Britain, Russia and ourselves." State Department officials agreed with Leahy's comments and declared that the United States might be forced to become an honest broker within the Grand Alliance, even when the two democracies held similar views on postwar issues. Some months later, in January 1945, a department briefing paper concerning Eastern Europe reaffirmed the administration's mediating role by concluding that, while American and British interests were "more or less the same in these questions, we prefer an independent approach to the Russians."[14]

The British naturally were troubled over America's approach to the Soviet Union. At best they considered it amateurish and naive, at worst disastrous. Eden advised his subordinates at the Foreign Office that the Roosevelt administration knew "very little of Europe and it would be unfortunate for the world if U.S. uninstructed views were to decide the future of the European continent." Roosevelt's confidence that he alone could deal with Stalin alarmed the British.

After observing the initial Tehran conversations in 1943, the chief of the imperial general staff, Field Marshal Sir Alan Brooke, admittedly a prophet of gloom concerning Anglo-American cooperation, commented to Lord Moran, Churchill's physician, that "this conference is over when it has only just begun. Stalin has got the President in his pocket." The permanent undersecretary of the Foreign Office, Sir Alexander Cadogan, worried about Roosevelt's growing suspicions of British intentions and his fundamental misunderstanding of Russia's. The idea that any joint representations to the Kremlin constituted "ganging up" seemed ludicrous to Frank K. Roberts, head of the Foreign Office's Central Department. A member of the embassy staff in Washington, Paul Gore-Booth, later said that this belief had been promoted by American liberals who had not grasped what Stalin was like.[15]

Churchill himself was worried about Roosevelt's policy toward the Soviet Union. As early as November 1943, en route to the Tehran conference, Churchill turned to Macmillan and said quietly, "Germany is finished, though it may take some time to clean up the mess. The real problem now is Russia. I can't get the Americans to see it."[16]

Britain's policy toward Russia, therefore, differed from that of the United States. British policy blended Churchill's intense anticommunism with his nation's traditional plans for dealing with the Continent. A descendant of the first duke of Marlborough, Churchill epitomized the prejudices of nineteenth-century Tory England. He assured the Spanish ambassador in 1943 that he was as anti-Communist as ever and that he would fight against communism all his life. The Anglo-Soviet wartime alliance was a marriage of convenience. As he had remarked with grim humor: "I have only one purpose, the destruction of Hitler.... If Hitler invaded Hell I would make at least a favourable reference to the Devil in the House of Commons."[17] British policy also reflected the efforts of nineteenth-century leaders from Castlereagh to Salisbury to ensure that no nation dominated the Continent. After the defeat of the Third Reich—as in 1815 after the collapse of Napoleonic France—Russia must be prevented from ruling Europe.

This conviction permeated the prime minister's thoughts, and some British officials agreed with their great wartime leader. While the Russians were fighting gallantly at Stalingrad, Churchill could still remark that it would be a measureless disaster if Russian barbarism were to dominate the ancient nations of Europe. He reminded his staff at Tehran that Britain must remain strong after the war for the eventual battle with the Soviet Union. In the postwar world, he warned, "Moscow will be as near to us as Berlin is now." Many military men and officials at the War Office had similar thoughts. As early as August 1944, while the Red Army advanced westward, signs appeared that the British chiefs of staff were thinking and speaking of Russia as "enemy number one and even of securing German assistance against her."[18]

British diplomats, however, generally were less anti-Soviet, less inclined to think that the Kremlin was bent on postwar expansion, and more hopeful that the West would have some influence in Eastern Europe. The foreign secretary and his colleagues were "horrified" when as early as October 1943 Churchill spoke to the cabinet for three hours stressing that Britain "mustn't weaken Germany too much—we may need her against Russia." Eden told Harvey that the prime minister was getting dangerously anti-Russian. Moreover, when Deputy Undersecretary Sir Orme Sargent learned that military leaders were making anti-Soviet remarks in their private conversations, he complained to Eden, claiming that such opinions would have a bad effect on relations with both allies. The foreign secretary agreed and promised to have a talk with Churchill's chief of staff, Gen. Sir Hastings Ismay.[19]

Regardless of the amount of anti-Soviet feeling held by the various British officials, they all agreed that there was only one way to negotiate with the Kremlin—on a quid-pro-quo basis. They felt that Roosevelt's idea of giving something and asking for nothing in return would not create trust but would convince leaders in Moscow that the West was powerless to stop the Russians in Europe. Churchill wanted to confront postwar issues during the war, especially early in the conflict while the Red Army was retreating. Soon after Germany attacked in the east, he proposed that the Big Three recognize

Russia's 1941 western borders, with the hope that after victory those frontiers would be the limit of Soviet expansion. When the Red Army at last took the offensive, Churchill's concern shifted from the enemy to the ally: the defeat of the Third Reich was inevitable, but not the Soviet domination of Eastern and Central Europe.

Yet Britain did not possess the power to halt the Soviet ideological and military advance. By the end of 1944 the Red Army was the most intimidating force on the Continent, attacking Germany with 13,000 tanks, 16,000 front-line aircraft, and 525 divisions totaling 5 million soldiers. While this massive horde rolled west, Churchill lamented that British troops made up only a quarter of the Anglo-American force on the western front, just 12 divisions comprising about 820,000 men.[20]

This, then, was Britain's dilemma: British goals for the Continent could only be obtained with the support of the United States, which had a much different policy toward the U.S.S.R. Churchill remarked late in 1943, "I realized at Teheran for the first time what a small nation we are. There I sat with the great Russian bear on one side of me, with paws outstretched, and on the other side the great American buffalo, and between the two sat the poor English donkey who was the only one, the only one of three, who knew the right way home."

Britain's relative weakness also meant that policy toward Washington was at least as important as that toward Moscow. Unlike the Americans, who occasionally might slight their democratic ally, the British could never afford to neglect the United States. Officials at the Foreign Office revealed their objectives in a March 1944 memorandum, "The Essentials of an American Policy." Great Britain must get the young, powerful American democracy involved in European affairs, influencing and guiding the Roosevelt administration to support British aims.

> It must be our purpose not to balance our power against that of America, but to make use of American power for the purposes which we regard as good.... If we go about our business in the right way we can help steer this great unwieldy barge, the

> United States of America, into the right harbour. If we don't, it
> is likely to continue to wallow in the ocean, an isolated menace to
> navigation.

To the British, then, Anglo-American collaboration and con-
sulation were mandatory, especially when dealing with the
Russians. The democracies must initiate a joint policy, for
only a united front would compel Moscow to accept Western
postwar goals. As early as 1942 Eden described the direction
of policy for the remainder of the war and during the ensuing
cold war: Great Britain "should always consult U.S. Government, but our object should be to bring them along with us."[21]

III

British-American differences over policy toward the Soviet
Union translated easily into disagreements about military
strategy and diplomacy on the Continent.

From early in the war, during the Atlantic Charter conference in August 1941, the Americans wanted to take the most
efficient route to knock out Germany—a thrust through
northern France. The British, however, wanted to lodge their
forces as far to the east as possible and advocated invading the
Balkans via the Mediterranean. Before the issue was settled it
had produced many heated debates. As late as the Cairo conference in November 1943, the chief of staff of the U.S.
Army, Gen. George C. Marshall, and Brooke, his British
counterpart, got into what the field marshal described as the
father and mother of a row over Mediterranean strategy. In
another session at the conference the American chief of naval
operations, Adm. Ernest J. King, burst into an almost uncon-
trollable rage at Brooke. Gen. "Vinegar Joe" Stilwell was there
and described the scene: "Christ. Brooke got nasty and King
got good and sore. King climbed over the table at Brooke.
God, he was mad. I wish he had socked him." Tempers flared
again during a January 1944 meeting in Algiers when Churchill urged the American commanders to support an invasion
of the island of Rhodes. Holding on to the lapels of his coat as
if making a speech in the House of Commons, the prime
minister proclaimed that "His Majesty's Government cannot

accept the consequence if we fail to make this operation against Rhodes!" Marshall snapped back: "No American is going to land on that goddam island!"

Like many of Churchill's ideas about military strategy, that of attacking Germany through the Balkans, the "soft underbelly" of Europe, struck Marshall as deplorably unrealistic. As he later recalled, the underbelly had "chrome-steel side boards. That was mountainous country. There was no question in my mind that the West was the place to hit. If we had accepted the Balkan thing, it would have scattered our shots." The general, of course, was arguing for immediate military goals, not long-range political objectives, and he summarized this outlook in a letter to Eisenhower concerning the proposed liberation of Prague in 1945: "Personally and aside from all the logistic, tactical or strategical implications I would be loath to hazard American lives for purely political purposes."[22] The eastern Mediterranean and the Balkans were diversions; Anglo-American forces would attack through northern France.

After the beachheads in Normany had been secured, Churchill began a campaign to use the Western armies to save Europe from the Russians. He urged that Anglo-American troops in Italy under the command of the British general, Harold R. L. G. Alexander, undertake a thrust over the Alps, northeast through the Ljubljana gap in Yugoslavia, and into Austria. The Americans were unenthusiastic about such a Hannibal-like maneuver, and instead planned Operation Anvil, the invasion of southern France. To Churchill, this operation was the last straw, and in late June he sent three long messages to Roosevelt advocating an Italian campaign. Ten days before Anvil began, Churchill and his military aides journeyed to Allied headquarters and attempted to force Eisenhower to abandon it. With FDR's support, Eisenhower refused, and in a tense scene "Ike said no, continued saying no all afternoon and ended by saying no in every form of the English language."[23]

Churchill momentarily relented, but the success of the summer campaign on the western front offered the British another opportunity to obtain their political goals. As demoralized and disorganized German forces retreated in France, Churchill and his commander on the battlefield, Field Marshal Bernard C. Montgomery, felt that Allied troops should take advantage of the confusion and make a stab into the heart of the Reich, not only defeating Germany but anticipating the Red Army's arrival in Central Europe. In September Montgomery telegraphed Eisenhower, claiming that "one really powerful and full-blooded thrust" would reach Berlin and end the war. He volunteered his army on the northern frontier to commence a single, annihilating strike. Montgomery later defined the British position: once it is clear you are going to be victorious, political considerations must influence the future course of war.

But Eisenhower disagreed: Montgomery's plan was premature, and a forward drive of all forces would involve fewer risks. American commanders were more acerbic about the proposal. Gen. Omar N. Bradley sarcastically complained that Montgomery wanted American troops to halt and resupply the British army so the field marshal could make his glorious "butter-knife thrust" into Germany. Gen. George Patton had even less respect for Montgomery. A tough man who carried two pearl-handled six-shooters, Patton claimed that Montgomery would take the offensive only if victory were guaranteed and labeled him "a tired little fart."[24]

Montgomery's demands to lead a strike into Germany and Churchill's numerous military proposals resulted only in irritating the Americans. Dissension increased on the front. A British general stationed at Supreme Allied Headquarters informed the Foreign Office that the atmosphere was tense and that Eisenhower found Montgomery "extremely difficult to handle." Churchill's plan to attack the soft underbelly of Europe, like his earlier designs for landing in Norway, invading Rhodes, and bringing Turkey into the war, had increased American suspicion. Roosevelt and other American officials respected and even admired Churchill as a man but suspected that he was trying to use American soldiers to secure British aims. At times, suspicion reached absurd proportions. On one occasion Marshall's staff objected to what they labeled a British proposal. The general did not see anything wrong with the idea, but his subordinates explained that London had an ulterior purpose. Marshall later discovered that the proposal was not British at all; his staff had been confused and had objected to their own plan![25]

Obviously, the British would not be able to persuade Americans to adopt their military strategy, and this failure prompted diplomatic maneuvers. There were two possibilities: organize a Western European bloc, or work out a deal for Eastern Europe with the Russians.

Whitehall officials favored the first scheme. The bloc idea had been proposed by the old South African field marshal, Jan C. Smuts, and was promoted by the foreign minister of the Belgian government-in-exile, Paul-Henri Spaak. Eden was considering the arrangement in May 1944 when the British representative to the French Committee of National Liberation, A. Duff Cooper, suggested that Great Britain could not rely on a world organization for security, and that a system of alliances with Western Europe should be established as a precaution against Russia. Arriving at this conclusion himself by July, Eden told Cooper that British policy should be directed toward establishing a defense system. Whitehall officials prepared a memorandum two months later declaring that it is "our policy to build up, even within the framework of a World Organization, a Western European security bloc which will involve close military collaboration with our European neighbors. There is every reason to suppose that the Russians will do the same in Eastern Europe."[26] The key to this arrangement was France, and the British supported de Gaulle, instructed Cooper to cultivate friendly ties in Paris, and urged the United States to recognize the general's regime.

Churchill, however, was more interested in the second possibility—a unilateral deal with Stalin. In May, the prime minister put the issue to Eden: "Are we going to acquiesce in the Communization of the Balkans and perhaps Italy?" The Foreign Office dutifully drew up a statement that the most feasible plan to counter the spread of Russian influence was to consolidate Britain's position in Greece and Turkey and to extend British power in such contested areas as Yugoslavia,

Albania, Rumania, and Bulgaria. Churchill then asked Roosevelt to accept a temporary arrangement in which the Soviets would have military responsibility for Rumania and Britain for Greece. The president, and especially Secretary of State Cordell Hull, disliked any agreement that sounded like spheres of influence, but after a second appeal FDR accepted the plan without informing the State Department. By early October, Churchill's anxieties had increased, and he urged Roosevelt to arrange a Big Three meeting. The president responded that he would not be able to attend before the November elections and the January 1945 inauguration. Churchill could not wait—the Red Army would not stand still until the American election returns came in—and he asked Stalin for a meeting in Moscow.

When Roosevelt learned that Churchill was going to Moscow he initially responded by offering "good luck," but the State Department showed more concern. The department's Russian expert and representative at the White House, Charles E. Bohlen, warned FDR's confidant Harry Hopkins that the meeting would "set a pattern, without American participation, for the future structure of Europe." According to Bohlen the conference would result in either a first-class British-Soviet row or a division of Europe into spheres of influence, both of which would hurt America. Hopkins persuaded Roosevelt to inform Stalin that Churchill was speaking for himself and that in this "global war there is literally no question, political or military, in which the United States is not interested."[27] The message apparently surprised the Russians, for Churchill, who had just returned from the conference with Roosevelt at Quebec, had given Stalin the impression that he would speak for both Britain and America. Roosevelt also wrote Churchill, asking him to allow the American ambassador to the Soviet Union, W. Averell Harriman, to sit in on the meetings in Moscow. Churchill reluctantly agreed.

Harriman only attended one meeting between Churchill and Stalin, but that was enough for him to perceive British intentions. He wrote Roosevelt that Churchill would try to work out some sort of spheres-of-influence deal with the Russians on the Balkan matters: the Russians would have a free hand in Rumania and perhaps in other countries, while the British were given carte blanche in Greece. Harriman was right, for on 10 October Churchill and Stalin arrived at the well-known percentage deal for dividing up Eastern Europe. The U.S.S.R. would have a 90 percent and Britain a 10 percent influence in Rumania, with a 75:25 ratio, favoring the Soviets, in Bulgaria. Yugoslavia and Hungary would be divided 50:50, and Britain would have 90 percent and Russia 10 percent influence in Greece. Churchill neglected to ask Harriman to attend this meeting.[28]

The prime minister's mission to Moscow actually had inconclusive results. Many officials in Washington saw it as a cynical deal, and it confirmed American suspicions that Churchill's diplomacy was a product of the nineteenth century—secret deals, balances of power, spheres of influence. Administration officials recalled Woodrow Wilson's statement during his second inaugural that there must be not a balance of power, but a community of power, not organized rivalries, but organized peace. The mission seemed to support the contention that British policy conflicted with American ideals, and many Americans were beginning to wonder if U.S. forces were fighting in Europe so that Britain and Russia could divide the spoils of war. The agreed-upon percentages were not even relevant to the situation on the Continent. How could democratic Britain have 25 or 10 percent control of an Eastern European nation occupied by the Red Army? The Soviet Union did not institute coalition governments based on parliamentary procedure.

Even Churchill realized the shortcomings of his deal, and on the following day, 11 October, he attempted to clarify the agreement. He wrote Stalin that the percentages were no more than a guide for the conduct of their affairs, and fearing America's response, that the figures should not be the basis of any public document since diplomats all over the world would consider them "crude and even callous."[29]

By October, then, just a few months after the successful landing at Normandy, British military and diplomatic behavior had contributed to a deterioration in Anglo-American relations. Churchill's numerous proposals, along with difficulties on the front with Montgomery, had such a deleterious effect that the Foreign Office supported a plan to "do more in the way of praising and buttering up General Eisenhower." They considered giving him an honorary Cambridge or Oxford degree but settled on having the prime minister award him the Freedom Medal of the City of London.[30] But such schemes did not relieve American suspicions, and relations continued to decline during the remainder of 1944.

IV

As their armies rolled toward Germany, Britain and America formed diverse policies toward the nations they liberated, and this marred Anglo-American relations. Of some importance was the situation in Belgium, which had been liberated by the British army in November. The British ordered local resistance groups to disarm and demobilize, alarming some Americans who charged that Britain was dictating policy to Belgium, a helpless nation that had suffered for five years under the Nazi yoke. In fact, the British commanders were merely following orders that had been originally issued by Eisenhower. When this was realized, and when Germany launched the Battle of the Bulge, Belgium no longer seemed so important.[31]

Much more significant were episodes concerning Greece and Italy.

London's wartime involvement in Greece had been complex. With British troops driven out in 1941, the Greek government-in-exile had been domiciled in London. The United States had agreed that Greece's future was a British responsibility since Whitehall had traditional interests in the eastern Mediterranean. The British naturally sought to reassert their influence and to curb the growth of communism, for Macmillan feared that after liberation the Greeks would accept the Communist argument that they should be "looking to the rising sun of the Kremlin, not to the setting orb of Downing Street." Churchill was concerned about a Communist coup after the occupying German troops departed and ordered preparations for the occupation of Athens and a naval demonstration off Piraeus. British troops entered the capital on 14 October 1944, and next day the government-in-exile returned. By these maneuvers Churchill gained time to install a shaky coalition regime, but the countryside remained in an even more precarious situation. As the Nazis withdrew, the pro-Communist EAM–ELAS guerrilla bands took control and challenged the regime in Athens. The central government attempted to maintain power by forming a national guard and by ordering demobilization of all guerrilla forces. Fearing reprisal and desiring control of the government, conservative and leftist groups both refused to lay down their arms. By November civil war was imminent as strikes ensued and the Communists quit the Athens coalition. On 3 December, Greeks were fighting Greeks. (1944)

Churchill responded quickly, instructing his diplomatic and military representatives, Amb. Reginald S. Leeper and Gen. Ronald M. Scobie, to use troops to maintain order and to force the British-sponsored Greek prime minister, Andreas Papandreou, to do his duty. If Papandreou wanted to resign, said Churchill, "he should be locked up till he comes to his senses." This was "no time to dabble in Greek politics. . . . The matter is one of life and death."[32] The British army was soon fighting the Greek underground.

Meanwhile Britain had become involved in an Italian imbroglio. Prime minister Ivanoe Bonomi faced a cabinet crisis in mid-November in which Count Carlo Sforza apparently was trying to make himself deputy prime minister or minister of foreign affairs. Sforza was popular in the United States. In the early 1920s he had served in many diplomatic posts including minister of foreign affairs. He had helped to lead the opposition to Mussolini; after Il Duce took power, Sforza left for France. In 1940 he arrived in New York, and until the liberation he lectured at American universities, accepting many honorary degrees. To most Americans he seemed a proven anti-Fascist, but the Foreign Office agreed with Churchill who labeled him an "intriguer and mischief-maker of the first order," a self-serving rascal who had complicated Anglo-Italian relations by opposing every British-supported Italian cabinet since liberation. Whitehall instructed the high commissioner in Rome, Sir Noel Charles, to prevent Sforza's entry into the government. Charles was told to take whatever action was necessary and not to inform the local American representative.[33]

But the British plan was soon common knowledge in Washington, and it distressed the U.S. government. The continuous civil strife in Athens had put the Roosevelt administration in an awkward position; liberal and left-wing Greeks had appeared in front of the American embassy with posters praising Roosevelt. The ambassador to Greece, Lincoln Mac-Veagh, explained to the State Department that he was doing all he could to avoid becoming involved in Greece's internal affairs while trying not to embarrass the British. To him, Churchill's actions in Greece were the "latest of a long line of blunders," and now the British had "a bear by the tail." In Rome the American representative, Alexander C. Kirk, deplored Britain's excursion into Italian politics and asked the State Department for instructions. Concerned about public opinion, the department carefully responded that the composition of the cabinet was an Italian problem and instructed its ambassador in London, John G. Winant, to communicate the department's regret that the British government had intervened in Italy without consultation.[34]

A growing public clamor forced the newly appointed secretary of state, Edward R. Stettinius, Jr., to release a statement that revealed the differences between British and American policies toward liberated nations. To the British, Italy was a defeated enemy; they felt justified in meddling in the affairs of Hitler's former ally. Americans disagreed; the administration felt that the Allies should only intervene when domestic policies jeopardized military operations. Stettinius's press release stated that the composition of the government in Rome was purely an Italian affair, that the Italians should work out their problems along democratic lines without influence from outside, and that Washington had no objection to Count Sforza.[35] It was not necessary, of course, for Stettinius to add that his criticism of Britain's policy in Italy had implications for the situation in Greece.

Stettinius's press release produced a heated response from

London. In a letter to Roosevelt, Churchill wrote that he was much hurt and "astonished at the acerbity" of the statement. He had loyally tried to support any American pronouncements and could not remember anything the State Department had ever said about Russia that compared with this document. Eden thought the release demonstrated calculated unfriendliness and complained to Halifax that if U.S. officials were unable to support Britain, at least they could have been vague and noncommittal, "a line which American policy seldom had difficulty in finding." He instructed Halifax to meet with Stettinius and talk to him "as roughly as you like."

The British press was also upset. In an article, "The American Snub," the *Manchester Guardian* commented that it was a "rude statement and it is meant to be rude." The *Guardian* felt that the United States and the American press had an absurd picture of English policy. The *Economist* criticized the "brusqueness of Mr. Stettinius' maiden performance," and the *Daily Herald* ran headlines that "States Disown British Policy" and "Stettinius Washes Hands of Crisis." Sir Norman Angell, a Nobel Prize winner, wrote the *New York Times* that the statement constituted a diplomatic bombing of Britain—an ally, he reminded Americans during the V-2 attacks on London, "whose nerves in the sixth year of war are perhaps a bit taut due to another kind of bombing."[36]

Anglo-American relations remained strained until the resolution of the Italian and Greek affairs, as the British attempted to induce the Roosevelt administration to assume a share of responsibility in Rome and Athens. Halifax called on Stettinius on 6 December and said again that London could have no confidence in a government that included Sforza and that British troops occupied Greece only to secure peace and not to establish an unpopular regime. The next day Michael R. Wright of the British embassy met Stettinius and delivered a forceful statement. He conceded that his government should have consulted the administration before taking action against Sforza, but he argued that the State Department should have informed the Foreign Office before issuing such a damaging statement. After all, he told Stettinius, "two wrongs did not make a right." The embarrassed secretary of state explained that he was new to the crisis and later that day sent a letter of apology to Eden. He was truly sorry, felt such situations should be avoided by consultation, and promised a friendly statement before the forthcoming foreign-affairs debate in Parliament. Indeed a press release from the State Department on 7 December emphasized Allied unity, and Stettinius gave Halifax a large Christmas turkey.[37]

In Rome, Kirk and Charles adopted similar policies to end the crisis. This was accomplished on 9 December when Bonomi formed a cabinet without Sforza. This time the State Department did not object.

As the situation in Greece deteriorated, Churchill urged American mediation. Stettinius argued against it: America should refuse to intervene with the British because public opinion was too hostile. Although Roosevelt wrote Churchill on 13 December that it would not be possible for the United States to take a stand with Britain, he suggested that King George II of Greece name a regent. The British felt that the archbishop of Athens, Damaskinos, was the best choice, and on 28 December, when Churchill was in Athens attempting to resolve the predicament, he urged FDR to send a message to the king supporting this plan. Roosevelt complied the same day. A regency was appointed on the first of January, a truce was signed at Varkiza in February, and Greece settled into an uneasy peace.[38]

Britain's behavior in Greece and Italy had stimulated an acute case of Anglophobia in America. Americans of all political persuasions had tired of British excuses for interfering in liberated countries and urged FDR to carry out a more forceful policy based on the terms of the Atlantic Charter. During the street fighting in Athens, the Anglophobic senator from Illinois, C. Wayland Brooks, stated in Congress that "Britain moves daily to expand her influence and establish puppet governments in Italy, Greece, Belgium, and France." Sen. Dennis Chavez of New Mexico agreed, expressing the feeling of many Americans by asking, "Are not the Greek boys who are now being killed on one pretext or another the same ones who put up a valiant fight against the Axis powers before the British forces entered into that part of the world?" To Pentagon officials, Britain had been playing politics while American troops fought in Europe. Stettinius had informed Halifax in mid-December that resentment was growing and that some military men were suggesting that with Germany on the brink of defeat it might be wise to evacuate the Continent, let Britain and Russia fight it out, and head for the war in the Pacific. The most vociferous response came from the press. An article in the *New York Times* charged that Churchill was a "product of nineteenth century thought fighting a twentieth century war for eighteenth century aims," and the *Chicago Daily Tribune* declared that he had betrayed the Atlantic Charter. A critic writing in *Nation* claimed that Britain occupied Greece not to chase out Germans, but to bolster their handpicked, spoon-fed Papandreou government. Churchill was labeled an arrogant, cocksure, unregenerate Tory who desired to dominate the Mediterranean, enlarge British postwar trade, and "build up a block of satellite nations in western Europe."[39]

In early December, Halifax reported from Washington that "no support of our position is discernible anywhere." The next week he remarked that the public suspected Churchill of attempting to erect reactionary governments in Europe. The "orgy of twisting the lion's tail," the ambassador later concluded, was more enthusiastic and sustained than on any occasion since the United States entered the war.[40]

American charges caused resentment in Britain, and in January 1945 the lion roared. The *Economist*—possessing connections with Churchill's minister of information, Brendan Bracken—declared that American criticism and abuse had been one of the most violent and sustained campaigns of the war; it was altogether out of place, especially when it came from a nation that had practiced cash-and-carry during the Battle of Britain. The article even suggested that, with "every outburst of righteous indignation in America, the ordinary Englishman gets one degree more ready to believe that the only reliable helping hand is in Soviet Russia." Americans, even Roosevelt, were appalled by this feeling that the United States had not made a sizable effort in the war against Hitler. When a British public-opinion poll asked what country had made the greatest contribution toward winning the war, only

3 percent of respondents said "America." Resentment was also voiced by the *Yorkshire Post,* owned by relatives of Eden's wife, which repeated a Foreign Office complaint that Washington's policy was "exaggeratedly moral, at least where non-American interests are concerned." The article demanded that the United States define its policies and assume its world responsibilities.[41]

It was clearly time for a truce. One Briton, a self-styled man in the street, wrote the *New York Times* that "all the mud-slinging and political rubbish printed in the press on both sides of the Atlantic does not interest the average Englishman. We shall have to live together when this war is over, so let us stop this childish nonsense and act like grown-ups. After all, we are both English-speaking nations, a 'to-mah-tow' is a 'to-may-toe' which ever way you eat it." An American agreed, responding that the great bulk of his countrymen held Britain in high esteem and durable devotion.[42]

V

Although the storm relented, much damage had been done. A State Department survey in late December 1944 found that 54 percent of those Americans dissatisfied with cooperation among the Big Three blamed Britain, while only 18 percent blamed Russia. Asked in February 1944 what country the United States might have to fight in the next fifty years, only 5 percent responded "Great Britain." By March 1945 that figure had risen to 9 percent—one point higher than that for the enemy Japan. During this cold winter many Americans, including the president, might well have felt that Britain, and especially Churchill, would be more of a problem in the postwar world than the Soviet Union.[43]

The British attributed the December–January crisis and the resulting decline in relations to American diplomatic adolescence. Halifax wrote the Foreign Office that as the United States moves into world affairs "we may expect many ups and downs of this kind and several bouts of growing pains."[44]

True, Stettinius's press release had been amateurish, and Roosevelt had a naive faith that he alone could deal with

Stalin. More serious, most American leaders were too sanguine about future Soviet-American friendship, especially if one considered the two nations' clashing ideologies and awkward prewar relations. The president's tendency to postpone postwar issues until the end of the war solved nothing and created apprehensions in London. From their vantage point just off the Continent, British officials grew more anxious every day as the Red Army rolled westward and as Roosevelt rejected proposals for an immediate Big Three conference. By autumn 1944 the British felt that they must act, and they urged the Supreme Allied Commander to accept military plans that would result in democratic armies lodged deep in Central Europe. When that failed, the British acted unilaterally in Italy and Greece—policies that might never have been initiated if American officials would have formulated a concrete, long-range plan toward Europe and the Soviet Union.

But the responsibility for the decline of relations cannot be placed solely on the Americans. Overwhelmed by a desire to prevent the communization of Europe, agonized by Roosevelt's refusal to confront the Soviets, Churchill acted rashly. His dramatic journey to Moscow and his machinations with the governments of Greece and Italy did not result in more British influence in Continental affairs, but only in increasing American suspicion. Officials in London should have realized that Roosevelt would not and could not support British actions that clashed with American beliefs as stated in the Atlantic Charter. Publicly supporting British policies in Greece and Italy a month after he had been reelected by a liberal constituency for a fourth term was politically difficult, if not impossible. Roosevelt might secretly help his democratic ally out of a difficult situation in the Mediterranean, but he was not willing to chance a breakdown of the Grand Alliance by openly supporting Churchill's anti-Soviet plans.

British policy toward the United States during 1944 had failed. They had hoped to influence officials in Washington—to guide the American ship of state, which Whitehall called the "great unwieldy barge," into London's harbor. With American support, the British government wanted to confront the Kremlin and prevent the Soviet domination of the Continent. But actions in Greece and Italy, along with continual military proposals, stimulated Anglophobia and were primarily responsible for the deterioration in Anglo-American relations. Most important, British behavior strengthened the Roosevelt administration's conviction that America had to deal independently with the Russians, just the opposite of what the Foreign Office had aimed to achieve.

Churchill had been premature. His diplomacy alone was not enough to convince the Americans to form a joint policy against their eastern ally. Britain would need help from the Soviet Union.

Chapter 2

Churchill and Roosevelt
The Transformation of American Policy

Overlooking the Black Sea, a former resort for the tsars, Yalta was chosen as the place where the Big Three leaders would compose a postwar settlement. By February 1945 there were a number of pressing issues, including the future of Germany, the establishment of a new world organization, the composition of governments in Eastern Europe, and the entrance of Russia into the war against Japan.

Roosevelt traveled to the Crimea intending to mediate between Britain and the Soviet Union, to be an honest broker between the Tory and Communist leaders. The initial results of the conference seemed hopeful to Churchill and especially to Roosevelt. But just a few weeks later Soviet behavior became as uncooperative as the prime minister had predicted. Communist regimes were being installed in Hungary, Rumania, Bulgaria, and the paramount issue—the composition of Poland's government—remained unresolved. The Foreign Office began one campaign in the United States to soothe Anglophobia and influence public opinion, and Churchill began another, by cable, to induce Roosevelt to accept a joint policy against the Kremlin. By late March, the president had been persuaded—he abandoned his attempt to mediate and joined the British.

I

During the weeks before the conference in the Crimea, British concern about America's policy toward the Soviet Union prompted one last attempt to convince the U.S. government to agree on a coordinated policy. Whitehall officials felt that the meeting would be fateful and that they must devise a definite plan and then "seek preliminary support for

our views from the President." Prior collaboration was mandatory, since it was at Big Three meetings that the "joint
influence of America and this country can effectively be used
to influence Stalin's mind." Churchill agreed and proposed
conferences between Eden and Stettinius and between the
Combined Chiefs of Staff on the island of Malta before meeting the Soviets at Yalta.[1]

The plan failed. Roosevelt vetoed the proposed Eden–
Stettinius conversations and military talks produced no
change in strategy. He and Churchill did meet on 2 February
aboard the U.S.S. *Quincy* at Valletta. Churchill told him that
Anglo-American troops must occupy Austria before the advance of the Red Army. But FDR was not interested in discussing military or diplomatic policy. As Harriman later said,
the president did not want to "feed Soviet suspicions that the
British and Americans would be operating in concert at
Yalta."[2] Next day the two leaders flew to the Crimea on separate planes.

American officials felt they could deal independently with
the Kremlin partly because of the trend in recent Allied relations. While British-American relations deteriorated during
1944, those between Washington and Moscow improved and
were even friendly. After Secretary of State Hull returned
from the 1943 Moscow conference he was convinced, as he
declared to a joint session of Congress, that there would no
longer be a need for spheres of influence, alliances, balances
of power, or any other old-world arrangements. Early in 1944
Hull felt that relations with the U.S.S.R. were closer than
ever, and they reached their zenith after American troops
landed in France. Some friction did develop in autumn 1944
when the Red Army took control of Poland. Stalin's refusal to
let American planes land on Russian airstrips during the
Warsaw uprising and his unilateral recognition of the Lublin
committee as the provisional Polish government momentarily
chilled American optimism. But in general relations remained warm. Americans realized the sacrifices the Russians
were making for Allied victory, and in every poll they named
the U.S.S.R. as the nation doing the most to win the war.
While Anglo-American troops faced fewer than 60 German

divisions on the beaches of Normandy, Soviet armies on the vast eastern front battled over 160. For every American killed in the war against the Axis, fifty Russians died. This heroic sacrifice, along with the Roosevelt administration's strictures on the need for unity within the Grand Alliance, discouraged criticism of the Communist ally. The State Department even tried to suppress publication of William L. White's *Report on the Russians* in which the author, son of William Allen White, compared conditions in the Soviet Union unfavorably with those in a Kansas penitentiary. The press dwelt on flattering similarities between Russians and Americans. A *Saturday Evening Post* article by Edgar Snow likened a Soviet general to a "good YMCA secretary," and an essay in *Collier's* assured readers that the average Russian family was "much like the Smiths or the Jones on your block."[3]

Never before or since have Americans been so optimistic, even utopian, about Soviet-American friendship, and this attitude reinforced Roosevelt's desire to act as a mediator between Churchill and Stalin instead of combining with the British at Yalta. Roosevelt later reported with some satisfaction that when differences arose at the conference, the protagonists would turn to him expecting a compromise.

Roosevelt's diplomacy naturally disturbed the British. Eden complained to Hopkins at Malta that Britain and America were going into a decisive conference without having agreed on what would be discussed or how to handle matters with Russia—the "bear who would certainly know his mind." To Whitehall officials, uncoordinated diplomacy would lead to Anglo-American confusion and would only benefit the Soviets.[4]

Despite British fears, Roosevelt apparently achieved significant accomplishments at the conference. Stalin yielded on some important issues and agreed to many Western proposals. He decided to help establish FDR's dream of a world organization, the United Nations, and he reduced his previous membership claims from sixteen (one for each Soviet republic) to three, while accepting an American claim for parity. The Allied leaders agreed to divide Germany into zones of occupation, and Stalin supported the British and American demand for French participation, as long as the French zone was in the western part of the defeated Reich. More important, the Russian leader signed the Declaration on Liberated Europe, in which the Allies pledged to support self-government and free elections throughout Eastern Europe, and he also consented to discussions on the composition of a postwar government in Warsaw. Finally, Stalin accepted the wishes of American military planners and promised to enter the war in the Pacific three months after victory in Europe.

The Yalta conference generated great optimism in the West. The agreement on Poland and the signing of the Declaration on Liberated Europe prompted Hopkins to write: "We really believe in our hearts that this was the dawn of the new day we had all been praying for and talking about for so many years. We were absolutely certain that we had won the first great victory for the peace—and, by 'we,' I mean all of us, the whole civilized human race." Most Americans felt that the conference was a success, justifying Roosevelt's independent diplomacy. Only 9 percent of those questioned in a poll said the results were unfavorable to the United States. Stalin's conciliatory acts did seem convincing. They even gave Churchill momentary hope: he told a member of the war cabinet, Hugh Dalton, that "Poor Neville Chamberlain believed he could trust Hitler. He was wrong. But I don't think I'm wrong about Stalin."[5] Parliament reflected the public's support of the Yalta accords by giving the government its largest vote of confidence in three years, 413 to 0.

Although Soviet-American friendship remained warm at Yalta, Anglo-American relations were still disturbed by suspicion. The evening before the conference adjourned, Roosevelt had informed Churchill that he was going to meet with three Arab kings on his return voyage to Washington. This plan was almost an insult to Churchill. Since the late nineteenth century, the British had considered the Middle East their private domain, and like many Englishmen during the Second World War, Churchill had grown apprehensive about his nation's economic future. Symbolic of British weakness was the decision of the Chicago aviation conference of December 1944 in which his government yielded to demands and granted American airlines postwar access to the colonies of the empire. It was reasonable to assume that because of lend-lease America eventually would acquire equal trading rights in Britain's possessions. The prime minister therefore was greatly disturbed by the president's announcement about meeting the Arab kings, since Mideast oil and the Suez Canal were vital to Britain's postwar reconstruction. Churchill approached Hopkins, asking him to explain Roosevelt's intentions. Hopkins was unsure, sensing that the trip was not a major event but just "a lot of horseplay." A presidential visit was a more serious gesture to the prime minister, who remained suspicious. "Nothing I said," Hopkins recorded, "was comforting to Churchill because he thought we had some deep laid plot to undermine the British Empire in these areas."[6] Next morning Churchill informed Roosevelt that he too intended to visit the Arab leaders, but since he had to go to Greece first, he would not arrive in Egypt until after the president had left.

This plan in turn aroused American suspicion. Leahy recorded that Churchill's trip was undertaken "undoubtedly with the purpose of neutralizing any accomplishment the President may have made during his talks with the three Kings." Other officials had similar thoughts, and perhaps the administration's opinion of the prime minister was summarized by Stettinius when he quipped in a cabinet meeting that Churchill "seems to be going through some sort of a menopause."[7] Roosevelt demonstrated his concern two weeks after returning from Yalta by ordering his special assistant Lauchlin Currie to London to interview officials and to ascertain British thinking. Roosevelt, however, did not live to read Currie's report.

II

Because the deterioration of Anglo-American relations had resulted in a marked decline of British influence on American policy, the Foreign Office undertook a virtual propaganda campaign in the United States.

Without a doubt, the American people knew very little

about Britain's diplomatic and military efforts. Chief of the British military mission in Washington, Field Marshal Sir Henry Maitland Wilson, was astonished that the vast majority of Americans did not know that the Royal Navy was fighting alongside the U.S. Navy in the Pacific and had met the enemy in the battle of Okinawa. During the war the British Information Service published and distributed a monthly journal, *Britain,* which included political and military speeches, facts about Great Britain, and laudatory statements by American generals about the hard-fighting Tommy. But Whitehall officials realized that they must have an even more forceful program that would assure close ties while guiding public opinion. In 1944 Halifax and Assistant Secretary of War John J. McCloy discussed how to keep the United States involved in world affairs after the war. They agreed that America was "still politically very immature and her public opinion needs not only education but the most careful nursing." For this reason, early in 1944 the Foreign Office proposed a joint board to deal with problems arising between American soldiers and British civilians and to begin an exchange of government officials. Whitehall diplomats advised their superiors that Parliament should invite large numbers of congressmen to Britain. In America Lord Halifax—an ambassador who visited every state in the Union—gave sixteen speeches during the year, explaining Britain's relations with the Dominions and India, describing democratic goals for world peace, and stressing the need for Anglo-American unity.[8]

America's unfavorable response to Britain's policies in Italy and Greece demonstrated that it was time to initiate a more active propaganda campaign. Donnelly reflected the feelings of many Whitehall officials when he wrote that "sooner or later American opinion and foreign policy prove to be the same thing. If we are to bring Administration policy with us, we must bring majority opinion with us as well." Increased contact among the British Information Service in New York, the embassy in Washington, and American journalists would ensure a friendly press, since policy could be explained before comments were made and newspapers printed. The Sforza crisis had been blown out of proportion, Donnelly surmised, because it had burst on the press "without warning and so all the ancestral and infantile prejudices (the Redcoats, the burning of Washington and so on) came into play." This sort of misunderstanding could be avoided with more "intelligent anticipation."[9]

The task of reconstructing American opinion was assumed by the versatile counselor of the embassy, Michael R. Wright. After an Oxford education, Wright had joined the diplomatic service in 1926. He had been sent first to Washington and, after assignments in Paris and Cairo, had returned to the United States in 1943. In mid-January 1945 he began his campaign, lunching with New York broadcasters and meeting with the editorial staffs of *Time, Life,* and *Fortune.* He talked with Scripps-Howard editors and with America's bitterest critic of Britain's policies in the Mediterranean, the commentator Johannes Steel, and even undertook to explain those actions on radio to Steel's three million listeners. During February and March he conferred with America's most important commentators, such as Joseph C. Harsh, Edward R. Murrow, Ernest K. Lindley, James Reston, and Walter Lippmann. In Detroit, Wright held discussions with a branch of the Council on Foreign Relations and also addressed a Rotary Club. He gave speeches at Fayetteville and Fort Bragg, North Carolina, and at Jackson, Michigan. By early February he had received invitations to Boston, Philadelphia, Buffalo, St. Louis, Minneapolis, Salt Lake City, San Francisco, Portland, and Seattle. Many of these invitations were accepted, and he also made speeches in Madison, Kansas City, Omaha, and Denver.[10]

During this rigorous campaign Wright adopted what he called the "frank approach." As he told the Foreign Office, he was trying to "divert criticism from ourselves to American policy" on the grounds that officials in the Roosevelt administration had "shirked their responsibility" in Europe; he also wanted to dispel the belief that Britain wanted to establish reactionary governments in Europe as a counter against Russia. Wright recognized that it was a "dangerous game for us here to inspire criticism of American policy. But risks have to be taken at times." In Jackson, Michigan, he attacked the State

Department's "tendency to decline responsibility" on the Continent and urged more collaboration: "In my opinion an Anglo-American force would have greatly diminished the difficulty" in Greece. He asked for America's help in repairing a war-torn world; as he said in Detroit, Englishmen felt that Americans would "fix a broken down car with your coats on when, as a matter of fact, you should take off your coats, roll up your sleeves and get your hands greasy in your efforts to do the repair job."[11]

Ambassador Halifax joined the campaign, holding a series of off-the-record individual and small-group conferences with Washington newspapermen in January. Next month he gave speeches in New Orleans and Jackson, Mississippi. He admitted British resentment over American charges about Greece, called for more understanding, and urged more American participation in European affairs. The ambassador declared that involvement was necessary to obtain a lasting peace, grimly reminding southerners that the United States had been unable to stay out of European quarrels in 1812 and 1917, and that in a decade or so America might be "separated from Europe only by the time it takes a projectile to reach its target."[12]

British themes were summarized by Wright in an essay for the American Academy of Political and Social Science that stressed Anglo-American bonds, the most important one being that both nations had common objectives—"a just and secure peace and expanding world markets." To achieve these goals he pledged that Britain would continue to be a "loyal and tenacious partner."[13]

Such remarks appeared to influence many Americans. Stettinius advised Roosevelt in January 1945 that the public now demanded a strong and positive approach to Europe. An *Economist* article attacking the administration's weak policy impressed the president. After discussing it with Halifax, Roosevelt announced a bolder policy, declaring in his inaugural address that the United States could not and would not shrink from its postwar responsibilities.[14]

Wright's campaign also seemed to have some impact, especially with American correspondents, and friendly reports began appearing in the press. Harsh wrote in the *Christian Science Monitor* about the situation in Yugoslavia, complaining about negative American diplomacy, declaring that the United States refrained from accepting joint responsibility with its allies. When the administration became more involved a month later, Reston noted that the involvement marked the beginning of a more active policy. Churchill's statement that Francisco Franco should not be allowed to attend a peace conference was applauded by Murrow and Lindley. British policy in Greece was praised late in February by the *Buffalo Courier Express,* and *Life* published an editorial titled "The Lessons of Greece," subtitled "It Showed That the Allied Occupation Policies Should Be Joint. That Means U.S. Troops." The editorial continued by saying that the administration could not criticize Churchill since it refused to become involved and that fear of being Britain's "cat's-paw" or devotion to nonintervention were no longer good reasons for abstaining from world responsibilities. A Scripps-Howard paper, the *Knoxville News-Sentinel,* proclaimed "Let Us Join with Britain," declaring that the way to assure liberty and democracy was to form a "greater union that will be imperishable."[15]

The Foreign Office was delighted with the results of this campaign. Donnelly felt that Wright had effectively defended British policy and had expressed Britain's craving for closer cooperation with the United States. Donnelly added with smug satisfaction that if the State Department has received "some of its own medicine in consequence, we need not be too distressed."[16]

III

Perhaps Whitehall officials overestimated their success. Anglophobia did seem to decline during February and March 1945, and some Americans supported closer cooperation with Great Britain. But as the British would see, this public support did not mean that the Roosevelt administration now favored adopting Churchill's anti-Soviet approach, especially before the first important test of Russia's postwar designs—Poland.

By 1944 Poland had become a sensitive issue. In the spring of that year, when the Red Army crossed the Vistula, Churchill and Stalin supported different Polish governments. Since 1939, the British had maintained relations with the prewar regime, and some of its members had fled to London. Britain's alliance with this government was the basis for its declaration of war on the Reich, and during the war 170,000 Poles fought alongside British troops. By 1944, however, Stalin's relations with the London Poles were tenuous, and as his armies swept westward he supported a Communist group organized in Lublin. Roosevelt's objectives for Poland had been similar to Churchill's; both desired a strong, independent, democratic nation. FDR's liberal heritage and a vocal group of six to seven million Polish-Americans, most of whom lived in northern cities and voted Democratic, convinced him that he could not tolerate a Moscow-controlled government in Warsaw. But he believed that a compromise of some sort between the British and Soviet positions could be obtained when the Big Three met at Yalta. The conference seemed to achieve this compromise: the Allies reaffirmed Poland's right to self-determination, and Stalin pledged that after the war he would allow the country to hold free elections.[17]

To carry out Stalin's pledge the Russians agreed to set up a commission for Poland's political reorganization, composed of Ambassador Harriman; British ambassador to the Soviet Union, Sir Archibald Clark Kerr; and the Soviet foreign minister, Vyacheslav Molotov—an interesting juxtaposition of personalities. Harriman was the son of the great American railroad magnate E. H. Harriman, a good friend of Roosevelt, and a sturdy member of the East's so-called liberal establishment. A scion of an established Scottish family, Clark Kerr had joined the diplomatic service in 1906 and during the next thirty-five years had distinguished himself as a troubleshooter and an intrepid negotiator. Serving in South America, Europe, and the Middle East, the tall, broad Scotsman had been transferred from China to handle a difficult assignment in Moscow in January 1942. The Russian foreign minister was the son of a store clerk and had assumed the name of Molotov (*molot* means "hammer") at the age of sixteen when he became involved in the Communist branch of the Social Democratic party. At nineteen he was exiled to Siberia, returning by 1912 to help Stalin edit a small newspaper called *Pravda*. Molotov was an excellent organizer, and after Stalin's rise, eventually became prime minister and then foreign minister where he proved to be a tough negotiator. At times he displayed such stubbornness that his associates privately referred to him as "rock bottom." (The Western version of the epithet was "iron pants" or "stone ass.")[18]

British policy had already been formulated when the commission convened on 23 February 1945 in Moscow. Whitehall had instructed Clark Kerr five days earlier that the new Polish government should contain a representation of non-Lublin Poles, that Russian harassment against the underground and non-Communist Poles must be stopped, and that all Polish groups should attend a meeting of the commission to allocate posts in the new cabinet. The new government would hold office until free elections could take place. The British assumed that Molotov would represent Lublin and that Clark Kerr and Harriman would represent the other Poles. The Foreign Office ordered Clark Kerr to arrange joint action with Harriman and then to make the "strongest possible stand" to ensure that the Polish government would function properly and freely.[19]

Harriman and Clark Kerr had a very close relationship, and their behavior exemplified the way Western diplomats in Eastern Europe would deal with the Russians for the remainder of the war and during the cold war. The more contact British and American representatives had with the Soviets, the sooner they arrived at the same conclusions about Russian behavior, cooperated with each other during negotiations, and advocated similar if not joint policies against the Kremlin. Perhaps this convergence was inevitable, for it resulted from a cultural and ideological clash between East and West.

This prominent theme in Anglo-American relations during the onset of the cold war first appeared during the Moscow conference. After three years of dealing with the Russians, Harriman was aware of Molotov's tenacity and the diplomatic advantage held by the Soviets because their troops occupied

Poland. Like their British counterparts, Harriman and his staff felt that an independent approach had less chance of obtaining a democratic Poland than a coordinated policy. Without informing the State Department, he and Clark Kerr discussed and agreed on common procedure before the first commission meeting. The two ambassadors then kept in almost daily contact, exchanging information, reading each other's cables, and discussing tactics before approaching Molotov.[20]

Russian obstinacy prevented agreement after two weeks of negotiation, frustrating Whitehall officials and inducing a new burst of Churchillian diplomacy toward the United States. Many British officials had disagreed with the prime minister's dreary estimate of Soviet intentions. Although Russia raised doubts in their minds by establishing the Lublin committee in spring 1944, their spirits revived after the invasion of Normandy, and a few British diplomats even anticipated a "honeymoon" in which Anglo-Soviet issues could be solved quickly. In August, Eden informed the war cabinet that the Russians would probably collaborate with the West in organizing the United Nations Organization. Whitehall officials were less sure after the Warsaw uprising and Moscow's announcement that it intended to recognize the Lublin committee as the provisional government of Poland; a British memorandum of December 1944 declared that the U.S.S.R.'s goal was security. Thoughts turned pessimistic during the stalemate of February 1945 in Moscow, and by March most British officials at last agreed with Churchill. Orme Sargent felt that Britain should be realistic and accept the fact that Rumania, Bulgaria, and probably Yugoslavia would have Soviet-dominated governments. The formerly optimistic Oliver Harvey recorded in his diary that relations with the Russians were deteriorating since they had "sabotaged" the Crimea accords. By early April the Russian expert of an earlier era, Sir R. H. Bruce Lockhart, wrote Sargent that "unless some curb is put on Russia's dreams of expansion, not only will cooperation between the three leading Allies become a sham but there will be no peace in Europe after the defeat of Germany."[21]

The stalled Moscow negotiations, along with the establish-ment of a Soviet-sponsored Rumanian government, prompt-ed Churchill to write Roosevelt. On 28 February he men-tioned many stories of "wholesale deportation by the Russians and of liquidations by the Lublin Poles of elements they do not like" and urged that all Polish factions meet at the Krem-lin and that British and American observers go to Poland. A few days later Whitehall followed up with a proposal to the State Department for a joint communication demanding that all political parties be represented in the Polish cabinet.[22]

The British proposal was consistent with long-range American objectives but not with short-range tactics, for the State Department still wanted to pursue an independent pol-icy.[23] Acting Secretary of State Joseph C. Grew suggested to Roosevelt on 3 March that, concerning the commission, there "should be no appearance given in any of their outward ac-tions that the United States and Great Britain are advocates of the non-Lublin Poles and the Soviet Union the sponsor of the Lublin Government." Having no intention of conspiring with Britain, the president concurred, and three days later Grew informed Harriman that a "joint communication at this stage in the negotiations is inadvisable and separate instructions would be preferable." Harriman was instructed not to sup-port Clark Kerr's plan to send Allied observers to Poland.[24]

IV

The Roosevelt administration's continued determination to pursue an independent policy not only irritated the British but prompted a diplomatic offensive during the last weeks of FDR's life. Churchill told his colleagues in a 6 March cabinet meeting that England was "entitled to expect the full support" of the United States, that "we must carry them with us," be-cause the British could not help the Poles without American aid. To gain support Churchill initiated an intensive cable campaign. From 8 March to 12 April, he sent Roosevelt thir-teen messages dealing with the Kremlin's behavior, six of them coming during the last ten days of March.[25]

Before examining that initiative, one should analyze the

themes Churchill stressed in his messages to Roosevelt. The topic was usually Poland, the "testing ground" of Moscow's intentions. Churchill generalized from the Polish situation to all areas in Europe liberated by the Soviets, making it seem logical that British and American troops should push into Central Europe. He alerted Roosevelt to any Russian behavior that could be construed as inconsistent with Anglo-American ideals, and if Stalin made a statement that seemed rude he suggested to the White House that it was a deliberate insult to the United States. Washington thus would receive the Soviet statement, followed by Churchill's unsolicited editorial and a suggested Anglo-American rebuttal. He used the pronouns "we" and "our" when referring to American and British policies, even if actions by the two nations were independent. He raised questions about subjects that he knew Roosevelt was sensitive about—whether Stalin's behavior would undermine the United Nations Organization, how Soviet actions in Poland might affect American opinion—and he always supplied the answers. In a sense he used public opinion to force the president to act: if the situation in Poland was not improved by a joint Anglo-American plan against the U.S.S.R., Churchill said, he would be forced to tell Parliament that Yalta had failed because Stalin could not be trusted. Because FDR's policy was based on personal cooperation with the Russian leader, the prime minister's statement was an implicit threat.

Churchill initiated his cable campaign on 8 March and during the next ten days sent Roosevelt six long messages concerning Eastern Europe. Russian policy in the Balkans, he wrote, was "absolutely contrary to all democratic ideas." In Rumania the Soviets had established the rule of a Communist minority by force and misrepresentation. Poland was much more important, for it was the test case between the West and the Russians. In Britain there was strong opinion against Soviet domination of Poland. Churchill asked: "How would the matter go in the United States?" It was a portentous question, and the prime minister knew the answer. Britain and America must prevent a totalitarian regime; if they did not, he warned, the world would see that they endorsed the

Crimea settlement—a "fraudulent prospectus." He thereupon revealed his design: Presidential action was required; both leaders must write Stalin, or Roosevelt alone must send a message with British support. Churchill even supplied a telegram that he thought would be appropriate.[26]

FDR was not alarmed. Harriman was instructed to restate the administration's position on free elections, to announce that the United States was "concerned" by the difficulties encountered at Moscow, and to inform the Soviets that America hoped for "political tranquility" inside Poland.[27]

After seeing Harriman's instructions, Churchill again urged presidential action. It suited the Soviets very well to have a long period of delay, he warned on 10 March, "so that the process of liquidation of elements unfavorable to their puppets may run its full course." It was folly to expect political tranquility or a truce between the Lublin and non-Communist Poles; their mutual hatreds would "eat into live steel." Churchill begged Roosevelt to consider his previous telegram. On the same day he sent FDR a startling report, a long summary of the situation in Poland based on information acquired from the Polish underground, contending that Soviet secret police were tormenting non-Lublin Poles. The Russians "beat prisoners, tortured them morally [and] keep them in the cold without clothes." Males between the ages of sixteen and sixty-five had to register with the authorities, and all Poles had to surrender their firearms and declare typewriters, printing presses, duplicators, and radios. The underground told representatives in London: "Please inform the British. Allied intervention necessary." Although the accuracy of this report was uncertain, Churchill informed Roosevelt that the information was stated with restraint and that it "emphasized the need for sending our own observers into the country."[28]

Roosevelt was becoming more concerned by 11 and 12 March, when he sent three replies, agreeing that public opinion was important and informing Churchill that Americans would not support a Polish cabinet that was either a "fraud or a mere whitewash of the Lublin Government." He assured his British friend that he also wanted a democratic Poland and noted that the difference between Washington and London was one of tactics. That difference was profound, for Churchill desired to confront Stalin while Roosevelt wanted to avoid conflict. As FDR informed Churchill, he felt that "achieving our common objective would be immeasurably increased if it were done under the guise of a general political truce." Roosevelt was more alarmed on 12 March when he responded to the report from Poland: it "points directly to an urgent necessity of our taking every practicable means of accomplishing the corrective measures in Poland that are envisaged in the agreements reached at Yalta."[29]

Clearly, Churchill had made progress. Harriman received instructions to work with Clark Kerr and to inform Molotov of similar Anglo-American aims. Meanwhile the president would await any results his ambassador might obtain concerning the Warsaw government. As for the Polish people, Roosevelt believed that "we may have to appeal to Marshal Stalin for relief for the oppressed inhabitants of Poland."[30]

Next day, 13 March, Churchill summarized his themes. Britain could not stand alone against the Soviet Union, nor make progress at Moscow without the support of the United States. The British had "not the necessary strength to carry the matter further and . . . the limits of our capacity to act have been reached." Churchill outlined his plan, a united policy, and warned that "if we get out of step the doom of Poland is sealed." Roosevelt should accept his proposed message to Stalin. Anglo-American action, or in Churchillian parlance, "combined dogged pressure and persistence," must be immediate. Time was on the side of the Lublin group, which was establishing an impregnable authority. Again the prime minister invoked public opinion. Was Poland "now to lose her freedom?" That would be the question asked by the public. Progress must be achieved soon, he warned, for if called before Parliament "I shall be forced to tell them the truth."[31]

The bombardment of messages must have tired Roosevelt, and it assuredly concerned the State Department. Churchill suspected that, except for occasional flashes of courage and insight, Roosevelt left the writing of his replies to his aides. Apparently Churchill was right: cables were usually prepared by Leahy and the State Department's White House liaison, Charles E. Bohlen, and were only approved in the Oval Office. It seems reasonable to assume that as the president's health declined he would rely more on advisers. Bohlen reports that he drafted many replies and that the State Department was leery of Churchill's influence on Roosevelt. The department, Bohlen explained, had been "disturbed by the apparent British acceptance of failure before any such failure had occurred and also the implication in the Prime Minister's message that the British were preparing the ground to place the blame on us." His superiors instructed Bohlen to examine Churchill's cable of 12 March "point by point" with the president. After leaving the White House, Bohlen reported to Stettinius that Roosevelt "thoroughly understands the great importance we attach to this matter."[32]

The State Department's concern was apparent in the next Roosevelt–Churchill exchange. The president tersely replied: "I cannot agree that we are confronted with a breakdown of the Yalta agreement until we have made the effort to overcome the obstacles incurred in the negotiations at Moscow." Roosevelt shifted blame for the stalemate at Moscow from the Russians, complaining that Harriman received his instructions on 9 March but had not acted because of Churchill's request. This was true; the negotiations were at a standstill because Whitehall desired to coordinate Anglo-American policy before instructing Clark Kerr. Churchill sent a more subdued reply the next day, reminding FDR that "our great desire is to keep in step with you and we realize how hopeless the position would become for Poland if it were seen that we were not in full accord." The issue remained: the British could not endorse the independent American "truce proposal, for we think it actively dangerous." Churchill reiterated his goals, stating that such aims would become realities if the United States adopted British tactics and presented the Russians with the "same, or at least very similar, communication."[33]

That same day, 17 March, Halifax applied pressure in Washington. He had informed the Foreign Office during the previous week that State Department officials desired to "wait and see" on the Polish and Rumanian issues since they were "keen to avoid any public controversy which might complicate relations with the Russians." He now visited the department armed with a plan for working out a uniform basis of approach. American officials agreed to compose corresponding instructions that could be sent to the ambassadors in Moscow. That evening Halifax visited Stettinius, and next morning he telephoned the White House to ask Leahy to make a "special effort" for presidential approval of a joint communication. Roosevelt gave way, and Harriman was informed that he and Clark Kerr were to send "separate, but identical" statements to Molotov. The ensuing Anglo-American message restated the British goals of introducing democratic elements into the Lublin government, sending Western observers to Poland, and establishing free elections.[34]

The joint message was delivered on 19 March, and the British were delighted. The cabinet congratulated the ambassadors in Moscow and Washington, and Eden wrote Halifax: "I am most grateful to you for all you have done in bringing the United States Government along. Thank you so much."[35]

The joint message marked an important step in British diplomacy, because Roosevelt had reevaluated his independent approach. For the first time, his administration had abandoned its objections to "ganging up" and had collaborated with London in confronting Moscow. Washington officials were beginning to realize that the British might be right, that joint tactics might be the best, indeed the only, way to win concessions from the Kremlin. The British had moved the "great unwieldy barge"—with help from the obstinant Russians.

V

Five days later, on 23 March, Molotov rejected the Anglo-American proposals, and Churchill again turned to the United States. On the same day the Soviet embassy in Washington informed the State Department that the Russian delegation to the San Francisco conference of the United Nations Organization would be led by the ambassador to the United States, Andrei A. Gromyko, and not by Foreign Minister Molotov, minimizing the importance of Roosevelt's world organization. Churchill informed Eden that nothing was more likely to bring the Americans "into line with us than any idea of the San Francisco Conference being imperilled." He wrote Roosevelt on 27 March that Molotov's absence would make a deplorable impression and would jeopardize the new organization. "Does it mean," he asked, "that the Russians are going to run out or are they trying to blackmail us?" He sharply criticized Russian behavior in Poland, stating that it was "as plain as a pike staff" that the policy was to stall while the Lublin group consolidated its power. The alternative to confessing total failure was to confront the Soviet leader: "is it not now the moment for a message from us both on Poland to Stalin?"[36]

The same day Churchill also sent suggestions for a joint message: the two leaders should tell Stalin to allow Western-supported Poles in the Warsaw regime and to accept the terms of the 19 March joint communication.[37]

Roosevelt had refused to use this tactic, but during the last days of March the behavior of the Russians, together with Harriman's reports, reinforced Churchill's strategy. A day after the Soviets announced that Gromyko would lead the delegation to San Francisco, Harriman wrote the president restating difficulties at Moscow. The ambassador and his minister-counselor, George F. Kennan, shared Churchill's pessimism over Poland and agreed with the British that only an Anglo-American policy of quid pro quo could produce a democratic Poland. Along with Clark Kerr, Harriman felt that the Russians were stalling so the Lublin group could secure power in Warsaw and that they were responsible for the lack of success at the Moscow conference. As early as 4 March, he wrote the State Department that if discussions were "unduly protracted to the point of public criticism our record should be very clear that it is due to the Soviet Government or the Poles and not the fault of the British or ourselves." The discouraging situation had changed little after the Western ambassadors presented the Soviets with the identical statements on Poland. Harriman reported on 25 March that Molotov objected to the Anglo-American interpretation of the Crimea declaration and had no intention of inviting the Western-supported Poles to join the Warsaw regime. The message seems to have provoked Roosevelt, who banged his fist on his wheelchair and proclaimed, "Averell is right; we can't do business with Stalin. He has broken every one of the promises he made at Yalta."[38]

Meanwhile action on another front further endangered a stable understanding with Russia. In March German commanders in Italy extended peace feelers to Anglo-American forces. Hoping that the Wehrmacht desired to surrender unconditionally, Americans met with German representatives in Switzerland. The Soviets were suspicious of the meeting in Bern, and Molotov indelicately confronted Clark Kerr on 22 March accusing Western forces of negotiating with the Germans "behind the backs of the Soviet Union." Whitehall, full of consternation, relayed Molotov's remark to the State Department. Stalin remained suspicious and on 3 April wrote Roosevelt: "Some of my advisers find it difficult to explain the rapidity of the advance of the Anglo-American armies in Germany unless there is some underlying agreement with the Nazis." This remark angered FDR. Bohlen reported that the president was sitting at his desk with "his eyes flashing, his face flushed, outraged that he should be accused of dealing with the Germans behind Stalin's back."[39]

Russian contentions, Harriman's reports, and British diplomacy all persuaded the weary president to accept Churchill's proposal for the "strongest possible appeal" to Stalin. On 29 March Roosevelt replied that he desired to tell the Russian leader, "I must make it quite plain to you that any ... solution which would result in a thinly disguised continuance of the present Warsaw regime would be unacceptable and would cause the people of the United States to regard the Yalta agreements as having failed." Churchill was delighted, calling the message a "grave and weighty document." The two Western leaders compared notes, and on the last day of March the prime minister sent the president a four-page cable that he proposed to send to Stalin. "Please let me know what you think," he said, "I will not send it off till I hear from you." Roosevelt replied that he was making additions to his draft to conform to Churchill's suggestions. Both leaders sent their messages on 1 April.[40]

Having achieved diplomatic unity, the British now resumed their attempt to influence military policy.

By March 1945 it was obvious that the Third Reich was defeated. The position of the Allied armies at the armistice would be important to the political settlement in Europe. Britain could win the peace, according to Montgomery, by getting possession of important political centers—notably, Vienna, Prague, and Berlin—before the Russians. Churchill agreed and on 1 April he reminded Roosevelt of Berlin's strategic importance. The Soviets would soon enter Vienna, he said, and if they captured Berlin they would think they were the "overwhelming contributor to our common victory." Would not this mood raise grave and formidable difficulties? As usual, Churchill answered his own question, demanding that the Western armies march as far east as possible and that they capture the German capital. He assured Roosevelt that Anglo-American differences over strategy were "small, and as usual, not of principle but of emphasis."[41]

This assurance was far from the truth. Although differences over diplomatic tactics might be ones of emphasis, disagreements over military strategy were profound and had been throughout the war. Having influenced Roosevelt's diplomacy, Churchill now sought to minimize all problems between Britain and America, hoping to create the appearance of total unity against the Kremlin.

While Roosevelt might accept British tactics to obtain common goals in Poland, he would not jeopardize Soviet-American relations or the remnants of his ties with Stalin for a few more miles of German rubble. After victory in Europe, Roosevelt still would face two more problems that demanded Soviet cooperation: continuation of the war in the Pacific and the making of world peace. His response to Churchill expressed confidence in Eisenhower's battle plan, which was based on the assumption that the purpose of strategy was not political but military—to destroy the forces of the enemy. In a later interview, Eisenhower elaborated on American reasoning. Political decisions had divided Germany for occupation purposes, and there was no possibility that Anglo-Americans would capture and hold Berlin. When he issued his final orders, Western troops were about two hundred miles from the capital; the Red Army was only thirty miles away with a bridgehead west of the Oder. "It didn't seem to be good sense to try, both of us, to throw in forces toward Berlin and get mixed up—two armies that couldn't talk the same language."[42]

VI

Although there would be no race for Berlin, the Roosevelt administration's diplomatic policies were changing. The president had reconsidered his conciliatory and independent approach toward Russia and now spoke in a stronger way about the Communist ally. On 6 April Roosevelt wrote Churchill calling for a "firm and blunt stand" against the Kremlin, going so far as to write: "We must not permit anybody to entertain a false impression that we are afraid. Our armies will in a very few days be in a position that will permit us to become 'tougher' than has heretofore appeared advantageous to the war effort."[43] The message was significant because it demonstrated a stiffer approach toward the Soviet Union and a greater desire to combine with the British than at any other time during the war. The message's blunt tone and use of "we," "our," and "us" make one wonder if Churchill wrote it himself.

Another example that Roosevelt's policies were changing concerned Greece. In the middle of March he suggested to the prime minister that an Anglo-Soviet-American investigating mission go to Athens and attempt to bring about a workable government. Churchill was not enthusiastic about sending Russians to Greece while his troops were there fighting Communists, and he did not respond for two weeks. On 3 April he expressed his reservations to the president; by then Roosevelt had changed his mind and agreed.[44]

State Department officials also had retreated from their earlier insistence on an independent approach. A memorandum of 10 April urged the president to write Churchill: "We shall have to consider most carefully the implications of Stalin's attitude and what is to be our next step. I shall, of course, take no action of any kind, nor make any statement without consulting you, and I know you will do the same." Halifax described the changing mood to the Foreign Office, reporting that anxiety about the international situation was widespread in official Washington circles and that the administration was "engaged in toning down exaggerated expectations concerning San Francisco conference."[45]

"Under Churchill's prodding," Harriman later wrote, "Roosevelt conceded that the time had come for a personal approach to Stalin."[46] The result was the similar 1 April messages to the Kremlin. The prime minister had persuaded the president that mediating between London and Moscow was an unrealistic policy. Roosevelt abandoned his independent approach and joined the British.

Other factors, of course, promoted the change. Harriman's continual warnings impressed Roosevelt and reinforced Churchill's plans for a tougher policy. More important, Russian obstinacy over Poland and repression of non-Communists in other occupied nations conflicted with American aims for Eastern Europe, decreased the administration's desire and ability to mediate a democratic peace, and made London's attack on Soviet policies more plausible. All this contributed to a decline in Roosevelt's opinion of the Russian leader. When leaving for Warm Springs he told journalist Anne O'Hare McCormick that either Stalin was not in control of the Soviet government or was "not a man of his word."[47]

Thus Soviet behavior made Churchill's approach more attractive to Roosevelt and increased the probability that FDR would accept British policy. When the friendship between Washington and Moscow cooled in March and April, there appeared an inverse ratio that would become more apparent in future months: as Soviet-American relations declined, Anglo-American relations improved. This "allied ratio" would become an indicator of the onset of the cold war.

The weather along the Atlantic coast was unseasonably warm when the president arrived at Warm Springs. He was aged; his hands shook so much that he had difficulty holding and reading a message. He was tired and wanted to relax in the sulphur pools. On 11 April Churchill stimulated him with two cables. FDR responded immediately, minimizing the Soviet problem and restating his new position: "We must be firm, however, and our course thus far is correct." According to Roosevelt's speech writer, Samuel I. Rosenman, who was at Warm Springs, "there is no question from the correspondence that the 'course' the President was referring to was not the general wartime policy toward the Soviet Union but the firm, even tough, position that he and Churchill had taken with Stalin on Poland."[48]

Roosevelt's optimism was fading. After all, during the preceding fifty days he had received a constant barrage of messages concerning Russian obstinacy, a daily stream of discouraging, negative news, all leading to the same sad conclusion: Stalin would not accept a Western peace for Eastern Europe. Therefore it seems logical to suppose that had Roosevelt lived, and had Soviet behavior remained unchanged, then he would have continued and even strengthened the tough British-American approach. The collapse of the wartime alliance and the rise of the cold war probably would have developed sooner than they actually did.[49]

While that conclusion is supposition, it is certain that during those April days Anglo-American diplomacy toward Russia was more united than at any other time during the war. But on the twelfth day of that month the president—and that policy—died.

Chapter 3

Truman and Churchill
The Reversal

War had been cruel to Europe. The once great cultural centers had been reduced to miles of rubble. Industries had been bombed, bombed again, and factories had become heaps of smoldering, twisted steel. Transportation stood still. Fields and pastures had become junkyards filled with the rusting refuse of battle. In human dimensions, forced labor, death camps, the Holocaust all reflected the horror of Nazi rule. And as the Wehrmacht retreated, streams of refugees followed, searching for the necessities of life. Homes had been devastated, clothing was scarce, and the people wore the hollow face of starvation.

But relief was coming. During the spring of 1945 the Thousand-Year Reich died prematurely. The Allies crushed the monster of Europe, and over the summer they turned the full brunt of their military machine against a faltering enemy in the Pacific. At the same time they began the complex task of peacemaking.

In Washington a new president, Harry S. Truman, faced a myriad of international problems. Historians have long debated his administration's policies, especially those toward the Soviet Union. Traditionalists declare that Truman was reacting to Russian aggression when he formed his "get tough" approach toward the Kremlin in 1946. Many revisionists, however, find that Truman abruptly changed Roosevelt's policy of wartime cooperation with Russia to one of confrontation; thus, they say that Truman bears the major responsibility for the cold war.[1] But the first three months of Truman's policy toward both allies have not been analyzed with the aid of British documents. Now, special attention must be given to Anglo-American relations from 12 April to the meeting at Potsdam—and to the reversal of American foreign policy.

I

Harry S. Truman was born in 1884 on a farm near Lamar, Missouri; the family moved to Independence in 1890. Harry worked at odd jobs in nearby Kansas City and returned to farming until America entered the First World War when he joined the army and served in France. He was thirty-four when the war ended, and with an army friend, he opened a haberdashery in Kansas City. After the store failed during the postwar recession, Truman became interested in politics, and in 1922, supported by Boss Thomas Pendergast's Democratic political machine, he ran for office and won. Four years later, he became presiding judge (actually county commissioner) of Jackson County. In 1934, after achieving a reputation for efficiency and honesty, he ran for and won a seat in the U.S. Senate.

Although he moved east, Truman held on to many characteristically provincial ideas. "I'm just a farmer boy from Jackson County," he would declare, and one of his favorite sayings was, "I'm from Missouri—show me." Honest and direct, he delivered straight talk and expected fair play. He liked to compromise on an issue, or as he called it, horse trade, and possessed the ability to make decisions quickly; once he made them, they were seldom reversed. He felt that democracy and free enterprise had made America great and set an example for other nations. He once agreed with a memorandum from Secretary of War Henry L. Stimson arguing that before peace could be secure Russia's autocratic government would have to become a democracy, and that before the United States gave the Soviets atomic secrets Stalin should establish a constitution and bill of rights. Truman held narrow views about other political and economic systems. In a press conference in May 1947, after two years in the presidency, he stated that there "isn't any difference in totalitarian states. I don't care what you call them, Nazi, Communist, or Fascist."[2]

Yet Truman clearly did not hold the isolationist beliefs that had been so common in the Midwest. He had long believed in free trade and called the liberal Trade Agreements Act of 1934 an outstanding achievement. As early as March 1938, he told a meeting of the American Legion that the nation had erred when it rejected the Versailles Treaty and the League of Nations and refused to accept responsibility as a world power. After war broke out in Europe, he supported Roosevelt's internationalist policies, voting for the extension of the Selective Service Act, lend-lease, various military-revenue measures, and repeal of neutrality legislation. By 1942 he had come to the conclusion, as he told an audience in Jackson County, that one reason for the Second World War was America's failure to remain involved in world affairs. Truman had accepted Wilsonian ideals, announcing his support for a congressional resolution for postwar Allied collaboration, favoring the establishment of an international organization, and thinking in terms of an American mission abroad. As he stated while campaigning for the vice-presidency in October 1944, "I think Almighty God intends for this nation to assume leadership in world affairs to preserve the peace."[3]

Truman held such convictions when he was sworn in as president on 12 April 1945. Unfortunately, Roosevelt had failed to groom his vice-president for the office. Truman had seen FDR about a half-dozen times during the preceding year, and except for some cabinet meetings the two men had met only twice since the inauguration in January. The Missourian had not been told about the Manhattan Project or admitted to the map room of the White House. Now, as the new president, he was concerned about foreign policy and worried about his inexperience. "I was sworn in one night," he recalled, "and the next morning I had to get right on the job at hand. I was plenty scared." Visitors easily sensed his apprehension; Paul-Henri Spaak of Belgium recalled that Truman spoke of anxiety about his new responsibilities, a feeling that had not disappeared after the first month in office. In mid-May he admitted to Joseph E. Davies that foreign policy was a "terrible responsibility and I am the last man fitted to handle it and it happens to me." But, he continued in a characteristic vein, "I shall do my best."[4]

It was natural that the new president would rely on his predecessor's advisers and would continue Roosevelt's policies. Truman had no intention of immediately revising FDR's plans. The speech writer for both men, Samuel I. Rosenman, remembered that when the new chief executive made a decision "he would say to himself: 'I wonder what Roosevelt would have done? Would he think this was the right thing?' You know, he had a picture on the wall of Roosevelt that he could see just by turning, and he frequently said to me, 'I'm trying to do what he would like.'"[5]

Yet continuing Roosevelt's policy toward the Soviet Union was not an easy task. Truman's advisers disagreed on what to continue—wartime cooperation or the British idea of joint confrontation. Harriman, Leahy, Grew, Secretary of the Navy James V. Forrestal, and the chief of the American military mission in Moscow, Gen. John R. Deane all felt that the administration should maintain the tough Anglo-American stance against the Kremlin. Harriman returned to Washington after six weeks of frustrating negotiation over Poland and told Truman that Russian conduct would be based on the "principles of power politics in its crudest and most primitive form." He warned Forrestal that "half and maybe all of Europe might be communist by the end of next winter." Grew, a devoted anti-Communist, advocated a policy that adjusted American aid to Soviet cooperation. Leahy agreed. Grew became more apprehensive in May, when he wrote that the Kremlin was endeavoring to have Western troops hold back while the Red Army occupied the remaining enemy-held territory and was using occupation to further their political aims.[6]

Other advisers disagreed. More optimistic, Davies advocated cooperation and emphasized that the Russians wanted collaboration with the West and a firm, unshakable peace, not another war. Marshall did not want a breakdown in the alliance while war was still going on in Europe and Asia. Stimson felt that the United States should use a friendly but direct approach to the Kremlin; policy should be stated with cold-blooded firmness but without showing any temper.[7]

Truman shared Roosevelt's mixed feelings about the Soviets. He desired—or at least hoped for—cooperation but was distressed by the reports from Eastern Europe. He adopted his predecessor's policy of military cooperation with the Red Army while supporting the British on Poland.

The British liked the new president. They saw a novice in foreign affairs but were impressed with his character and hoped for the future of Anglo-American relations. Churchill realized that Truman was new to the international situation and would rely on his advisers, and Eden agreed with Hopkins's advice not to have the prime minister visit Washington because the Missourian knew absolutely nothing of world affairs and would be terrified. Yet the British were impressed with this new personality. Halifax met him and felt that he would be a friend. In Halifax's opinion, Truman was a man of principle, courage, pertinacity, and sound judgment. Eden saw an honest and friendly person who would be a loyal collaborator. Cadogan met Truman in May and wrote his wife, "You say people in London don't think much of Truman. As a matter of fact . . . he seems to me awfully good—very practical and quick and helpful, with a mind of his own." In these ways he was "rather unlike his dear predecessor."[8]

II

As Anglo-Russian relations deteriorated, the British continued the policy that had been somewhat successful during Roosevelt's last days: they urged the new administration to join them in opposing the Kremlin's aims on the Continent. The tactics were also familiar. In the first forty days of the new presidency, Churchill sent about forty cables to Truman, half dealing with the Russian problem. That figure reached ninety by the meeting at Potsdam. When Foreign Office officials met American diplomats, they emphasized Anglo-American cooperation, exposed Soviet actions inconsistent with democratic ideals, and advocated the use of troops to obtain Western political goals in Europe.

Anglo-Soviet relations degenerated rapidly during April and May when Whitehall officials felt a "sudden truculence" in Russia's attitude as Western troops entered Germany and Austria. Frank K. Roberts described his pessimism and frustration, writing to colleagues in the Foreign Office's central division that after working so hard to establish good relations with Moscow it was "very galling to be confronted with example after example of power politics in their crudest form." Roberts admitted that it might be an exaggeration to compare postwar Russia to Germany in 1939, but there could be little wishful thinking as long as Kremlin policy was controlled by the "tough, tricky, and untrustworthy personalities who comprise the Politburo." He felt that worsening relations meant that the British must approach the Russians carefully and realistically. Eden and Cadogan agreed, even if that policy resulted in a showdown with the Kremlin.[9]

That task was left to Churchill, who on 18 May confronted the Soviet ambassador to London, Feodor T. Gousev. In language so emphatic that Clark Kerr could not reproduce it in the official minutes, the prime minister took Gousev on a tour of East European capitals and demanded an explanation for Soviet policy. He accused the Soviet government of "dropping an iron screen across Europe from Lubeck to Trieste," setting up puppet regimes, and failing to keep the promises made at Yalta. The situation was incomprehensible and intolerable, and the British government objected in the strongest way to being treated as if they had no say in the postwar world. Britain would not be pushed around, Churchill barked at the ambassador, and to prevent this possibility he had postponed the demobilization of the Royal Air Force.[10]

Simultaneously Britain continued to seek American support. During April and May the undersecretary of the northern department of the Foreign Office, Christopher F. A. Warner, often discussed Allied relations with Gallman, urging that now was the time to talk very frankly and firmly to the Russians. It was a mistake, Warner said, to make democracy the issue because the term meant something quite different to the Soviets, and it was a similar error to make an issue of free elections in Eastern Europe and the Balkans. Those areas never had free and fair elections and "nothing can be gained by insisting on the impossible." He argued that the West must challenge Russia on issues of power politics, leaving no doubt about American and British interest in each question. This sort of talk might mean spheres of influence, but recognizing each other's interest in certain areas eventually would lead to understanding.[11]

Warner's evaluation was poignant. Before the war almost all Eastern European nations had been dictatorships, not democracies. Why should the Western allies irritate the Soviets by trying to establish capitalistic democracies in Russia's front yard? Warner and a few other British officials realized that such a situation could never be accepted by the Kremlin.

Britain's principal diplomatic effort, of course, was put forth by the prime minister. Churchill's correspondence with Truman began when he expressed his sympathy at Roosevelt's death and his hope that he and Truman could build an intimate relationship. The new president responded that he was aware of "urgent problems requiring our immediate and joint consideration," especially the pressing and dangerous issue of Poland and the Soviet attitude toward the Moscow negotiations. After stating that he knew what his predecessor had in mind, he told Churchill: "You can count on me to continue the loyal and close collaboration" that had existed between the two Western leaders.[12]

The new administration continued to cooperate with the British on Poland. On 13 April, the day after Roosevelt died, Truman informed Churchill that he was very aware of the warnings about Soviet obstructionism and proposed a joint message to Stalin. The rapidity of this action suggests that it may have been the next plan of Roosevelt and the State Department. Churchill was amazed that Truman committed himself to joint action a few hours after assuming the office and was delighted to continue the tactic he had sponsored. On 15 April the two leaders sent a joint message that restated the aims enunciated two weeks earlier by Churchill and Roosevelt.[13]

Cooperation was demonstrated again when Eden suggested to Stettinius that they meet with Molotov in Washington to discuss Poland before the San Francisco conference. Stettinius agreed, and Eden wrote Churchill that even if nothing resulted from meeting the Russian, it would still be "stimulating to have a chance to get to grips with the animal." Eden and Cadogan then saw Stettinius and Grew and discussed how to handle Molotov on Poland. Eden also discussed the topic on 22 April when he met Truman, urging him to talk to Molotov. Truman said that he intended to be firm when discussing the Polish situation with Molotov, words that delighted Eden. The same day, and again on 23 April, the ministers held three meetings, the Anglo-Americans lining up against the Soviet foreign minister. Eden and Stettinius expressed their displeasure at the mutual assistance pact the U.S.S.R. had signed with the Lublin Poles. But nothing came out of these conversations, for the Russian remained mulish.[14]

On 22 April Truman met Molotov. The president said that Poland was a symbol of future Soviet-American relations. He hoped that the three ministers would be able to work out their differences while negotiating in Washington.[15]

But the next conversations of the foreign ministers also lacked progress, prompting Truman to meet again with Molotov. The session of 23 April was stormy. Truman lectured Molotov as if he were a junior official in Jackson County, demanding in words of one syllable that the Soviets keep their Yalta promises. Molotov protested, "I have never been talked to like that in my life," whereupon the president warned, "Carry out your agreements and you won't get talked to like that."[16]

Roosevelt's policy continued in substance, but certainly not in style. Diplomacy is an art of the personality; the charming gentleman from the estate on the Hudson would not have behaved like the man from Missouri. Truman's actions resulted from his character; his inexperience in diplomacy; the influence of such men as Harriman, Leahy, Grew, Deane, Eden, and Churchill; and from his desire to continue the tougher approach Roosevelt established in March and April. After being in office for just ten days, Truman did not have the intent or confidence to alter policy. True, he had talked strongly to Molotov, but as he told his staff, he hoped for good results. As Molotov was leaving, Truman gave him a note urging Stalin to accept the terms of the 15 April Anglo-American cable. In other words, the new president again asked the Russians to accept Western aims for Eastern

Europe, the same policy that had been enunciated in the 1
April message written by Churchill and Roosevelt.[17]

Later that month the three ministers arrived in San Francisco to establish the United Nations. Eden and Stettinius,
continuing the joint policy, confronted Molotov on the Polish
issue. In an off-the-record press conference Eden told about
twenty reporters that the British and Americans "intended to
stand firm on the fulfillment of the Yalta agreement—*no matter what the consequences.*"[18] But Eden's plan to gain concessions
from the Soviets again failed to get results from the intrac-
table Russian.

The Soviets were irritated by the Anglo-American front
against their policy in Poland. Their position had not changed
since June 1941 when the Wehrmacht invaded their homeland. Neither Stalin nor any other Russian leader could permit an unfriendly government in Poland; it must become a
Russian preserve, a defense bastion against more attacks from
Central and Western Europe. Ideology reinforced this concern for national security; far from accepting capitalism,
Kremlin officials were products of a Marxist revolution
against such systems. Stalin's attitude toward democracy had
been obvious to Western representatives in Moscow, and later
he would say that any government that was not Fascist was
democratic. The Soviets suspected that their allies were attempting to coerce them into accepting an unfriendly government in a neighboring territory vital to their defense. Stalin
rejected the Anglo-American message of 24 April, complaining to Truman: "Such conditions must be recognized as
unusual when two governments—those of the United States
and Great Britain—beforehand settle with the Polish question" and then dictate policy to the U.S.S.R.[19]

Truman's actions naturally pleased the British. Churchill
wrote the president that the cabinet "authorizes me to inform
you of their entire agreement to the course you have
adopted" and then transmitted those feelings to Stalin. Truman, Churchill said to Eden, "is not to be bullied by the
Soviets." When the Russian leader rejected the Anglo-
American note, Churchill restated the democratic position to
the Kremlin and asked Truman for support. The president
complied on 4 May by sending a message to Stalin.[20]

Meanwhile, the British continued to urge the use of Western troops to obtain political goals on the Continent. Three days after Roosevelt's death Cadogan met with Ambassador Winant in London and pointed out the political advantage if American forces liberated Prague. On 18 April Churchill introduced Truman to the subject of occupation zones by stating that "we should retire with dignity" to the prearranged zones, and that some "crude assertion of a local Russian General" should not force the troops back from their forward positions. Churchill implied that an Allied commission should be set up in Berlin to settle complications with the Russians. British concern later shifted to Anglo-American control of the Adriatic port of Trieste. Cabling on 27 April that Roosevelt had attached great importance to the city and that the American commanding general in Italy, Mark W. Clark, supported the British plan, Churchill encouraged Truman to order the port's capture before it was occupied by Yugoslav Communists. He defended this brusque action with a phrase that Stalin would make better known at Potsdam and that might, indeed, be termed the foundation of the postwar settlement: "Possession is nine points of the law."[21]

By the end of April the Americans had not responded to any of these proposals, and the British pressed again. After the 22–23 April talks with Molotov on Poland, Eden reminded Stettinius that liberation of western Czechoslovakia would affect the fate of nearby countries. If Britain and America did not liberate Prague, Eden warned, Czechoslovakia would go the way of Yugoslavia. Stettinius agreed, for he understood what the Soviets meant by the "Yugoslavian precedent" in referring to the postwar governments of Eastern Europe. He had been informed by the American ambassador in Belgrade, Richard Patterson, that Yugoslavia was under almost complete Russian control. Patterson was alarmed by Soviet behavior, favored the stiff policy urged by the British, and wrote Stettinius that the only chance for democracy was pressure on Moscow from Washington and London. Desiring more than diplomatic pressure, on 30 April Churchill urged Truman to prevent the communizatation of Czechoslovakia by ordering the liberation of Prague.[22]

But continuing Roosevelt's military policy, Truman refused to liberate the German or Czech capital. He later explained that although he would have liked to see the lines extended as far east as possible he could not reverse the zonal arrangement Roosevelt had agreed to, and he was preoccupied with deploying troops to Asia. Moreover, American commanders did not desire a change in strategy. General Bradley calculated that capturing Berlin would cost 100,000 casualties, and Eisenhower and his staff felt that military interest dictated cooperation with the Red Army. Murphy later observed that the desire for this policy was so strong that during his first months in office Truman "could hardly have reversed Roosevelt's policy even if he desired." British plans again elicited caustic remarks from Americans such as Admiral King who complained that Churchill was "fudging" his commitments.[23]

Soviet actions then caused Churchill to become more alarmed. Stalin's reply to the Churchill-Truman message of 15 April rejected the Western interpretation of the Yalta accords. The Soviet foreign minister admitted early in May that the Red Army had arrested fifteen non-Communist Polish politicians for alleged anti-Soviet activities. Such behavior suggested to Churchill that a more forceful approach was needed. He informed Eden that nothing could "save us from the great catastrophe but a meeting and showdown." The only way to gain concessions from the Kremlin was to threaten Stalin at the conference table, saying that if Moscow failed to honor its agreements, the Western armies—now at their peak of strength in Europe—would not withdraw into their own zones. On 6 May Churchill proposed to Truman an immediate Big Three conference, urging that the two nations consider their attitudes toward the Soviets and "show them how much we have to offer or withhold."[24]

III

Three days later Truman accepted Churchill's proposal. Then for the first time, the new president began to evaluate policy toward Britain and the Soviet Union.

Now that the war was ending in Europe, there were many Anglo-American issues that had to be confronted by the new administration. Military men discussed an expanding role for British forces in the Pacific, but nonmilitary issues were more important. The United States wanted a final agreement satisfying its desire for preferential trading rights in British colonies, and as Allied armies liberated former possessions, Americans renewed their interest in ending imperialism, demanding the decolonization of the British Empire. Great Britain wanted a reconstruction loan or gift, and their officials would soon be knocking at the door of the U.S. Treasury. On the horizon loomed another question of potentially catastrophic proportions—the international control of atomic energy.

But in May 1945 Truman's most immediate concern was the postwar aims of the two allies, including Britain's designs for the Continent. Like most Americans, Truman held the common biases against Great Britain—the distaste for empire, imperialism, and old-world diplomacy—and had suspicions that Churchill would attempt to use American power to secure British goals in Europe, the Mediterranean, and the Middle East. During his first day in office, Truman had received an assessment from the State Department emphasizing that Great Britain desired security, was deeply conscious of its declining power in the Big Three, hoped to exert leadership over Western Europe, and wanted to maintain close contact with the Commonwealth. The department received a report later from Lauchlin Currie, Roosevelt's special assistant who had held interviews in March with Eden, Richard Law, and Ronald Nigel of the Foreign Office. Currie described the creation of a West European bloc as one of the "leading controversial, though undercover, issues in British government circles." He said that Britain had a scheme to take the lead in forming an alliance with Scandinavia, the Low Countries, and France. Such a policy and, more important, Churchill's pleas to keep U.S. troops on the Continent also concerned other officials. Leahy suspected that the prime minister wanted to use the American army to sustain Britain's position in Europe. Stimson was apprehensive, and during the Anglo-Yugoslavian conflict over the occupation of Trieste he feared that Great Britain—by accident or design—might drag the United States into war against Belgrade and Moscow.[25]

The administration also examined policy toward Russia. Like his predecessor, Truman was irritated with Soviet behavior. The Missourian prided himself on honesty and was frustrated by Stalin's refusal to install coalition governments in Eastern Europe. On 14 May he discussed this situation with Leahy, Grew, and Halifax, referring bitterly to Russia's failure to implement the Yalta accords. Truman also realized that Americans were becoming pessimistic about relations with the U.S.S.R. In May opinion polls revealed that more Americans doubted the Kremlin's willingness to cooperate than at any time since March 1942.[26]

It was time to reevaluate policy. During his first three weeks in office, Truman had continued Roosevelt's last approach, collaborating with Britain to form a democratic front against the Russians. But what had been gained? Joint messages to Stalin and straight talk to Molotov had not produced cooperation, had not induced Moscow leaders to accept Western aims. On the contrary, British tactics had failed and perhaps had even heightened Soviet obstinacy.

Thus, in mid-May Truman began to consider another approach toward the U.S.S.R. He realized that there were two American assets that might influence the Russians—money and bombs.

As early as 1943 the Soviets had shown interest in aid for reconstruction. Molotov handed Harriman the first request for $6 billion in assistance in January 1945, and Harriman later informed Washington that Russia placed profound importance on a large postwar credit. Harriman, William L. Clayton, and others thought the loan should be used as a "concrete bargaining lever" and advised Truman to accept this approach. During May the president apparently arrived at the same conclusion.[27]

Meanwhile, on 25 April, Secretary of War Stimson met Truman and told him of "the most terrible weapon ever known in human history"—the atomic bomb. The administrator of the Manhattan Project, Gen. Leslie R. Groves, participated in the discussion, which soon shifted from military to diplomatic implications of the new weapon, especially the effect it could have on the Soviet Union. Three weeks later Stimson concluded that the bomb could be used as a "way of persuading Russia to play ball." Truman accepted this idea. On 6 May when Churchill urged convening the Big Three meeting immediately, Truman stalled. The bomb was scheduled for testing in mid-July, and Truman informed Churchill that he could not attend the conference until then because of the budget. The "budget," the president told Davies, actually meant "atomic bomb experiments" being held in a western state.[28]

In mid-May the realization that America might be able to use atomic and economic power to influence the Russians, the unsuccessful results of Anglo-American diplomatic efforts, and apprehension about Britain's designs for the Continent all convinced Truman to change policy toward the Allies. He must act independently toward the European powers, for he now felt, as he told Davies, that both Stalin and Churchill were "trying to make me the paw for the cat that pulled the chestnuts out of the fire." But it was too early for the novice to initiate his own approach. As late as 26 May he was still finding it difficult to believe he was chief executive, commenting to his staff about "how funny things work out"; "I'm the one American who didn't expect to be President." Truman's course was to resurrect Roosevelt's earlier policy—America would mediate between Britain and Russia and would again deal independently with Stalin.[29]

This plan became apparent in mid-May during a round of exchanges between Churchill and Truman. In four days the prime minister sent six messages, beginning 11 May when he urged that both Western leaders should meet in London before their rendezvous with Stalin at Potsdam. He proposed that the next tactic should be to keep troops in the Soviet zone of Germany "until we are satisfied about Poland" and suggested offering the Russians free transit out of the Black Sea and the Baltic in exchange for evacuating Eastern Europe. The president's response was brief: he simply informed Churchill that he did not favor a preliminary meeting in London. After collaborating with the British for a month, Truman now desired to avoid arousing Soviet suspicions that the West was "ganging up" on Russia. Churchill sent two messages on 12 May stating profound concern about the Kremlin's behavior. He proposed a joint message to Stalin concerning the Red Army's refusal to allow Western representatives into Vienna and suggested that American troops in Europe not be sent to the Pacific until a satisfactory peace was secured on the Continent. In a now historic cable, he declared that the Russians had lowered an iron curtain across the center of Europe. Here for the first time Churchill used the term that he would announce to the world ten months later at Fulton, Missouri. (The phrase, incidentally, was not created by Churchill; Joseph Goebbels, the Nazi propaganda chief, had used it during the last weeks of the war in a futile attempt to convince the Western allies to side with Germany against Bolshevik Russia.) Churchill thought his message portentous, writing that "of all the public documents I have written on this issue I would rather be judged by this." At the time, however, Truman, unimpressed, merely thanked him for his estimate of the situation and said it was impossible to forecast the future of Europe.[30]

The mediating policy appeared again on 19 May when Truman suggested to Stalin that Hopkins talk to him in Moscow. While the British had been advised of previous proposals to the Russian leader, this time the president did not tell them until the Kremlin had accepted; then on 22 May he asked if Davies could confer in London. Along with Leahy, Marshall, and Stettinius, Truman needed information about Stalin and Churchill, wanted to revive an independent approach toward Russia, and sought cooperation among the Big Three. He was forming his idea of a just postwar settlement; employing an awkward phrase, he felt that the world must rest on a "balanced tripod of power." Harmony demanded confidence and trust. America could not appease Russian demands contrary to those of the West and especially to Britain's interest in Europe, nor could it gang up with London against Moscow. Hopkins was to inform Stalin of the policy change and of Truman's eagerness for a fair understanding. Truman told Hopkins to pound this message into Stalin's head by the most appropriate means—diplomatic language or a baseball bat.[31]

Hopkins's mission, lasting from 26 May to 6 June, produced encouraging results. Six conversations with Stalin concerned the forthcoming tripartite meeting, the future of Germany, and the government of Poland. By 1 June Hopkins had apparently succeeded in gaining what British tactics had failed to accomplish: the Russian leader agreed to invite non-Lublin Poles to Moscow for consultation and possible inclusion in a Warsaw cabinet. After months of obstinacy, Soviet policy seemed to be shifting. Perhaps Hopkins, who symbolized the era of wartime cooperation, had convinced the Russians that their security would not be jeopardized by a handful of non-Communists in Warsaw. After all, the Kremlin had no intention of withdrawing the Red Army. Another possible reason was that for the first time since mid-March the Soviets did not face an Anglo-American front. Stalin might well have thought that agreeing to Hopkins's terms might encourage future unilateral American actions. Truman's interest in mediating was to Russia's advantage because without the support of the United States there was little probability that the British would obtain their goals on the Continent. Stalin told Hopkins during a dinner at the Kremlin that Churchill was the culprit who had misled the Americans, and that Britain desired to dominate Poland. Hopkins seems to have accepted part of the argument, later informing colleagues that "Uncle Joe's" concessions discredited the prime minister's warnings about Soviet intentions.

Hopkins was very pleased that the Russian leader had accepted his list of non-Lublin Poles and on 1 June cabled the president: "I believe that this is a satisfactory list and I urge that you approve it, if you do, then the correct time is Now!" Truman informed Churchill of the breakthrough, adding that it "represents a very encouraging positive step." On his return from Moscow, Hopkins stopped at Eisenhower's headquarters in Frankfurt, full of enthusiasm. He informed the staff, "We can do business with Stalin! He will cooperate!"[32]

Relations with Moscow remained cordial in June, strengthening the hopes and desires of administration officials that they could deal independently with the Soviets and obtain a just peace at Potsdam. In Germany, where the victors were preparing for the conference and setting up an Allied control commission, the Americans were impressed with the cooperation of the Red Army. Agreements were quickly made concerning food, currency, and transport. Murphy felt the Soviets were anxious to collaborate in Germany. The situation in Poland seemed promising as on 21 June Poles from all the principal parties established a provisional government. Stanislaw Mikolajczyk, leader of the London Poles, was appointed minister of agriculture and deputy prime minister. Harriman sensed a warmer climate in Moscow after the Hopkins visit, writing Truman on 9 June that "since Harry's departure I find Soviet officials and senior army officials less constrained than they have been in recent months and much more cordial." About this time Stalin personally gave Harriman, a polo player, and his daughter two well-trained Red Army cavalry horses.[33]

The British did not share American enthusiasm. Whitehall officials complained privately that Hopkins's mission demonstrated that the United States would be content with "papering over the cracks" in the alliance, not forcing the Soviets to live up to their agreements. The British felt that Stalin's conciliation over Poland was a temporary maneuver; the Russians now would conclude that America was less willing than Britain to take a stand, and that they could drive a wedge between the democracies simply by making their usual lavish promises. Clark Kerr felt that closer Soviet-American relations would leave Britain with a diminished role in the Big Three, and Churchill admitted to Truman that Stalin seemed conciliatory but the Russian's actions were no more than a "milestone in a long hill we ought never to have been asked to climb."[34]

Feeling that difficulties with Churchill were "very nearly as exasperating as they are with the Russians," Truman meanwhile had decided to send Davies to London. Davies had been ambassador to the Soviet Union in the late 1930s and was a known Russian sympathizer. In his *Mission to Moscow* he had described the Soviet government as a system of state socialism operating on capitalistic principles and Stalin as such a kind and gentle man that a child would like to sit on his lap and a dog would sidle up to him. During a heated debate at the Potsdam conference Davies later showed his strange faith in the Russian when he sent Truman a note that said, "I think Stalin's feelings are hurt, please be nice to him." The Kremlin recognized Davies's work on behalf of Soviet-American relations by awarding him the Order of Lenin. Thus, he was hardly the man to give an unbiased evaluation of Churchill's attitude toward the Russians, especially since the British disliked him, feeling that he was an appeaser. As Davies recorded in his diary, Truman "particularly wanted me to go to London because I was known to be a friend of Stalin's, and Hopkins to go to Moscow because he was known to be a friend of Churchill's. That would keep the balance and the record straight." Truman instructed Davies on 22 May to explore the situation with Churchill and Eden and if possible to obtain their approval for a Stalin–Truman meeting before the Big Three conference at Potsdam, so that the two leaders could size each other up. Davies was to make sure the prime minister understood that there could be no question of any "double-crossing" in relations among the Allies.[35]

Davies arrived in London on 26 May and was driven out to the prime minister's country home at Chequers where Churchill greeted him warmly. The first and most important conversation began that night at 11:00 P.M. with a colorful and moving statement by the host. Brandy snifter in hand, Churchill recapitulated the dismal political situation in Europe, summarizing with a denunciation of Russia. He began to ramble, attacking de Gaulle, Tito's failure to appreciate British generosity in rescuing Yugoslavia, and unconditional surrender, asserting that he could have made peace with Hitler. Working himself into a frenzy, he wailed that American armies must not evacuate the Continent, that they must be used for "trading purposes," that if they were deployed to

Asia, Europe would be left to the mercy of the Red Army. Davies broke in, stating that he was "immeasurably shocked." He felt that he was "listening to Goebbels, Goering, and Hitler" and asked if the prime minister was willing to proclaim that Britain had bet on the wrong horse—whether the British had not "made a mistake in not joining up with Hitler to establish a joint rule over Europe and the Seven Seas, and save the Western Civilization from the 'Bear.'" Churchill cooled, and shifting the conversation to the Truman administration's desire for Allied unity, Davies introduced the president's plan to meet alone with Stalin before the Big Three sessions. At first Churchill seemed to agree, but after more consideration he became agitated and "blew off," intimating that Truman wanted a meeting behind his back. Davies retorted that such a statement insulted the president of the United States and that, if Churchill was serious, Davies would have to leave. Churchill apologized, admitting that he had spoken heatedly, but he would not agree to any meeting in which Britain was not represented. Davies then began a discourse on the Soviet Union. He described how Russia had fought gallantly and suffered tremendously during the war, how suspiciously the Soviets had always regarded the West since their country was an island surrounded by capitalist enemies, how sincerely the Kremlin's leaders desired peace as long as it did not jeopardize security. Churchill listened, and the conversation became friendly, lasting into the early morning hours. At 4:30 A.M. he escorted Davies to his bedroom and offered goodnight to a "great American envoy." Touched, Davies responded, "Goodnight to you, Sir, the greatest Englishman of all times, who lived what Shakespeare dreamed, and who translated into deeds what England's greatest had taught."[36]

Davies and Churchill held two more conversations, and on both occasions the prime minister vehemently attacked the Russians.

Davies's report described Churchill as nervous, agitated, bitter. Since autumn 1944 the prime minister's anxiety had increased over Europe's future, but in late May he seemed uncharacteristically impulsive for a man who had led his country through five perilous years of war. Burdened with the duties of the prime ministry and the ministry of defense, Churchill was tired. Eden had told Harvey as early as March 1944 that it was doubtful that the prime minister would live through the rest of the year. Lord Moran, his physician, later wrote that the end of the war found him spent; by the time of the Potsdam conference, the seventy-year-old leader was "sliding almost imperceptibly into old age." Ambassador Winant told Truman that Churchill appeared overworked. An election approached; possibly Churchill's anti-Communist pronouncements were intended to gain the independent votes he needed to retain control of the government. But the collapse of the Axis made a Tory victory probable, and in any case, political expediency fails to explain why he made such statements in private conversations with Davies. Perhaps a contributing factor was a special aspect of Churchill's personality. The prime minister suffered from recurrent and prolonged episodes of depression; in psychological terms he has been described as a depressive personality. This melancholia had appeared in five of the last seven dukes of Marlborough, and it had been markedly present in the first duke and in Churchill's father. Moran was aware of the condition, which was such a familiar companion that Churchill himself had given it the nickname of Black Dog. This type of depression can make an individual irritable, despondent, fatigued, and perhaps the prime minister was suffering from the malady during Davies's visit.[37]

Whatever the case, Davies's report on Churchill and, more important, Hopkins's success in Moscow strengthened Truman's desire to mediate between the Allies. After receiving the good news about Poland, the president turned to Secretary of the Treasury Henry Morgenthau, Jr., and said, "I just finished talking to Harry Hopkins, and I am the happiest man in the world over what I have been able to accomplish." Now Truman felt that he could secure concessions from the Russians—without the help of the British and without the risk of being used by the wily Churchill. Furthermore, the Davies mission had supported apprehensions held by the president, Leahy, and the newly designated secretary of state, James F.

Byrnes, that the prime minister's primary aim was to obtain British goals on the Continent, not to secure a lasting peace. Truman's feelings were revealed on 13 June at a breakfast conversation on postwar Pacific issues at the White House. When Hopkins commented that it was vital that the president announce his intent to cooperate with Britain, Leahy interjected: "Why the British? As a matter of fact, our relations with Russia are much more important." Davies agreed. Truman settled the matter by stating that he would make clear that he was not in "cahoots" with either one—that it was necessary for all three Allies to cooperate to have peace.[38]

IV

The British continued their attempts to influence the United States before the Big Three conference. Churchill urged that before a postwar settlement American troops in Europe should remain as far east as possible; the sooner they went home, the sooner they would have to return. He informed Truman again on 4 June of misgivings about the retreat into zones, repeating that this retreat would bring Soviet power into the "heart of Western Europe and the descent of an iron curtain between us and everything to the eastward." The British were concerned about American plans to redeploy U.S. forces to Asia and during a dinner conversation in late June Alexander asked Ambassador Kirk if the administration could be persuaded to retain troops on the Continent. London desired a common policy concerning the satellite peace treaties—Finland, Bulgaria, Rumania, and Hungary. After the Polish cabinet was formed, Whitehall officials argued that both democracies should withhold recognition until it declared its intent to hold a free election. In early July Halifax reminded Truman that when the Anglo-Americans said the same thing to the Russians, they got the "right answer from Moscow."[39]

The British succeeded on two issues. For months they had been urging American involvement in Yugoslavia. In early May, Tito's troops occupied the disputed territory of Italy, Venezia Giulia, and some Austrian territory without Allied permission. As Truman informed Churchill on 12 May territorial issues were going to be settled by orderly process at the conference table, not by "uncontrolled land-grabbing." On 15 May both governments presented identical notes to Tito demanding withdrawal. Truman told Grew that the United States should "throw them out." This solution occurred to Churchill, too, and on 2 June he suggested to Truman that a military operation against the interlopers would be "sharp and short." Truman did not desire bloodshed in the Balkans but agreed to repeat the joint demand for withdrawal. It proved sufficient, and the Yugoslavs evacuated in mid-June.[40]

Meanwhile British concern mounted about the situation in Austria, occupied by the Red Army since spring. Unlike Germany, Austria had not been divided into zones, and the Russian commander soon became uncooperative, limiting the rights of the British and American missions. Churchill wrote Truman on 12 May that the exclusion of Anglo-American representatives from Vienna was unacceptable and sent the draft of a joint message for Stalin. A month later he told Truman that Western forces should not withdraw from their advanced positions until the Soviets respected their agreements. Truman's reply that arrangements should continue to be made by local commanders was unsatisfactory to the British and painful to Churchill who recorded that it "struck a knell" in his breast. He urged that occupation of zones, establishment of an Allied control commission, and creation of Western garrisons all take place simultaneously in Germany and Austria. Truman was more receptive to this plan; it appealed to his sense of fair play and compromise, and he incorporated it almost verbatim in a message to Stalin.[41] The Russians accepted, and zonal positions were occupied on 1 July in both Germany and Austria.

But British overtures generally were rejected, and the Truman administration continued its independent course. Stettinius announced on 28 May that the primary objective was to continue and strengthen collaboration with the Soviet Union. In June Truman rebuffed Churchill's warning to keep the armies as far to the east as possible, did not respond to pleas to retain troops in Europe, and continued redeployment. Washington refused to resume relations with German satellites, and the president told Stalin that he desired to discuss the situation at Potsdam. Americans broke an understanding with the British on Poland by establishing telegraphic communication with the Warsaw regime, and they neglected Churchill's plea to withhold recognition.[42] On 5 July both Britain and America recognized the new Polish government.

Other American actions raised British resentment. Churchill received Truman's proposal to talk with Stalin before the Big Three meeting with justified indignation. As the ally at war with Germany the longest, the British felt they should be represented at all sessions of the peace conference. The president refused to visit London before Potsdam but said he intended to stop in Paris; Whitehall considered this symbolic gesture to France, a nation that had capitulated to the Third Reich, insulting. (Truman later recognized the validity of Churchill's complaint and did not visit the French capital.) Other actions perturbed the prime minister—Truman's refusal to allow Hopkins to stop in London after the talks with Stalin, cutbacks in lend-lease supplies, America's hurried recognition of the provisional government of Poland. Britons considered the redeployment of American troops shortsighted and irresponsible, and Churchill noted his apprehensions and helplessness in a minute to the Foreign Office: "It is beyond the power of this country to prevent all sorts of things crashing at the present time. The responsibility lies with the United States and my desire it is to give them all the support in our power. If they do not feel able to do anything, then we must let matters take their course—indeed that is what they are doing."[43]

As America became less cooperative, Britain again became interested in establishing a West European bloc. Roberts had written the Foreign Office late in April that, because the Kremlin was dominating and organizing Eastern Europe, Britain should "ensure that our half of Europe remained the stronger half." By V-E Day the bloc was against Russia, and some influential Britons wanted to include Germany. The proposed functions of the bloc were numerous, foreshadowing the North Atlantic Treaty Organization and Common Market. Whitehall considered a common foreign, military, and economic policy with Belgium, the Netherlands, Denmark, and France. Under British leadership those countries would have a combined chiefs of staff, a customs union with a common currency, and boards to manage raw materials, production, and transport.[44]

Interestingly, many American officials disliked Truman's policy. Grew had agreed with the British earlier that America and Britain must develop a more unyielding approach toward the Kremlin. As he informed the president, Socialists and Communists were arguing that the United States and Britain could no longer oppose the Soviet Union in Europe. Along with Kennan and Deane, Grew felt that Washington and London should work in cooperation since the Russians "feared more than anything else the prospect of confronting a united West." Harriman agreed and still shared Churchill's pessimism over Poland. The prime minister, he said, "labored under no illusions."[45]

The American ambassadors, ministers, and other representatives in many other European nations, especially in areas controlled by the Red Army, disapproved of an independent, conciliatory approach. These men's constant contact with their British and Russian counterparts had convinced them that, while Anglo-American aims were almost identical, the Kremlin's interpretation of the Yalta accords clashed with that of the democracies. They cooperated closely with the British, and representatives from both countries concluded that collaboration was the most productive way to obtain Western aims. The U.S. representative in Bulgaria, Maynard B. Barnes, had reported in March that he and his military adviser approved a British plan for joint policy toward the local Allied control commission. Barnes called for stronger policy and by late May was reporting that the Communists were conducting a bloodbath, purging some twenty thousand people. Patterson in Yugoslavia felt that the Yalta agreements could be saved only by a staunch Anglo-American policy and reported in mid-May that Communists were arresting anyone

seen with an Englishman or American. The representative in
Hungary, H. F. Arthur Schoenfeld, complained about Russian designs to institute a dictatorship and on 16 June called
for action. A month earlier the British had urged a joint policy in Hungary, but the appeal received no response from
Washington. The Foreign Office was giving up on Hungary,
and Schoenfeld reported that without a joint effort there was
no hope of securing Anglo-American representation on the
Hungarian control commission. The chief of the Allied commission in Italy, Rear Adm. Ellery W. Stone, reported that,
unless Italy received help and guidance from the United
States and Britain—and five divisions of troops—it would become a Communist police state. On 5 May the director of the
Office of Strategic Services, William O. Donovan, sent Truman a memorandum based on information received from
agents in Europe. Sounding an alarm similar to that from
Britain, Donovan stated that after victory the United States
would be confronted with a dangerous situation since Russia
would be strong enough to dominate Europe and establish
hegemony over Asia. The Soviets would like to avoid war for
ten to fifteen years, and during this time the administration
should assert its rights in Europe, seek to avoid conflicts, and
support the democratic and economic development of Western Europe. These nations, in cooperation with Britain,
would serve as a bulwark against Soviet expansion, and they
must be supported because it was "better to fight abroad"
than to "fall back on our hemisphere defense."[46]

   Such foreboding reports would have more effect on the
administration in early 1946, but after the Hopkins mission
and before Potsdam, the president and his closest advisers
believed, or at least hoped, that they could mediate a peace
for the Continent. Soviet actions in Eastern Europe angered
Truman, but he tended to delay decisions until the tripartite
meeting and had no intention of reverting to the Anglo-
American stand of some weeks before. It now was of vital
importance, Hopkins commented, that Americans not be
maneuvered into a position where Britain had them lined up
against the U.S.S.R. Byrnes felt that the United States should
make every effort to preserve Allied unity and to maintain

Stalin's trust. Truman was not ready to listen to those diplomats who advocated cooperation with Britain, and he did not
invite them to Potsdam. His feelings appeared on 7 June in
his press secretary's diary: "The President made the comment
that when you deal with the striped pants boys, you have to be
careful—referring to the diplomats."[47]

V

At the Cecilienhof, the Potsdam estate of the last Hohenzol-
lern crown prince, the Big Three held their last wartime
meeting. From 17 July to 2 August, the Allied leaders discussed the future of Germany, reparations, Poland's borders,
the governments of Eastern Europe, and the defeat of Japan.

The British and Americans had considered the sort of policy each would initiate at the conference. Halifax had informed Churchill that the Americans were still suspicious
about British support of right-wing governments in Europe,
would represent themselves as the mediator between London
and Moscow, and would try to promote cooperation. The
Truman administration, he warned, would not be receptive to
warnings about the spread of communism. The Americans in
turn had some idea of what to expect from Britain. According
to State Department briefing papers, Churchill would give
the impression that he was the spokesman not only for Great
Britain but for the entire Commonwealth. He tended to in-
flate his position and offended the Dominions by "forgetting
that the British Empire had changed since Kipling's day."
The British would urge American support to blunt Soviet
designs while attempting a regional arrangement with West
Europe.[48]

In the first meeting with Truman the prime minister got
right to the point: "Were all these States which had passed
into Russian control to be free and independent or not?"

No, the president did not want Soviet satellites in Eastern
Europe, but he was not going to be pressured by Churchill
into adopting an anti-Russian front. Potsdam was Truman's
first meeting with Stalin, and he wanted to demonstrate that
under his leadership the United States could mediate between

the European allies and bring about a fair and lasting peace. Thus, the president decided to talk privately with the Russian leader, and during a dinner party on 21 July he approached Stalin and gave him an earful, saying that he was on the level, that he had no hostile purpose, that Americans wanted nothing but "security and peace with friendship and neighborliness in a free world." Afterward, he strolled over to Davies and said, "I spread it on thick, and I think he believed me. I meant every word of it."[49]

But Truman's approach failed, for as the British had warned, the position of the Allied armies determined the outcome of the issues. Over Churchill's protest, Polish borders were moved to the line of the Oder and western Neisse. When the president proposed internationalization of the Danube, a plan the British had suggested to the Americans as early as October 1944, Stalin vetoed it. The situation in Rumania, Bulgaria, Hungary, and Finland was discussed, and the Soviets proclaimed that these former German allies were democratic and fulfilled the requirement of the Yalta declaration on liberated areas. The Big Three issued a call for Japan's surrender and established the Council of Foreign Ministers to complete the task of peacemaking.

Some American officials had hoped that the United States could use the atomic bomb and offers of reconstruction aid to gain concessions from Stalin. News of the explosion of an atomic device near Los Alamos, New Mexico, elated Truman and his advisers. Stimson recorded that the president was "tremendously pepped up" and now had an "entirely new feeling of confidence," and indeed Truman's approach stiffened in later negotiations. The issue of the postwar loan, however, was not discussed at Potsdam, and by the end of the conference it appeared that neither the atomic nor economic lever would pry the Russians out of Eastern Europe.[50]

The British had other ideas about the bomb. Churchill was overjoyed; Brooke, who was not impressed with the weapon, remarked scornfully in his diary that the prime minister let himself be "carried away by the very first and rather scanty reports of the first atomic explosion. He was already seeing himself capable of eliminating all the Russian centres of industry and population. . . . He at once painted a wonderful picture of himself as the sole possessor of these bombs and capable of dumping them where he wished, thus all-powerful and capable of dictating to Stalin!" Stimson saw Churchill's elation and felt that he was inclined to use it in negotiation. Foreign Office officials were more realistic, hoping that, since the bomb was a joint project, it would jolt the United States out of isolationism for good and would improve Anglo-American relations. But at Potsdam the bomb had no effect on British diplomacy; Churchill's enthusiasm could not be transformed into action.[51]

The Americans left Potsdam with mixed emotions about future relations with the Allies. By the end of the conference some American officials were discouraged by Soviet obstinacy and determined not to share control of Japan or atomic secrets with the Kremlin. After a frustrating session on 1 August, Leahy complained in the presidential limousine that the Russians could not be trusted and that "Stalin was a liar and a crook." Byrnes was not so sure, feeling that the Soviets were hard bargainers but that the negotiations had established a basis for "maintaining our war-born unity." Truman was disappointed that Stalin had not been more agreeable. Asked on the voyage home what he thought of the Russian leader the president responded with salty language, "I think he's a son of a bitch," and continued with a smile, "I guess he thinks I'm one too." After returning to Washington he seemed more optimistic. He told his White House staff he was impressed with Stalin, a man who could be depended on. During the conference, the Labourites had ousted Churchill's cabinet and Truman seemed pleased with Britain's new government. He wrote his mother, "It is too bad about Churchill but it may turn out to be all right for the world." He hoped for more cooperation with the new prime minister, Clement Attlee. The president, however, had formed a low opinion of an individual who would be so important in future Anglo-American relations, the new foreign secretary, Ernest Bevin. Truman compared Bevin with John L. Lewis, labeling him "crude and uncouth." Stalin and Molotov might be rough men but they knew common courtesies, whereas the new foreign secretary lacked all of them. Bevin, he said, was a boor.[52]

VI

During May 1945 Truman reversed Roosevelt's last policy toward Russia—joining the British and confronting the Kremlin—and rejuvenated the independent wartime approach. This change resulted from the apparent failure of the joint policy to secure a democratic Poland, apprehension about British designs in Europe, and the president's hope that American atomic and economic power would gain concessions from Stalin.

The reversal distressed the British; they felt that this plan was the same one that had produced idealistic declarations but few tangible results at Yalta. Considering that the long-range goals of the Western democracies were almost identical, they felt that American mediation between Britain and Russia was "heresy." Sargent noted in a Foreign Office minute that the United States would neither be dragged into a quarrel between London and Moscow nor allow the British government to dictate America's policy for Europe, but would assume the role of an independent mediator, "tough to both the Soviet Union and Great Britain until both became reasonable and cooperative." Clark Kerr stated that the "renewed American-Soviet flirtation" meant that the administration was hoping to reestablish a relationship with Moscow that would avert the dangers of an Anglo-American bloc.[53]

British ideas on how to deal with Russia did not change after the defeat of Germany; Balfour wrote that "every ounce of Anglo-American cooperation will be needed if the Bear is brought to a halt."[54]

The administration disagreed. Like Roosevelt at Yalta, Truman went to Potsdam hoping to deal independently with Stalin and to mediate a compromise peace. Although he and his advisers left the conference with mixed feelings, they were not prepared to alter policy. They would hope, wait, and see.

Chapter 4

Lepidus and the Lumbering Giant
Britain and the Origins of a New American Policy

Suddenly, the war was over. The new atomic weapon devastated the enemy in the Pacific, and in early September 1945 Japan surrendered.

Now the victors were confronted with peacemaking on two continents, and the Big Three debated many issues in the half-year following V-J Day. Yugoslavia's borders, Japan's administration, peace treaties with and recognition of Germany's former allies, reparations, Eastern European elections, atomic energy, and the occupation of Germany, Austria, Korea, and Iran—all were discussed at the London and Moscow meetings and at the conference of the United Nations Organization.

During the meeting at Potsdam a new Labour government came to power in Britain, but they did not change British policy toward the Allies. In the nine months following that conference, American policy did change. At first, concerned with domestic problems, the Truman administration let foreign affairs drift, resulting in an unsure and ill-defined policy during the remainder of 1945. There remained a hope—not a policy—of cooperating and compromising with Moscow while mediating between the European allies. Not until early 1946, after becoming frustrated and alarmed by Soviet actions, did American officials begin to form long-range ideas for the postwar era. British leaders then provoked the United States, especially in the United Nations and at Fulton, Missouri, and accelerated the administration's adoption of an Anglo-American partnership.

I

Clement Attlee was Britain's new prime minister. In contrast to his flamboyant predecessor, he was more comfortable

81

working in the background with cabinet committees than making public speeches. He enjoyed the administrative chores of government, once saying that "the job of a prime minister is to lead and coordinate a team, not to seek to be an omnipotent minister."[1] Personal diplomacy almost ended between the prime minister and the president, except for the atomic-energy conference of November 1945 in Washington. From 1945 to 1947 Attlee wrote a handful of messages to Truman, and not one concerned policy toward Russia.

Attlee left foreign policy to Ernest Bevin, a man of impeccably lower-class background. The illegitimate son of a farm laborer, he was born in 1881. His father died a few months before his birth, and his mother, the village midwife, died when he was six years old. He grew up with a married sister in rural Devon, leaving school at the age of eleven to work in the fields. Two years later he was doing odd jobs in Bristol, and when work was hard to find, he pilfered an occasional loaf of bread. During these lean years Bevin began what proved to be a lifelong affiliation with the nascent trade-union movement. In 1910, after six years of organization, he became the first secretary of the Dockers Union. In 1915 the Trades Union Congress elected him as their representative to the American Federation of Labor convention in San Francisco. After the First World War Bevin moved to London where he served as a mediator for the great railroad strike of 1919, and the next year delivered his famous eleven-hour speech before the Shaw commission which resulted in the standard minimum wage for the dockers. During 1920 he helped to organize about twenty unions into the Transport and General Workers' Union (TGWU), which by the late 1940s had become the world's largest union. He meanwhile had assumed the post of general secretary of the TGWU and by 1937 reached the summit of the labor movement by being elected chairman of the Trades Union Congress.

In May 1940 Bevin accepted the post of minister of labor and national service in Churchill's war government. When the Labour party won the elections in 1945, although he desired to become chancellor of the exchequer, he accepted the foreign secretary's portfolio. Bevin wielded great influence with

Attlee. Once the prime minister summoned him and Patrick Gordon Walker, the Commonwealth secretary, who arrived first. The prime minister said he wanted to take a strong line against a Commonwealth policy urged by the United States. Bevin then arrived. Slumping into a chair he immediately stated: "Clem, we must stand by America in this." Without discussion, Attlee agreed. The prime minister later remarked that because of Bevin's "genius for organisation and his confidence in his own strength, he did not fear—he embraced—power. . . . If he agreed that power corrupts, he would have said that it corrupted only the men not big enough to use it. And power was given to Ernest."[2]

Bevin proved an engaging if unusual figure in the Foreign Office. His 240 pounds included a large belly and wide shoulders; he had a broad face and a flat nose. His voice was harsh, heavily inflected with a Devonshire accent. He was blunt and at times rude. His cabinet colleague Aneurin Bevan commented that Bevin would make a good diplomat because he never finished a sentence. The new foreign secretary did not care for theater or sporting events, preferring an evening reminiscing with trade-union cronies over a whiskey and soda, and he lunched at his desk, with a sandwich and beer. The *Observer* rightly labeled him the first British statesman born a working man who remained one. But Bevin's personality transcended class. Churchill and Eden praised him. The professionals at Whitehall, whom he called his "trade union," held their boss in unparalleled respect. After forty years of diplomatic service Paul Gore-Booth noted that no secretary engaged the loyalty and affection of the whole diplomatic service as did Bevin, an imaginative leader with "tremendous force, tremendous courage." Frank K. Roberts went even further—Bevin was as great as Churchill.[3]

But other factors besides courage determined Britain's postwar foreign policy. The country was in economic crisis, a legacy of the Second World War. Bombing had destroyed or damaged four million houses and thousands of factories. Torpedoes had cut merchant shipping in half and exports in 1945 were less than a third of the 1938 depression figures. To finance the war Englishmen sold $5,000,000,000 worth of overseas investments, cutting the income from this source to less than half the prewar amount. As national income declined, external debt accumulated, reaching a figure in 1945 of nearly $12,000,000,000. The war's total cost was an appalling $30,000,000,000—a fourth of Britain's wealth. After six years of war, there was an enormous popular desire to turn to domestic problems. In a poll of May 1945 a vast majority of the British people demonstrated that they had tired of international affairs and wanted the government to address such internal issues as housing and employment before June elections. "Let us face the future" was Labour's campaign slogan, and by autumn the party had initiated a program of economic and social reform. The government began to demobilize the armed forces, to reconvert forty-five thousand factories to peacetime operation, and to start the awesome job of reconstruction.[4]

These domestic factors contributed to the decline of Britain's international importance in the postwar era. It had been obvious for some time that Britain was becoming a secondary power. Churchill sadly watched his influence dwindle during the last year of the war, noting that Britain had supplied only a quarter of the forces invading Germany from the west and had no chance to regain naval equality with the United States. Of course the world saw this decline; in August 1945 only 5 percent of those polled in the United States, Canada, France, Denmark, and Australia felt that Britain would be the most influential member of the Big Three in the future. When Orme Sargent received the result of the poll, he succinctly defined his nation's position vis-à-vis Russia and America— Britain was "Lepidus in the triumvirate with Mark Antony and Augustus."[5]

Whitehall would have to rely on the strength and support of the United States, but without any pretense of an equal relationship. After a century at the pinnacle of world power the British had to swallow their pride and attempt to become America's "junior partner." The prospect, although unattractive to Whitehall officials, at least meant that the Western democracies had ideals and goals different from the Soviet Union's.

During the winter of 1945–1946 British diplomats gloomily discussed their new status and future policy. A member of the North American Department, Berkeley E. F. Gage, wrote: "We need not be discontented with the American conception of our role as a 'junior partner' . . . as long as we can continue to influence our senior." Britain's task was to encourage America "to shoulder the burden of wider responsibility— even if this means pocketing our 'ego' to some extent in areas where we have hitherto considered our interest to be paramount." Halifax wrote the Foreign Office in December that it "should be a major task for His Majesty's Government to encourage America to shoulder the burden of wider responsibilities that is now hers." According to the Foreign Office, the United States was a lumbering giant, a powerful nation but a novice in foreign affairs, lacking leadership, aimlessly wandering down international paths. Whitehall must guide this colossus by demonstrating sound leadership, emphasizing common diplomatic aims, urging consultation on policy toward Russia, and reminding Washington that American power partly depended on the resources and strategic location of the Commonwealth. Donnelly of the North American Department wrote that "we may yet be able to turn their immensely superior power to our benefit as well as to that of the world as a whole," and Gage added with a touch of hope that in "due course it will no doubt be borne upon Americans that we, with our long experience, can be of some assistance to them in the proper application of their power."[6]

The Labour government, therefore, did not change the Conservatives' policy toward Russia. Before the June elections some Labourites had emphasized that they could ease Anglo-Soviet tensions and revive the cooperation that had waned during the last months of the Churchill government. There would be an ideological bond, or as Bevin informed the electorate, "Left will be able to speak to Left." By the time the new foreign secretary arrived at Potsdam he realized that in foreign affairs ideology was secondary to traditional interest. "I'm not going to have Britain barged about," he told General Ismay, and continued Churchill's opposition to Stalin's design for enlarging Poland. After Potsdam he outlined his policy to Joseph E. Davies—he desired to work for peace but Britain would stand up to the Soviet Union. This policy was confirmed two weeks later when he complained in Parliament about the Red Army's behavior in Eastern Europe. The new regimes there did not represent the people, he said, one kind of totalitarianism was being replaced by another.[7]

II

The end of the war against Japan brought peace to the whole world, and Americans turned to domestic problems: food and housing shortages, reconversion, unemployment, wage-and-price controls, demobilization, strikes. Asked in a poll during August what would be the most important problems during the upcoming year Americans discounted foreign issues and overwhelmingly answered unemployment and reconversion. Only 6 percent replied occupation of defeated and liberated countries and keeping the peace.[8]

The Truman administration responded quickly, and a few days after Japan's surrender, Truman sent Congress a twenty-one-point domestic program. The president called for expanded social-security coverage, raising the minimum wage, full and fair employment, public housing, and more scientific research. Within ten weeks he sent additional recommendations concerning aid to education, national health insurance, and the St. Lawrence Seaway. Such proposals aroused loud cries from the members of Congress, especially Republicans, and the nation was soon embroiled in "politics as usual." At the same time the administration faced mounting unrest caused by reconversion and demobilization. The number of idle man-days caused by strikes increased from 1.5 million on V-J Day to 8 million by the end of September. Such problems burdened the president during the remainder of the year. He complained to his mother in October that "pressure here is becoming so great I can hardly get my meals in," and by December he admitted wearily that "peace is hell."[9]

Preoccupation with domestic issues resulted in an unsure and ill-defined policy toward the Allies. There were the expected pronouncements of friendship and calls for cooperation. The United States also pledged to support the United Nations. As Truman told Stettinius, he felt strongly that the U.N.O. "must be made to work" and that he intended to "*make* it work." Such empty rhetoric showed no more than wishful thinking; although the world had changed enormously since Germany's collapse, America had not formed a postwar policy. The state–war–navy coordinating committee revealed the administration's stagnant thinking in a paper of December 1945 that outlined the same policy used throughout most of the war—the United States "must act as mediator and conciliator between Britain and Russia."[10]

British diplomats described America's foreign policy as "floundering," and nowhere was this more apparent than in the Truman administration's relations with the Soviet Union. No one seemed to know quite what to do. There were many signs of friendship toward the Communist ally. When General Eisenhower visited Russia in August he received a cordial welcome and an unprecedented honor for an American—he was allowed to review a Red Square parade with Stalin from the top of Lenin's tomb. Stalin sent Truman a framed photograph inscribed with "very best wishes from his friend." Thereupon the Soviet war hero, Marshal Georgi K. Zhukov, was invited to the United States. Clearly administration officials desired to be friendly, yet at the same time they wanted to show firmness, especially concerning democracy in Eastern Europe.[11] Which approach would America choose? The question went unanswered during the remainder of 1945. Like Buridan's ass the administration stood between two bales of hay—friendly and firm—and starved.

Policy toward Britain was not much better defined. The administration expected Bevin's cooperation and saw no reason to anticipate a change in British international goals. These expectations did not mean that Americans thought well of Great Britain. John D. Hickerson, head of the State Department's European division, told John Balfour of the British embassy that the American people expected the future to be determined by Washington and Moscow with London in a secondary role and the Commonwealth surviving only through aid from the United States. Americans remained suspicious of the mother country, "as full of tricks as a monkey" and apt to drag them into something not in their interest. According to Balfour there were two groups in the administration. The first "ignores us altogether, or regards us as a hindrance to American interest. The second accepts us as a valuable junior partner in an Anglo-American concern."[12]

While the men at the White House were occupied with domestic issues, James F. Byrnes became the central figure in American foreign policy. Born in 1879, the son of an Irish immigrant, Byrnes had grown up in South Carolina and by the end of his twenties was an enterprising lawyer entering on a political career. He was elected district attorney and in 1910 won a narrow victory for a seat in the U.S. House of Representatives. "I campaigned on nothing but gall," he commented, "and gall won by 57 votes." In 1930 he was elected to the Senate, holding his seat until 1941 when he accepted appointment to the U.S. Supreme Court. Because of the war, he cut short his judicial career, becoming director of the Office of Economic Stabilization and later director of war mobilization, a post that Roosevelt described as assistant president on the home front. Byrnes's ambition for higher office was frustrated in 1944 when FDR passed him over for the vice-presidency and later for secretary of state. Dejected, Byrnes resigned from the administration until July 1945 when President Truman asked him to head the State Department.[13]

Although an astute domestic politician, Byrnes was a novice to foreign relations. Shortly after becoming secretary of state, he told his special assistant Walter Brown, "this is another world to me." Despite this disadvantage, he did not lack confidence, but he gradually revealed certain defects of judgment and tactics. During his first six months he relied little on professionals in the State Department and often was unprepared in negotiations. Harriman later complained about the cavalier way Byrnes treated advisers—and the British—and Kennan noted that Byrnes played negotiations by ear with no clear or fixed plan, no definite set of objectives. Byrnes had the narrow perspective that has handicapped many Americans involved in international relations. As Bohlen explained, the South Carolinian had always dealt with Congress where compromises worked "because we're all under the same tent—common law, common constitution—and this doesn't operate in foreign affairs, particularly with an outfit like the Russians." Another of Byrnes's problems arose from his frequent trips abroad during 1945 and 1946. Of 562 days in office he spent 350 away from the department, mainly negotiating a postwar settlement. These long absences, along with his self-reliance, produced disorientation and dissension in the department; one official complained that "the State Department fiddles while Byrnes roams."[14]

III

Bevin and Byrnes got their first chance to face the Russians on their own in September 1945 at the Council of Foreign Ministers meeting in London which was convened to consider peace treaties for the former satellites—Finland, Hungary, Rumania, and Bulgaria. The leaders in both democracies wondered how the Communist ally would behave in this first test of postwar negotiations.

Molotov promptly stalled the conference with a series of disruptive statements—Russia should receive Italy's colonies; the West was supporting anti-Soviet elements in areas controlled by the Red Army; the Rumanian and Bulgarian governments were more representative than the regime in Greece; he would not accept an Anglo-American treaty with Italy unless the West accepted Russia's arrangements for Eastern Europe. On 22 September, after sixteen sessions, apparently to improve his bargaining position, Molotov called for the exclusion of France and China from further discussion, on the grounds that their participation violated the agreement at Potsdam. Two days later he advocated the end of American rule in Japan and the establishment of an Allied control council with Soviet representation.

These demands irritated the Americans and British. Bevin became angry and, after much bickering at the negotiating table, decided to "'ave it out" with the dour Russian. Heated sessions followed in which the Labourite's grammar declined as his emotions rose. At one point Bevin declared that

Molotov's arguments resembled "Hitlerite philosophy." The Russian became infuriated, and only Bevin's apology prevented him from stomping out of the room.[15]

Before the conference Bevin had warned Byrnes about Soviet designs in Eastern Europe. He suggested that Britain and America should attempt to induce those governments to "look to the West rather than to the East." He warned of danger in uncoordinated methods and urged that both nations "combine their policies" to obtain the greatest advantage when negotiating with the Russians. When the conference deadlocked, Bevin approached Byrnes again and urged that America follow his lead and issue a statement refusing to recognize the new governments of Rumania and Bulgaria.[16]

Byrnes rejected the overtures. A veteran of compromise, he was confident he could manage the Russians. En route to the meeting he had informed a reporter that it would take him "about three weeks" to make the Soviets "see some sense." Perhaps he felt the threat of the atomic bomb and the offer of reconstruction aid could be used as diplomatic levers. Whatever the case, Byrnes soon realized that negotiating with the Russians was no easy task. After many private meetings with Molotov, Byrnes reached the limit of his tolerance. During a 20 September session he walked out and informed his assistant that he had no confidence in peace with Molotov. Unlike the British who saw the deadlock as planned by the Kremlin, Byrnes blamed the stubborn foreign minister. He told his assistant that Molotov was "trying to do in a slick dip way what Hitler had tried to do in domineering smaller countries by force." There was "no hope of stopping M except by appealing to Stalin." The next meeting must be held in Moscow where he could deal with the Russian leader.[17]

As his single-handed diplomacy appeared to be failing, Byrnes began to search for other methods, including a brief attempt to cooperate with the British. Again demonstrating interest in economic diplomacy, Byrnes informed Bevin that the State Department would determine if Russia would receive a postwar reconstruction loan and inquired if the British thought it feasible to initiate an Anglo-American economic policy "as a means of pressure" on Moscow. The plan tantalized British officials, but at the same time they were skeptical, doubting that the U.S.S.R. could be bribed into accepting Western aims. Britain had no funds to contribute, and diplomats feared that if the scheme leaked out to the press, it would appear that Great Britain was using American dollars to secure British goals, which only could damage relations. Bevin informed Byrnes that his government could not participate.[18]

Nevertheless, during the third week in September, a noticeable shift appeared in American tactics toward the Allies. Three days after Byrnes's heated meeting with Molotov a British diplomat observed a "marked tendency on the part of the U.S. delegation . . . to get together with the British delegation and coordinate our respective views." This cooperation was especially true for issues such as Austria, Yugoslavia, and Europe's inland waterways, where Anglo-American aims usually had been similar. American desire for cooperation was again demonstrated at the end of September when Byrnes accepted Bevin's policy toward Yugoslavia, saying he would "gladly join" the British and press Tito to reduce the Yugoslavian army. The secretary of state would conspire against Tito, but not yet against Stalin.[19]

Thus, the alignment of late March and April 1945 reappeared at the London conference. On the earlier occasion Roosevelt, frustrated by Soviet obstinacy had discarded his independent approach and formed an Anglo-American policy with Churchill. Now, Byrnes was considering a similar course.

This shift was apparent to the British. At Whitehall, Donnelly noted that Russian obstinacy tended to unify the United States behind a firm policy and to kill "the heresy of mediation." He felt that Britain was now in a stronger position and unless "the Russians swiftly see the way of wisdom, it is likely that as time passes the Americans will become even more aware of their need for the British Commonwealth as a strong partner." Halifax certainly agreed, stating the simple allied ratio: Britain's "stocks in the United States appreciate when those of the Soviet Union decline."[20]

This allied ratio would become more common in 1946, but

at the London conference, Byrnes's initial desire to cooperate with the British proved ephemeral. After deciding that talks were useless, he persuaded the chairman of the council to declare the conference at an end. He acted on his own without consulting his staff, the president, or the British. Byrnes had not given up hope for cooperating with the Russians and still desired a diplomatic victory. His last remarks before he left England were conciliatory, stating that after elections America would be willing to recognize the government of Hungary and that he would reconsider Moscow's request for an Allied control commission in Japan. Returning to Washington he told Davies that the United States had compromised before with the Russians concerning Poland, Finland, and Hungary and now would try to do the same on Rumania and Bulgaria. The president was not yet pessimistic and told Stettinius that he was not seriously concerned with the suspension of the foreign ministers' conference. After victory, he said, it was inevitable that America should have difficulties with Russia. In a cabinet meeting of 21 October, Truman emphasized mutual trust to achieve peace, one of the themes announced the next day in his Navy Day speech. Byrnes affirmed friendship on Halloween by assuring Moscow that "the U.S. would never join any group of states hostile to U.S.S.R." By the first week in November the United States demonstrated its desire for cooperation by recognizing the provisional governments of Austria and Hungary and by sending to the Kremlin a proposal to guarantee Russia's access to the Mediterranean.[21]

After the London conference, then, America's policy was still in flux. At times Washington cooperated with London, such as when both demanded the implementation of the Declaration on Liberated Europe. More often the United States acted unilaterally on issues that were of interest to the British. Without consulting Whitehall, Byrnes sent the editor of the *Louisville Courier-Journal*, Mark F. Ethridge, on a fact-finding mission to the Balkans and abandoned a proposed Anglo-American commission to investigate conditions on the Greek-Yugoslav border. Concerning Yugoslavia Byrnes reversed earlier plans, privately consulted Stalin about Tito, and urged postponement of Yugoslavia's elections. He also approached the Russians regarding a Hungarian-Soviet economic agreement.[22]

This uncertain policy irritated the British. In Moscow, Roberts worried over the American tendency to rush ahead with unilateral representations to the Russians on questions of joint interest, referring to issues in Central and Eastern Europe on which Britain and America "think alike and are both trying to get some satisfaction out of the Soviet Government." Kremlin leaders were bound to attribute less importance to Western and especially British demands when policy was uncoordinated. While the reason for America's impulsiveness was not clear to Roberts, Lord Halifax reported in mid-November from Washington that the United States was displaying the "familiar anxiety to avoid the appearance of ganging up on the Russians," coupled with a desire to demonstrate that the "policy of the State Department is an American policy." In London Lord Gore-Booth later remembered that "Byrnes took over and sailed off in a way that terrified us." BBC correspondent Leonard Miall was suspicious, later recalling a fear that the United States and the Soviet Union were going to "carve the world into spheres of influence to suit each other, leaving Britain out in the cold."[23]

The continued deterioration of Anglo-Soviet relations after the London failure stimulated the British to approach the Americans. In October the Russians stepped up their campaign against "British imperialism" and sent the assistant military governor of Germany, Air Marshal Sholto Douglas, a note accusing his government of maintaining large units of the former Luftwaffe in the British zone. This complaint, which Douglas called utterly senseless, was the first time one ally had criticized the conduct of another in the control council. That month Sargent talked with members of the American embassy in London, reminding them that the Russians desired to cause discord between the democracies so they could "gain for themselves a freer hand in Europe." He warned that Moscow wanted to drive bargains while it still had great military strength in Europe. Two weeks later Whitehall officials informed Gallman that the Soviets would continue their effort to split the West, a tactic designed to force a last-minute compromise on Balkan issues. How to meet the challenge was the topic of a 19 October memorandum that Halifax delivered to the State Department. The Labour government informed the United States that it agreed with the Conservatives' wartime plan. Britain and America must deal with the Kremlin tógether on a quid-pro-quo basis. A month later Balfour brought the department a long memorandum exposing the Russian threat to the Balkans. Soviet pressure on Rumania enraged the British. According to reports, many Rumanians were being tried for subversive activities, a charge given to anyone connected with the Western missions. Trials were a sham. The judges, men whom the Allies had considered war criminals, were imposing stiff prison sentences under a law abrogated a year earlier. The memorandum complained that the Russians had removed quantities of equipment from British-owned oil companies, failed to return British ships confined on the Danube, and hindered trade between the Balkans and the West. Such acts against Allied interests, the memorandum declared, were "entirely inconsistent with the duty owed by one Ally to another."[24]

An increasing number of American officials agreed with the British. Harriman warned the State Department in October that Soviet aims for the Middle East were "security and aggrandizement": the endless pursuit of power was a habit of Russian statesmanship, not only in the tradition of the Russian state but in the ideology of the party, which viewed all advanced nations as Russia's enemies and backward nations as pawns in the struggle. American diplomats in Eastern Europe agreed. Regardless of country, their reports outlined a Soviet policy that disregarded democratic objectives and used totalitarian methods to establish Communist regimes; the only chance of frustrating Russian aims lay in an Anglo-American stand. The American representative in Bulgaria wrote Byrnes that the "hopes of southeastern Europe . . . are based almost entirely on what you, supported by Mr. Bevin, may be able to do as spokesman for world democratic leadership." Such messages, along with British prodding, convinced officials at the State Department's European desk to reevaluate the

U.S.S.R. By 27 November they had reached similar conclusions: the Kremlin had taken steps that made it difficult, if not impossible, for the administration to convince the American people that Russia wanted a satisfactory postwar settlement.[25]

Thus by the end of November 1945 many State Department officials favored more coordination with Britain and a tougher approach toward Russia, but the secretary of state was not yet ready to adopt this policy. Byrnes paid little attention to the department or, for that matter, to the president. After the first session of the London conference, a diplomatic aide, Theodore Achilles, typed a report to be sent back to the department and took it to Byrnes. He looked at it and asked, "What's this?" After Achilles explained, Byrnes exclaimed, "God Almighty, I might tell the President sometime what happened, but I'm never going to tell those little bastards at the State Department anything about it." Byrnes also neglected the president. On 8 December he received a report from Ethridge about Russian behavior in the Balkans. When Truman finally received the report on 5 January, he complained that Byrnes had "put it in his pocket and took it with him to Moscow." He failed to inform Truman before making an announcement on 11 December concerning economic policy toward Germany—Truman learned of the plan the next morning when he read the *New York Times.* Upset, the president complained bitterly that there "ought to have been some discussion with the man who has to approve it"; he "should not have to read the newspapers to get the U.S. foreign policy."[26] Byrnes apparently had decided that he alone should determine America's policy toward the Soviet Union. After his failure with Molotov in London, he would attempt a compromise with Stalin in Moscow.

IV

In addition to Soviet behavior, the negotiation of a postwar loan for Britain and atomic energy were prominent issues during the autumn of 1945.

Britain was concerned about American control of atomic secrets. During the war Churchill had urged the United States to share information with London but not with Moscow. The Americans hesitated, unsure of the policy they should adopt. Roosevelt finally agreed to meet Churchill at Quebec, and in August 1943 the two leaders pledged full and effective collaboration in research and development. Thirteen months later at Hyde Park they signed a memorandum again pledging cooperation for military and commercial purposes. In neither agreement, however, did the United States agree to share secrets concerning production of atomic weapons.

Anxious to define and expand this cooperation after the war, Prime Minister Attlee personally informed Truman in August that he desired collaboration, information, and talks. Although Truman endorsed the suggestion, he and his advisers had not yet defined policy, so they procrastinated. On 25 September Attlee sent the White House a nine-page letter outlining his thoughts on the bomb, calling for cooperation, and inquiring how the president's "mind is moving." Truman agreed to hold discussions, but his reply on 5 October set no date. At an "old fashioned bull session" with reporters during a fishing trip at Tiponville, Tennessee, he announced that the United States had no intention of sharing atomic "engineering secrets." The British were startled; this statement seemed nothing less than a breach of good faith, a transgression of the spirit if not the letter of the Quebec and Hyde Park agreements. Attlee sent a more urgent letter in which he again urged the president to set a date for talks and volunteered to come to Washington, adding that he was facing parliamentary pressure for a statement. Truman's reply came on 27 October in New York during his Navy Day speech. He announced that British-Canadian-American discussions were imminent but emphasized that talks would not concern the manufacturing of atomic weapons. Possession of the new power, the president continued, "we regard as a sacred trust." The prime minister realized a critical situation and asked for a face-to-face meeting. That request could not be ignored, and on 10 November Attlee and the Canadian prime minister, Mackenzie King, arrived in Washington.[27]

Discussions began on 11 November aboard the presidential yacht *Sequoia*. Attlee's position apparently was that atomic secrets should be shared with the United Nations, but only after the West had received an acceptable statement of Russia's political, economic, and territorial objectives. The British felt that the Soviets must pledge to abide by the U.N. charter and without this guarantee the democracies should monopolize atomic secrets. During later negotiations it became obvious that the British wanted full collaboration—what amounted to an Anglo-American atomic partnership. The Americans had just recently formed their position. A week before the conference, after Attlee was invited to Washington, Byrnes asked the director of the Office of Scientific Research and Development, Vannevar Bush, to devise a policy. The scientist was appalled at the haphazard method used to develop the proposal, writing Stimson that he had "never participated in anything that was so completely unorganized or so irregular. I have had experiences in the past week that would make a chapter in 'Alice in Wonderland.'" The resulting American plan called for a U.N. commission to deal with atomic issues and continual sharing of information with the British, excluding the means of production.[28]

The British and Americans signed a document of intent that replaced wartime atomic agreements, and Truman, Attlee, and King on 16 November signed a pledge of cooperation.

Attlee's visit had paid handsome dividends, especially for the British. The Truman administration had agreed to continue wartime cooperation, albeit excluding the means of production. More important, it now seemed that the United States had formed a joint policy with Great Britain. The democracies had agreed on a proposal that they planned to present to the Russians at the upcoming United Nations meeting. Many people wondered if the conference had formed an Anglo-American bloc—complete with atomic arsenal.

In fact, there was no atomic alliance in the West, and one might wonder if the possession of the bomb made any difference in the peacemaking process. This question is difficult to answer without access to Soviet documents, but the weapon did not seem to have much impact on Kremlin leaders. After all, the Russians did not change their policies after Hiroshima and Nagasaki. What effect did the bomb have? Roberts answered that question from Moscow as early as October 1945, writing the Foreign Office that with the possible exception of increasing Soviet suspicion there is "no reason to suppose that the atomic bomb has influenced current international problems one way or the other." About that time many American officials, including Llewellyn Thompson, Bohlen, even Byrnes and the president, were forming the same opinion.[29]

Nevertheless, the Truman–Attlee–King meeting concerned many people in the United States, especially congressmen who had promoted friendly Soviet-American relations and scientists who had constructed the bomb. With the support of almost every one of those scientists, Helen G. Douglas of California introduced a resolution urging the president to invite both Britain and the Soviet Union to confer on a Big Three atomic-energy proposal that would be introduced in the first meeting of the United Nations. At the State Department Benjamin Cohen and Leo Pavolsky feared the meeting hurt Russian-American relations, and they urged Byrnes not to wait as planned until the January meeting of the General Assembly to discuss atomic issues with the Soviets.[30]

V

Atomic energy concerned the secretary of state, but he was more interested in concluding the stalled peace treaties with Germany's former allies. During the third week in November he approached the Kremlin, and a conference was set for mid-December.

There was another reason why Byrnes desired a conference—for the first time since the end of the war Americans were questioning their country's foreign policy. Since Japan's surrender the president had given one address concerning international affairs, the Navy Day speech. On that occasion he reviewed the fleet in New York harbor, and after a thousand planes had zoomed overhead he advocated Wilsonian ideals. To British diplomats the scene "created the impression that America is behaving like a lumbering young giant, racked by indecision, troubled by a guilty conscience, and uncertain about how long his strength will endure." To Donnelly America was "floundering"; to Halifax its foreign policy was "without purpose or direction" and reached the "nadir of confusion" during December. Many Americans agreed. Edwin L. James of the *New York Times* complained about vacillations and "lack of preparation," and the *Saturday Evening Post* published an article titled "Our Foreign Policy Needs Clarifying." Byrnes now desired to show the public that the administration had a policy.[31]

The secretary of state did not tell the British that he was arranging another meeting, and when they found out they urged a coordinated approach toward the Soviet Union. Whitehall officials discussed the situation with Ambassador Winant, who told Byrnes that Bevin was "desperately anxious to talk with you before the Moscow Conference." But Byrnes refused to cooperate, replying that it was not necessary or desirable for the democracies to reach agreement before the discussion.[32]

The British then became unwilling to participate. They doubted the wisdom of the meeting and felt that the Americans had arranged it in their usual haphazard manner. While Byrnes was organizing the conference late in November, Truman had commented that no more talks would be necessary, since any differences could be discussed at the January session of the United Nations. Byrnes had then proceeded to secure Soviet approval for the conference before he mentioned it to the British. He had not even told them whether it would be restricted to an exploratory exchange of views or would attempt to secure a final agreement. In either case, they objected to discussing the issues without the Chinese or the French and questioned the timing of the meeting; they feared that the Russians would stall until the Western diplomats became impatient to return home for the Christmas holidays and would then try to rush through a settlement. Bevin summoned Winant and told him that American policy was bewildering and that the cabinet had twice discussed the conference unfavorably.[33]

Byrnes was in no mood to see his plans foiled and applied pressure to Whitehall, threatening to go to Moscow alone.

Bevin then agreed to join him, and on 15 December both men arrived in the Soviet capital. Bevin was still perturbed, complaining to Bohlen that Byrnes had called the unexpected meeting without any consultations with the British. Bohlen could sympathize; on vacation in South Carolina, he had to rush back to Washington and catch a plane for Moscow. He too thought the conference "hastily improvised and . . . thoroughly disorganized. Items were put on the agenda without adequate preparations."[34] The issues were atomic energy, peace treaties and future relations with Germany's former satellites, and the governments and occupation of Bulgaria, Rumania, Greece, Korea, Japan, and Iran.

Britain and America shared the same aims, but again they differed in their tactics for gaining concessions from the Russians. After the opening session Bevin asked for a private conversation with Byrnes, and on 17 December they met at the American embassy. Bevin immediately commented that Soviet policy was disturbing and that the Kremlin was attempting to undermine Britain's position in the Middle East. If the troops were withdrawn from Greece, Moscow would increase pressure and manufacture some incident. He wanted to return the Dodecanese islands to the Greeks but hesitated because of the Russian threat. Nor could the British government be indifferent to the Kremlin's recent demand for a base in the Turkish straits. Britain would stand by the government in Ankara. Shifting the discussion to Iran, Bevin suggested that Soviet aims were either to secure more oil or to annex the northern province of Azerbaidzhan—attempting to form a sphere of influence, or what he curiously labeled a "Monroe area." Anticipating Churchill's "iron curtain" speech, Bevin declared that the Kremlin expected this area to extend "from the Baltic to the Adriatic on the west to Port Arthur or beyond on the east."

Doubtless Bevin hoped for more than an exchange of views with Byrnes. The British had regularly given the Americans their opinion of Soviet intentions; now he was attempting to convince Byrnes that joint policy was the only way to meet the Soviet threat. But the plan failed, for in the words of an eyewitness, Kennan, Byrnes was determined "to achieve some sort of an agreement, he doesn't much care what. The realities behind this agreement, since they concern only such people as Koreans, Rumanians, and Iranians, about whom he knows nothing, do not concern him. He wants an agreement for its political effect at home."[35]

The resulting American diplomacy was amateurish. Harriman complained that Byrnes was "stiff and unwilling to listen" to advisers, and Kennan noted that during negotiation the secretary of state had no set objectives; often unprepared, he relied on his "agility and presence of mind." The British complained. Halifax had informed Whitehall in July that Byrnes saw himself as an "idealistic honest broker" and was a "self-confessed addict to courses of honourable compromise." Now, after two foreign ministers' meetings, the British delegation formed similar opinions. After sitting through several Moscow sessions Roberts labeled Byrnes a "prima donna," and Cadogan wrote that determining his slippery policy was "like trying to tickle a trout with highly oiled gloves."[36]

Without coordinated Western tactics, Bevin had no recourse but to approach the Russians alone; his discussions with Molotov on 18 December and the next day with Stalin outlined the issues separating the European powers. The first conversation quickly arrived at the occupation and governments of Greece, Rumania, and Bulgaria. Each side called on the other to withdraw its occupation forces. Molotov was blunt, stating that "the Greeks were not masters in Greece," whereupon Bevin replied that conditions were the same in Bulgaria where the Russians were masters. Next day the Labourite met Stalin to discuss the occupation of Iran and recent Soviet demands on Turkey. Bevin got right to the point, asking when the Red Army was going to withdraw from Azerbaidzhan. Stalin responded that he did not propose an early withdrawal, since he desired to protect the oil wells at Baku. Bevin asked if the Russians feared an attack from Iran. Stalin said no, but he was "afraid of acts of sabotage." The conversation shifted to Turkey. Russia had demanded a military base in the Dardanelles and annexation of the Georgian and Armenian provinces of northern Turkey. Bevin suggested that Moscow seemed to be conducting a "war of nerves" against the government in Ankara. He reminded Stalin that Britain had an alliance with Turkey, which had mobilized its army. Stalin replied that Turkey need not fear the Soviet Union, that problems should be settled by negotiation.[37] The issues remained unresolved.

Byrnes then approached the Russians, meeting them on Christmas Eve. After some discussion Stalin became conciliatory. He approved a list of nations that could participate in peace negotiations and agreed to the establishment of a United Nations atomic energy commission, an Allied council for Japan, and a commission for Korea. Byrnes felt that his most important achievement concerned the Balkans. Stalin said he would allow two non-Communists to join the Bulgarian government and a three-power commission to visit Rumania. The agreements were vague, but Byrnes felt he had ended the impasse created during the London conference. So did the Soviet and American press. *Izvestia* called the meeting a "new step" toward Allied collaboration, and the *New York Times* labeled the Moscow communiqué the most hopeful document presented to the world since the capitulation of Germany and Japan.[38]

The British were less enthusiastic. The *Economist* voiced a growing feeling about American diplomacy: because of the "inexperience of Mr. Byrnes as a negotiator and America's general diplomatic myopia when any area other than the Far East is in question, the Russians have succeeded in separating their two allies and Britain has been left isolated." A similar theme was expressed by the former permanent undersecretary of the Foreign Office and chief diplomatic adviser to the British government, Lord Vansittart. In a long letter to the *Manchester Guardian* he labeled the conference a "milestone in the wrong direction." Vansittart blamed "naive Mr. Byrnes," who first slighted the British by not informing them of the meeting until it had been set up with the Russians and then sought diplomatic success for domestic reasons. As a result "Russia gained everything and gave practically nothing in return." This sad result was not Bevin's fault: "Byrnes produced this show and Russia 'stole' it."[39]

Many Americans also felt that Byrnes's achievements were

superficial. Bohlen called the Bulgarian accord a mistake because it prevented the United States from gaining membership in the Sofia government for "two men who had every
right to be there." Byrnes had signed the agreement against
the advice of almost all members of the American delegation.
Back in Washington, Leahy entered in his diary that Russia
had been granted every demand that had wrecked the London conference, thanks to the "refusal of the U.K. and the
U.S. to agree at the time." Perturbed, Harriman felt that the
secretary of state was "letting the British slip away from us,
not because of any disagreement on policy but purely by of-
fending them through his unwillingness to consult and what
Bevin considers his somewhat overbearing attitude." Byrnes
had let the Soviets avoid the problem that British and American diplomats felt was most critical—evacuation of Soviet
troops from Iran. An angry Truman later wrote that it was
"abundantly clear to me that the successes of the Moscow
conference were unreal." The joint communiqué contained
"not a word about Iran or any other place where the Soviets
were on the march. We had gained only an empty promise for
future talks."[40]

VI

The United States finally announced a long-range policy
toward Russia three months after the Moscow conference.
After months of floundering, the Truman administration finally discarded its independent attempt to mediate and began
to cooperate with Britain in a tough approach toward the
Kremlin.[41]

There were many reasons for the change, and it must be
stated clearly that most originated in the United States or
Russia. Soviet behavior had angered the president. Russia's
refusal to withdraw from Azerbaidzhan, totalitarian methods
in Eastern Europe, and demands on Turkey were all incompatible with his idea of international relations. As he told his
staff, nations should live by the golden rule, which meant
keeping agreements such as the treaty with Iran and the Declaration on Liberated Europe. Historians have noted that

Truman showed his first sign of displeasure and his inclination toward a stronger policy after Byrnes returned from Moscow. But even before then, on 17 December, Truman made a revealing statement during a White House conversation with his press secretary Charles Ross. The president said that the Russians "confront us with an accomplished fact and then there is little we can do. They did that in the case of Poland. Now they have 500,000 men in Bulgaria and some day they are going to move down and take the Black Sea straits and that will be an accomplished fact again. There's only one thing they understand." "Divisions?" Ross asked. The president nodded, adding that "we can't send any divisions over to prevent them from moving from Bulgaria. I don't know what we're going to do." He had a better idea of what to do after Byrnes returned from Moscow. The two men met on 5 January and Truman signaled the changing direction of policy with the now famous statement: "I'm tired of babying the Soviets."[42]

In all likelihood, Truman honestly believed that he had been babying the Russians. During his first eight months in office this potentially impulsive man had been patient. For the most part, he had treated both allies in a similar fashion while attempting to mediate between them. In return, the British had expressed a strong desire to cooperate on international issues and Anglo-American problems. But not the Soviets. After one Big Three conference and two meetings of the foreign ministers the president's independent approach had not persuaded Kremlin leaders to cooperate or compromise over the occupation of Eastern Europe, Iran, Korea, and many other issues. Truman had not yet comprehended what Roosevelt had learned late in March 1945: because the Western democracies had similar long-term aims, London would cooperate with Washington against Moscow. The Russians would not collaborate; the "compromise" settlement offered by the administration was unacceptable. As Truman told Stalin at Potsdam, all the United States wanted was "security and peace with friendship and neighborliness in a free world." To Americans, a free world meant capitalistic democracies, not Communist dictatorships. Kremlin leaders could not accept this definition in areas that their army occupied any more than the president could accept the status quo. Truman had misjudged his former allies throughout 1945; there was no reason to mediate between the Continental powers, for a fundamental difference existed on a global scale—between East and West.

Truman became more distressed as Soviet-American relations continued to deteriorate during February 1946. He informed Leahy of his "sharp disapproval" of appeasement toward the Kremlin, stating that he was "convinced of the necessity for the U.S. to adopt a strong diplomatic opposition to the Soviet program of expansion." Later in the month he showed more concern; Ayers recorded that the president "pulled a number of telegrams or cablegrams out of the folder on his desk . . . with the comment that we were going to war with Russia or words to that effect."[43]

Perhaps in the stack on Truman's desk was an eight-thousand-word, five-part message from Kennan, not the first expression of this talented diplomat's views on Soviet behavior. Like many American representatives in Eastern Europe, and like the British, Kennan had been warning the administration for over a year about the Kremlin's intentions. On 10 January he reminded Washington that Soviet aims were to "confuse the West and expand their power." His reports stirred little interest until after a speech by Stalin on 9 February stressing the incompatibility of communism and capitalism. Two days later H. Freeman Matthews wrote Acheson and Byrnes that the address was an important and authoritative guide to postwar Soviet policy, that it made an interesting companion piece to Ethridge's report on the Balkans, and that it provided "full confirmation of the soundness of George Kennan's excellent recent telegrams evaluating Soviet policy." Matthews recommended that Stalin's address be made required reading for everyone in the department. A few days later Kennan sent his now famous 22 February message to Washington. He portrayed the Soviet Union as an aggressive nation bent on expansion for traditional and ideological reasons. He believed that Russian success would depend on the failure of cohesion, firmness, and vigor in the Western world.[44]

British diplomats, of course, had long agreed with this analysis. Roberts, Kennan's counterpart in Moscow, respected the American's intellect and knowledge of Russian history. The two men had often discussed Soviet behavior and found "very few things in which we were in disagreement." America must form a realistic policy; Russia was much less likely to expand if confronted with a united West. Kennan's proposals, later labeled "containment," were not new to the British. They had been containing Russia since the Congress of Vienna. Churchill's military and diplomatic aims after 1943 were an application of this concept. The British did not call it containment, but "holding the line"; Attlee later wrote that his government's foreign policy during the Stalin era had been based on holding the line against Soviet expansion.[45] While America was discussing and slowly adopting this idea during the remainder of 1946, Britain was acting, holding the line against the spread of communism in Greece.

Kennan's telegram had a considerable effect on the administration. Frustrated by months of Soviet behavior, officials were now ready to listen to such reasoning. Secretary of War Patterson was impressed, and Forrestal strengthened his opinion that "communist doctrine creates a fanatical and mystic support in its adherents" and that the Soviets were aiming for world revolution. Truman and Leahy were forming the same conclusion, and the message probably reinforced the president's desire to take a stand against Russia.[46]

By this time the American people were discouraged with the situation at home and abroad. Opinion polls after V-J Day showed that 54 percent of those asked felt that the U.S.S.R. could be trusted to cooperate with the United States after the war; by March 1946 that figure dropped to 35 percent. In April only 7 percent of those asked approved of Russia's foreign policy; by June almost 60 percent believed that the Kremlin wanted to rule the world. The public was also wondering about Truman's ability to lead the nation. Deteriorating relations with Moscow, along with a domestic situation that seemed to be slipping out of control, produced a marked decline in the president's popularity. Polls before Potsdam showed that 87 percent of those surveyed approved of the way Truman was handling his job. A year later that figure had plunged to 43 percent. Congressional attacks followed, especially from Republicans looking forward to the November elections. Sensing the growing disillusionment, Halifax wrote in February that not since the Hoover era had Congress been "so completely out of White House control. To serious observers it seems painfully obvious that the man at the helm is no longer the master of the ship."[47]

British diplomacy also contributed to the reorientation of American foreign policy, for London continued its attempt to influence Washington. In January the Lord President of the Council, Herbert Morrison, arrived in the United States and met with journalists, senators, and diplomats to explain Britain's economic and foreign policies. The next month in London, Whitehall officials told Winant that the difficulties of Britain and other colonial powers would create a vacuum in many areas that the Russians hoped to fill. Paraphrasing Lenin's epigram they told the ambassador the Soviets did not care how many eggs they broke if they could make their own kind of omelette. Undersecretary Christopher F. A. Warner informed Gallman early in March that it was the time for "firm, plain speaking" because Britain and America's failure to speak out now would only multiply misunderstandings between East and West.[48]

A more significant Anglo-American contact was provided in mid-January when the U.N. General Assembly and Security Council convened for the first time in London. Bevin represented Britain. Byrnes attended only the first week, and Stettinius became the chief negotiator. The Soviet Union was represented by its first deputy minister for foreign affairs, Andrei Vyshinsky, a man known throughout his country as one of the creators of the Soviet judicial system and the famed prosecutor of the purge trials during the 1930s. But on 19 January 1946, before the Russian lawyer had a chance to negotiate the issues, the government of Iran submitted a complaint to the Security Council concerning Soviet occupation of Azerbaidzhan. A controversy quickly broke out between Britain and Russia, in which the Americans carefully took no part. Iran's charges were discussed on 25 January. Vyshinsky argued that for procedural reasons the issue should not be on the agenda but Bevin disagreed, and Iran stated its case. The council adjourned until 30 January, when Bevin again confronted the Russians with an incisive speech discounting Soviet reasons for occupation: "I cannot imagine the Iranian army or anybody else attacking the Soviet army and endangering the Baku oil fields; I really cannot." Russian behavior constituted nothing less than a war of nerves. Vyshinsky later countered with a complaint about Britain's occupation of Greece. He charged that British troops were exerting pressure on internal affairs and that Greece was a menace to world peace; jabbing his pencil at the British delegation, he demanded immediate withdrawal. Bevin retorted that his government had power to do in Greece what the Soviets did in Eastern Europe. "We could have put in a minority government, but we did not do that." With flushed face he added, "We believe that democracy must come from the bottom, not from the top."[49]

British diplomacy had two aims at the United Nations: to marshal world opinion, which would force the Soviets out of Iran, and to influence America. Whitehall officials reasoned that in order to prick the lumbering giant into action, they must take a clear, strong position, demonstrating to the world their "consistent, constructive and principled statesmanship" against the United States' "vacillation and lack of principle." They felt that Bevin's remarks would succeed if they could prepare the American public and the "unstable Mr. Byrnes for the one method of handling the Russians which had not yet been tried consistently, namely, an united British-American stand."[50]

Bevin's "gloves off, cards on the table" diplomacy generated support in the United States. It appealed to America's sense of realism, for mustering world opinion was the most practical way of forcing Russia out of Iran. Also, Bevin's tactic engaged American enthusiasm for the United Nations, whose charter, signed by all members at San Francisco, stated that nations would respect treaties and international law and refrain from threats or use of force against any country. To the Western mind, the Soviet refusal to withdraw from Azerbaidzhan was a violation of the wartime treaty with Iran and of the charter. Bevin's attack identified him as champion of the charter and, since the organization was based on American ideals, as a statesman upholding U.S. policy.

Bevin received wide coverage in America's press. *Newsweek* placed him on the cover of the 11 February issue, commenting that the Bevin–Vyshinsky exchange had few parallels in the history of diplomacy and that he was the freshest and most controversial figure in British foreign affairs since Lord Palmerston. After the foreign secretary had exposed the issues and taken a stand, Americans began to question their policy. The *New York Times* commented on abundant evidence that the people of the United States and of many other nations needed and would welcome a long-range policy. They wanted something "beyond a general declaration that we favored peace, prosperity, progress and freedom in the world. They wanted to know our definite aims and interests." The article asked a question pondered for months in Britain: "What, for example, is our Russian policy?"[51]

Bevin had stimulated concern and won many friends in America. The ordinarily anti-British Dallas *Times Herald* published an article entitled "Let's Lend-Lease Jimmy for Ernie." It gave a "friendly suggestion" to the president: "swap Jimmy Byrnes to the British for Ernie Bevin and toss in any number of old destroyers it takes to clinch the deal."[52]

Bevin's diplomacy appealed to the two Republican members of the American delegation at the United Nations meeting—John Foster Dulles and especially Sen. Arthur H. Vandenberg of Michigan. On returning to America, Dulles complained about the administration's meek policy, stating at Princeton that the delegation "received no substantive task to perform, no great objective to achieve." He later urged that before the next conference the United States develop realistic and significant plans. A member of the Foreign Relations Committee, Vandenberg spent thirty-seven days in Britain before and during the conference. The British government paid many of his expenses while he talked with officials. During the debate over Iran in the Security Council he was appalled by America's timid approach and impressed by Bevin. To Vandenberg's satisfaction, the foreign secretary continued his attacks in Parliament and, turning to the situation in Poland, accused the Polish police of complicity in political murders, demanded an end to the crimes, and called for free elections. This speech aroused Vandenberg's anticommunism as well as his ever-present concern for the Polish vote in Michigan. He asked Byrnes to support Bevin and then criticized the secretary of state's statement requesting the Polish government to ensure freedom as "deplorably mild." Returning to Washington Vandenberg called for a more active American role; rising in the Senate on 27 February, he stated that there should be a line beyond which no compromise was possible— "let America take her stand." He praised the performances of some members of the American delegation to the U.N.O. meeting and the "sturdy" manner of Bevin.[53] He conspicuously failed to mention Stettinius or Byrnes.

Vandenberg's speech was applauded by the press. The Houston *Post* declared it the most important speech since the declaration of war, and the Omaha *World-Herald* heard the "voice of responsibility, the voice of statesmanship, the voice that America has been longing to hear." *Newsweek*'s headline declared what British diplomats longed to hear: "Period of Appeasement Ends with Strong Criticism of Soviet by Returning UNO Delegates."[54]

VII

The climax of the British campaign to influence America was Winston S. Churchill's "iron curtain" speech of 5 March 1946. When the former prime minister announced that he was going to spend the winter months relaxing in Florida, the president of Westminster College in Fulton, Missouri, Frank McCluer, saw an opportunity for a speaking engagement. He sought out his friend, the presidential aide, Harry H. Vaughan, and the two men approached the president. Truman favored the idea and wrote at the bottom of the invitation:

"Dear Winnie: This is a fine old school out in my state. If you come and make a speech there, I'll introduce you."[55]

Churchill had not planned speaking engagements while in the United States, but the offer attracted him. During the war he had been concerned about the power of America, thinking it "benevolent without doubt but no less certainly in need of guidance." As he told Americans at Harvard in 1943, the best hope for Britain was the unity of the English-speaking peoples. Truman's invitation offered a chance to repeat these thoughts, to comment on the precarious world situation, and to make proposals for future relations between Britain and the United States. He cleverly replied to Truman: "If you would like me to visit your home State and would introduce me, I should feel it my duty—and it would also be a great pleasure—to deliver an Address to the Westminster University on the world situation, *under your aegis.* This might possibly be advantageous from several points of view."[56]

Churchill made it clear to the president that he wanted to use the occasion to publicize the policy he had advocated privately since 1944. Sunning himself in Miami late in January, he wrote Truman: "I need to talk with you a good while before the Fulton date. I have a Message to deliver to your country and to the world and I think it very likely that we shall be in full agreement about it. Under your auspices anything I say will command some attention and there is an opportunity for doing some good to this bewildered, baffled and breathless world." Soon after receiving an encouraging response from Truman, Churchill left for Havana. While dining at the American embassy, he gave a preview of his address. Speaking of Russia, the threatening "Bear that walks like a man," he feared that it would soon master atomic power. If that occurred, he wryly remarked, the U.N.O. would perish with the epitaph of "United Nations Orphan." The way to escape disaster was for him to issue "clarion calls" regarding the Soviet menace—as he had done against the Nazis—and for Britain and America to develop a "definite working agreement." As Churchill expected, the ambassador reported to the president. When Churchill met Truman at the White House on 10 February, the two men discussed the address for two hours.

Admiral Leahy, who was present and described the interview in his diary, recorded no presidential objections.[57]

After a jovial trip to Missouri, the presidential entourage arrived in Fulton. Not since 1875, when Jefferson Davis urged the citizenry to patch up the wounds of the Civil War, had such noted figures visited the sleepy little college town. To an audience of seven thousand, Truman introduced his guest as a man who would have "something constructive to say." Churchill quipped that the name Westminster was somehow familiar and began his now famous address. He analyzed Soviet policy, the situation in Europe, and declared: "From Stettin in the Baltic to Trieste in the Adriatic, an iron curtain has descended across the Continent. Behind that line lie all the capitals of the ancient states of Central and Eastern Europe. Warsaw, Berlin, Vienna, Budapest, Belgrade, Bucharest, and Sofia, all these famous cities, and the populations around them lie in what I must call the Soviet Sphere, and all are subject in one form or another, not only to Soviet influence but to a very high and, in many cases, increasing measure of control from Moscow." While he could not forecast Russian intentions or the limits of their "expansive and proselytizing tendencies," he could offer a path of wisdom. Since there was nothing Moscow admired so much as military strength, he urged that America and Britain stand together and continue their military association and joint defense arrangement. Then there would be "no quivering, precarious balance of power to offer its temptation to ambition or adventure." There would be an "overwhelming assurance of security": the future would be clear, "not only for us but for all, not only for our time, but for a century to come."

Three days later Churchill confronted Americans in a lesser known address to the Virginia General Assembly. He warned that he might "blurt out a lot of things people know in their hearts are true" about the international situation but were "shy of saying in public" and concluded that for the rest of his life he would be the bearer of a simple message: "we should stand together."[58]

The Fulton speech received a mixed response in Britain. Moderate papers such as the London *Daily Mail* and the *Man-*

chester Guardian welcomed the address, the latter stating the theme was "never more timely." The *Observer* agreed with Churchill's analysis, declaring that the only way to stop Russia was a "show of overwhelming strength; and there is nothing on earth left to make that show except the British-American combination." The left-wing press criticized the speech. The Labour party's *Daily Herald* commented that his atomic bombardment of rhetoric was untimely and irresponsible, and the Communist *Daily Worker* noted that Churchill had returned to his "anti-communist vomit." Radical Labour M.P.s signed a statement repudiating the policy of the Conservative leader and under this pressure Attlee, who had authorized Churchill's visit at government expense, reminded Parliament that the former prime minister spoke for himself.[59]

There was a different reaction from British diplomats. Although not consulted, the Foreign Office was delighted. Churchill had supported their attempts to provoke the lumbering giant into forming a long-range policy and providing democratic leadership for the world. Many Britons had long felt, as Donnelly noted, that Americans were "hedonistic escapists," hoping the U.N.O. would solve postwar issues. Churchill's speech had given the "sharpest jolt to American thinking" since the end of the war. Halifax reported a very profound impact. More than any utterances of Byrnes, Vandenberg, or Dulles, Churchill's speech had "made it difficult for the United States public to ignore the painful choices before them." Under pressure from leftists within his party, Bevin was less enthusiastic. He did not sign their protest, but he admitted to Gallman that the address had caused him a lot of work. In his opinion Churchill had shown poor judgment by saying the "right thing at the wrong time."[60]

Across the Atlantic the Truman administration privately agreed with British diplomats. Speaking off the record in New York, Harriman supported cooperation, stating that "whenever Russia was faced by an identical British and American policy her pressure abated." Leahy labeled the address a courageous statement. He and Truman had been aware of Churchill's intentions since February and after the president read the manuscript on the train to Missouri, he agreed with the accuracy of Churchill's evaluation. In the perceptive words of *Time* magazine, the speech was Truman's "magnificent trial balloon," for it seemed that he had let Churchill announce the administration's new view of the world situation and could await American reactions before assuming responsibility. It was thus an admirable speech, as Truman told Churchill en route to Fulton. It would do nothing but good, he added, although it would make a stir.[61]

Truman was right. The speech provoked great controversy. Congressional and press response revealed a divided public. The ranking minority member of the Foreign Relations Committee, Sen. Arthur Capper of Kansas, expressed Anglophobic indignation, calling the proposed fraternal association "a bid for us to furnish forces to help hold Gibraltar, Malta, Suez, Singapore, India and all the British colonial possessions." Other congressmen criticized the speech for undermining the United Nations. A sizable group supported the "realistic" evaluation of Russia, such as Rep. Charles A. Eaton of New Jersey. He felt that, in the face of the Soviet threat, if Britain and the United States were to "survive as free, democratic, capitalistic societies, they must stand together in complete unity," and Rep. William M. Colmer of Mississippi called Churchill's speech a "most profound and true exposition of world political conditions." The press reaction was similarly varied. The *Chicago Sun* stated that the president should reject such "poisonous doctrines," and Manhattan's pro-Russian *PM* angrily labeled the speech an "ideological declaration of war against Russia." The *Wall Street Journal* thought it brilliant with a "hard core of indisputable fact," and David Lawrence editorialized that there was a very good chance that Russia "will be stopped if the United States and Great Britain stick together."[62]

The reaction from the press and Congress was expected, but it is doubtful that the president was prepared for the response from grass-roots America. From Brookline, Massachusetts, to Torrance, California, letters and telegrams went to the White House. The message was clear—Americans were outraged. The speech had revived Anglophobia. A Seattle woman asked, "Does criticism of Russia negate the fact that

millions of Britain's colonials are living in slavery?" A man
from that city added that "Britain has subsidized not only the
pot-bellied reactionary rulers of India but every bloodthirsty
puppet ruler in the Middle East." A New York woman asked
if we must "again be forced to pull England's chestnuts out of
the fire, paying the bill as usual, while the British Empire
expands and strengthens itself for future conquests?" The
letters demonstrated that many Americans had little faith in
administration policy or in Truman as president. One Massachusetts woman declared that "we won the war but You and
Your state department are losing the peace," and a man on
the West Coast complained that the president's "genial tail
wagging behind British Toryism is none too gradually forcing
us into a suicidal course of action." A Salt Lake City lawyer
accused Truman of playing flunky for Churchill, and a New
Yorker wrote, "It seems that Mr. Churchill took you for a
sleigh ride." He added, "Let us be honest with the world. Let's
not be bullies. And above all let's not be England's Catspaw."
A New York woman excoriated the chief executive: "Where
do *you* get off at allowing your presidency to be made a stupid
mockery of? I keep telling myself you can't be as unen-
lightened and inane as you seem. I seem to recall that you
were a good senator. If the presidency is too difficult for you,
why the devil don't you resign?"[63]

Truman identified with the common people and flinched
from these attacks on his personality and policies. His administration dissociated itself from the speech. Byrnes had read
and discussed the address a month earlier, but he now denied
that the government had anything to do with it and insisted
that he had not been consulted. The straight talker from Missouri crumbled under pressure and lied to the American
people. In a 8 March news conference he stated, "I didn't
know what would be in Mr. Churchill's speech." Ross, Truman's press secretary, later added that the president had "no
advanced knowledge and didn't know what Mr. Churchill was
going to say." Before the former prime minister sailed from
New York, Undersecretary of State Dean Acheson, the administration's representative, canceled his appearance at
Churchill's farewell reception at the Waldorf. "Urgent but

unexplained matters" forced Acheson to remain in Washington.[64]

The denials did not mean that the administration no longer agreed with Churchill. The president and his advisers were convinced that the evaluation was accurate. Truman told Jonathan Daniels that the former prime minister had been right all along. "Churchill had tried to get me not to withdraw our troops from Prague. I told him we were bound to do that by our agreements with the Russians. But if I had known then what I know now, I would have ordered the troops to go to the western boundaries of Russia." A month after the speech the president met Air Marshal Douglas. During a White House conversation Truman made quite clear that he was "fully in agreement with what Churchill had said." Douglas recorded that Truman's ideas about Russian intransigence were much more closely in line with those of the British than had been the case in the recent past.[65] But in a storm of Anglophobia, the administration could not publicly adopt Churchill's policy. Truman would have to wait and later give English policy an American accent.

VIII

In the six months after Potsdam, the Truman administration adopted a new attitude toward the Allies that became apparent later in 1946. The Soviet Union promoted the change. Russian behavior appalled American diplomats in Eastern Europe, Iran, and Korea and outraged a public that had hoped for a world based on Wilsonian ideals. It was true, as Gage wrote in a Foreign Office minute, that Russian actions were "busily forging a strong demand in the U.S. for a strong policy and arousing unusual sympathy for the British position."[66] The allied ratio was in effect—as Soviet behavior became more offensive, Britain's friendship became more attractive.

British diplomacy also contributed to the evolution of policy. The immediate aim was to guide America into collaboration: the eventual hope was to provoke the United States into assuming responsibility for Western democracy. Foreign Office officials felt that America's "general awakening" to the international situation and the origin of a more realistic policy began with Bevin's stand at the United Nations. This idea contains some truth. On 11 March *Newsweek* published an article concerning the administration's new approach toward Russia and, after mentioning the foreign-policy speeches of Vandenberg, Dulles, and Byrnes, noted: "Beating them all to the punch had been Ernest Bevin, British Foreign Secretary, in his clashes with the Russian UNO delegate to London, Andrei Vyshinsky." Bevin provided the American people and especially their negotiators with a vivid example of leadership, confronting the Soviets over Iran and Eastern Europe. This crusade appealed to Western values. Americans began to wonder why their nation, the strongest in the world, was playing a secondary role to Britain and not taking the lead against the Kremlin. Vandenberg, impressed by Bevin's stout diplomacy, returned to the Senate and called for change. A week later Churchill aroused the American people, dramatically buried the Grand Alliance, proclaimed the iron curtain, and forced the giant to evaluate its position in the world. The address influenced opinion. Leahy wrote that it might "go down in history as one of the most profound influences in bringing about a close British-American collaboration to preserve world peace." Polls after the speech found that only one American in four approved of Churchill's suggestions, but by May, 83 percent of those asked favored a permanent military alliance with Britain.[67]

British diplomacy during the first three months of 1946 was a catalyst—Bevin's stand in the U.N.O. and Churchill's address accelerated the evolution of the administration's new attitude toward Russia. Both men, along with diplomats at Whitehall, helped to convince Americans that the best way to achieve democratic goals and to contain Russian expansion was to cooperate with a willing ally, Great Britain, and to confront an unwilling one, the Soviet Union.

Chapter 5

The Rise of a Partnership

Nineteen forty-six was a crucial year. During those twelve months the wounds of a world war began to heal. Men returned home, and women gave birth to a new and innocent generation. If destruction had tainted the past, construction would mark the future. People began rebuilding their homes, cities, nations, and their lives.

In international affairs, the people of the world witnessed a profound metamorphosis in Soviet-American-British relations. The Grand Alliance collapsed. The Big Three split into two blocs—East versus West—a situation that influenced international events for at least the next generation. The policies of Britain andRussia toward the allies changed little, but those of the United States shifted dramatically. The inclination to mediate and to act independently gave way to a "patient and firm" approach toward the Kremlin. The Americans demonstrated new leadership in negotiations, which eventually had implications for the British. They accepted the role of a "junior partner" in a Western alliance, staunchly supporting the Truman administration's initiatives.

Naturally, the rise of closer relations did not mean agreement on all issues between the democracies. Americans insisted on independence for colonial peoples and the demise of empires, a somber thought to many Britons. The United States supported liberal trade policies throughout the world. The British justly complained that they would not be able to compete and that they had paid enough since their industries had been targets for the Luftwaffe. American free trade sounded too much like economic imperialism. Britain also resented the Truman administration's policies monopolizing atomic secrets and the occupation of Japan. After all, Britain had participated in developing the bomb and in the Pacific war. The complex problem of Palestine raised animosity.

118

While the British were attempting to control an impossible situation and prevent war in the Middle East, Americans demanded the immediate establishment of a Jewish homeland.[1]

All these issues raised tension, especially between the people and press of the two nations, to a much lesser degree between officials in Washington and London. They realized that the paramount question of the postwar years was not decolonialization, free trade, or Israel. Instead, how would the West confront what they perceived as a threat from the Soviet Union? That question was answered in 1946 by the rise of a "parallel policy," which first appeared in the summer at the meetings of the Council of Foreign Ministers and later at the peace conference in Paris. By autumn, after Russian and Yugoslav provocations in August, the United States finally adopted the approach Britain had been advocating since 1944—an Anglo-American partnership.

I

The first public expression of a tougher American attitude toward the U.S.S.R. appeared two weeks after Churchill, Leahy, and Truman met at the White House and discussed Soviet behavior and Churchill's upcoming speech at Fulton. On 27 February, the night before Byrnes was to address the Overseas Press Club, Truman edited the speech and told him to "stiffen and try for the next three months not to make any compromises." In his speech the secretary of state declared that no nation had the right to station troops in the territory of another sovereign state, to prolong the making of peace, or to seize property before completing a reparation agreement. To support these words, the administration announced early in March that it would send a naval task force to the eastern Mediterranean. Ostensibly the navy was to take home the body of the late Turkish ambassador, or in the president's words, "to honor a dead Turk," but in reality this move demonstrated that Washington supported Ankara against Moscow. Unable to send a squadron because of demobilization, the president dispatched his favorite ship, the U.S.S. *Missouri*. While Truman and Churchill were at Fulton, Byrnes sent a stiff note to the Kremlin calling for immediate with-drawal of the Red Army from Iran. He commented to the new ambassador to Iran, George V. Allen, that if the Russians were denounced as violators of their treaty before the Security Council, the United States must "support Iran even if it meant an irreparable break with the U.S.S.R." Later in March the administration protested Soviet actions in Bulgaria, Manchuria, and Korea, and Byrnes proclaimed in New York City that the United States could not disarm while other nations remained armed. On Army Day the president urged Congress to unify the services, to extend the draft, and to adopt universal military training. In what was to become a familiar rhetorical phrase, he declared that the United States must "assume leadership and accept responsibility."[2]

Following Truman's instructions, Byrnes presented a more forceful policy at the Council of Foreign Ministers meeting in Paris. Before the conference the secretary of state was pessimistic, predicting in a cabinet meeting of 19 April that no agreement would be reached since there seemed to be no way of getting the Soviets to compromise. Even the Poles, he said, listened to proposals when they anticipated a loan, but money had no influence with the Russians. The first session, convened on 25 April and lasting until mid-May, was intended to resolve issues of peace treaties with the former satellites, the disarmament and demilitarization of Germany, and the status of Trieste and the Italian-Yugoslav border. Unlike his behavior at the Moscow conference, Byrnes did not seek a compromise. Instead he took the initiative and proposed the immediate reduction and eventual removal of occupation troops from Europe and a plebiscite to determine the fate of Trieste. He later surprised both the British and Russians by urging that the Allies sign a twenty-five-year, four-power treaty to keep Germany disarmed. The Russians would not accept the proposals, and the ministers adjourned until June. After returning to Washington, Byrnes explained to the American people that winning the peace required not only tolerance and understanding but also "patience and firmness."[3]

This diplomacy marked a new departure for the United States. The nation had traditionally abstained from long-term commitments in Continental affairs but now was willing to sign a twenty-five-year treaty. Nineteen nineteen would not be repeated; Americans would not leave Europeans to their own devices. Nor would the American people continue to accept hopeful statements about future cooperation with the Kremlin, for after more than a half-year of negotiations it was painfully clear that the Russians would not accept Western aims in areas occupied by the Red Army. Now, in spring 1946, the Truman administration began to unveil its long-range policies, ones that openly contradicted those of the Soviets. Future cooperation among the Big Three was an illusion. The Grand Alliance was being buried, and a new era in international relations was being born.

America's new diplomacy was noticed on both sides of the Atlantic. The *New York Times* called Byrnes's proposal a "most daring venture" and "one of the best-prepared that any American Secretary of State had ever attempted." Ernest Lindley wrote in *Newsweek* that Byrnes had gone to Paris with the "intention not only to stand firm but to seize and hold the initiative," and *Time* declared that the secretary of state "after months of feeble diplomacy, had boldly retrieved U.S. leadership." In London, the *Times* saw the United States "moving towards what seems likely to prove a decisive turning-point in American, and indeed in world affairs"; compared to the isolation that followed the First World War, the present attitude was "scarcely short of miraculous." Though less surprised, Whitehall officials were encouraged. As late as the first week in March the Americans seemed to have "devoted themselves to an orgy of escapism" but the Paris conference marked an entirely new phase; there the Americans were much tougher than at London or Moscow. Halifax informed the Foreign Office that there was almost no talk of power politics or the mediator role and that the public was aware of America's responsibilities as a great power. British diplomats saw Truman's Army Day speech as an indication that he planned to maintain the "recent firmer policy of his Administration."[4]

II

Throughout the remainder of 1946 British power declined as economic problems increased, and London's relations with

Moscow deteriorated. From Moscow Roberts wrote gloomily that Britain had no option but to accustom itself to "a constant atmosphere of tension," for any hope of achieving a general settlement seemed illusory. Most diplomats in London were at least this solemn; indeed, one Whitehall official, Thomas Brimelow, thought Roberts's analysis too optimistic.[5]

The path of British diplomacy was clear. Gage wrote in a Foreign Office minute: "Anglo-American relations were becoming increasingly the bedrock of our policy." During the Iran crisis, Whitehall officials agreed that the only means of resisting Russian pressure on the empire was solidarity and cooperation with the United States. To obtain American support these officials were prepared to make a major sacrifice: they now would welcome the Americans on equal terms in an area they had long considered their special preserve—the Middle East. Paul Mason wrote that Great Britain must "genuinely encourage, and not merely acknowledge in principle, American attempts to develop their own interest in these countries." Other officials supported this view and they called for "an extra effort on our side" to gain American collaboration.[6]

Thus Bevin and his subordinates carried out a constant exchange of views and ideas with the Americans during spring 1946, warning of Soviet intentions, proposing Anglo-American stratagems, and supporting the administration's new stand against Russia. Undersecretary Oliver Harvey told Gallman in late February that beyond any doubt Moscow's aim in Germany was a Communist state. British diplomats urged the State Department to join them in confronting the Kremlin about free navigation on the Danube. Undersecretary Warner reminded Gallman in mid-March that once the Soviets initiated a policy they could not modify it and would "crash on relentlessly regardless of effects elsewhere." That same month Bevin wrote a long message to Byrnes outlining a joint policy to oust the Red Army from Iran. He suggested that if the Soviets refused to attend the United Nations, or walked out when the issue was introduced, the Security Council should go ahead without them. Britain and America had to "face this issue squarely," attempting to resolve it and other postwar problems without the Soviet Union. In April the Foreign Office urged the State Department to take the initiative and resist Russian demands for reparations in Austria and to oppose the Kremlin's position on international waterways. Before the foreign ministers' meeting Bevin proposed that both nations agree on an agenda and send the list to Moscow. In May he asked Byrnes to consult on a joint economic plan for Eastern Europe and suggested that, if the Russians would not compromise on peace terms with the former belligerents, Britain and America should sign separate treaties.[7]

The campaign mounted. Harriman, now ambassador to London, met with Warner in May and was told that the Russians "would proceed in a wholly selfish way following an obstructionist and uncompromising course" to obtain their goals. After the Overseas Press Club speech, Bevin sent congratulations to Byrnes: "In the words of the cockney, 'Blimey, them's my sentiments.' Good Luck." Before sailing back to England, Churchill told Forrestal that he was very glad the U.S.S. *Missouri* was being sent to the Dardanelles, but that an entire fleet would be better. The Foreign Office and the Admiralty welcomed this show of force and support for Turkey. After the secretary of state reported on America's policy at the Council of Foreign Ministers meeting in a radio address of 20 May, Bevin wrote to him: "I want you to know that I am entirely with you in the firm and altogether admirable stand which you took in your speech." Bevin made his support public on 4 June when he addressed the House of Commons.[8]

Such tactics were intended to ensure an Anglo-American front; other factors made Britain an appealing junior partner to the United States. The Labour party had promised to transform the empire into a commonwealth—a complex transformation for more than forty territories spread around the globe, ranging in size and population from India to the Falkland Islands. The government had worked out a program during the winter, and in spring 1946 it announced that India would receive independence and that Britain would evacuate most of its troops from Syria and Egypt. Americans remembered 1776 and welcomed the news as a signal ending the age of colonialism. Balfour's reports from the British embassy in Washington of the favorable response aroused hope at the Foreign Office that Britain's chances for a $3.75 billion loan had increased.[9]

During summer 1946 Whitehall officials wanted to improve relations with the United States and put forth a variety of proposals to their superiors. They advocated close cultural contacts through speaking tours; student, professional, government, and motion-picture exchange programs; broadcasting the BBC from New York; and tours of England for American servicemen on leave from Germany. Other ideas included simplifying visa and passport regulations, talking with visiting American politicians and journalists, and encouraging investment by eliminating double taxation of American companies in Britain. Some suggestions were more bizarre, such as giving the United States embassy a country estate or commemorating the fifty destroyers traded to Britain in 1940 by sending a history of each destroyer and even its bell to the American town after which it had been named.[10]

These gestures, and the transformation of the empire, were minor considerations. The main reason Britain became a more appealing partner was Soviet behavior. The Truman administration feared the spread of communism in the Middle East, China, Southeast Asia, France, and Italy. The Kremlin's goals in Korea, Iran, Germany, Austria, Trieste, Greece, Turkey, and throughout Eastern Europe clashed with those of the White House. At the foreign ministers' meeting Molotov repeatedly dismissed American and British proposals with "nyet," until one delegate, Sen. Tom Connally, asked Molotov, "Isn't there a word in the Russian language meaning 'yes?'" Byrnes called Truman and said that the Soviets were getting "more difficult than ever," and Vandenberg felt that Russian-American relations had "fallen into a bottomless pit." Simultaneously Americans were forming a more endearing opinion of the mother country. British diplomats in Washington wrote home after the Paris conference that their country's stock in the United States was "higher this week than it has been for a long time past. It is generally agreed that the news from Paris disproved the allegation that Britain is as obstructive as the U.S.S.R., and showed that, on all key issues, it can be relied upon to assist America in her peace offensive."[11]

III

By the summer of 1946 Russian intransigence and British persuasion were producing a new Anglo-American partnership. After the failure at Paris the new U.S. policy was revealed in a booklet dated 15 May and apparently written by State Department officials and the special counsel to the president, Clark M. Clifford. Part one concerned American policy toward the Kremlin and stated that if it was impossible "to enlist Soviet cooperation in the solution of world problems, we must be prepared to join with the British and other Western countries" and recognize that the United States cannot pursue common aims with the Soviet Union. That same week Balfour met Acheson, who remarked that the failure at Paris "drove home the lesson that there can be no early adjustment of the differences between the Soviet Union and the West, and that we must anticipate an endless process of argument in which neither side will find it possible to reconcile its point of view with the other."[12]

The administration now began to adopt a "parallel policy" with Britain against the former ally, the Soviet Union. In June, Acheson wrote Byrnes about Bevin's proposal that the democracies initiate a joint economic policy toward Eastern Europe. The State Department desired informal consultation to achieve a general understanding on objectives but wanted to stop short of measures "which would give the appearance of joint action by UK and US." Similar views were expressed that same month in a discussion between Balfour of the British embassy and Kennan, Elbridge Durbrow, and Llewellyn Thompson of the department. Durbrow remarked that when reporters asked if America was conspiring with Britain against Russia he answered that the appearance of concerted action was the "inevitable outcome of our possessing a kindred concept of human liberties." Balfour concluded that American officials were "readier than ever before to accept the spectacle of parallel Anglo-American action towards the Soviet Union," but that as a diplomatic tactic, independent representations should be made to the Kremlin.[13] The administration did not want to encourage accusations that Russia faced a Western bloc.

There were many other indications of a new parallel policy. The most important issue at this time between the Anglo-Americans and the Soviet Union was how to get the Red Army out of Iran. On 5 March Byrnes sent a note to Moscow demanding an evacuation, and the next day a British message supporting the American demand arrived in the Soviet capital. Three days later Byrnes inquired if Bevin would "join the US in placing the Iranian question before the Security Council." Bevin agreed, and the two men corresponded on tactics for the next United Nations meeting; their collaboration continued until the Red Army evacuated Azerbaidzhan in May. During March Britain and America also sent similar notes to Moscow protesting the situation in Bulgaria and Manchuria. Before the Paris meeting of the Council of Foreign Ministers Bevin proposed that both nations exchange views and agree on agenda. Byrnes agreed but, fearing charges of conspiracy, suggested that Britain transmit the list to all allies, to "avoid any feelings that the British and Americans have any advance agreements." In a cabinet meeting of 19 April, Byrnes said that if the Russians would not compromise at Paris, then the United States, Britain, and France might "sign a separate treaty with Italy and later present it to the other nations for ratification." During the ensuing conference Byrnes and Bevin supported each other, especially concerning the Danube, Trieste, and Germany. In May they sent protests to the Kremlin concerning the situation in Rumania, and the administration approved an earlier British proposal to publish captured German documents, including those leading to the 1939 Nazi-Soviet pact.[14]

Britain and America also collaborated on Yugoslavia and Austria. Tension was growing between Yugoslav and Western forces in Venezia Giulia. While the control of the border area was being considered, Tito increased anti-Western propaganda and hinted that his army might take the region by force. Border incidents became more common, prompting an Anglo-American response. Western commanders warned the Yugoslavs in April that they would defend their position, and in mid-May the British and American representatives in Belgrade presented virtually identical protests to Tito. That same month in Vienna both democracies were working on a draft peace treaty for Austria. The Americans accepted the British plan and in June agreed that German assets in Austria and the withdrawal of occupation forces should be discussed at the next meeting of the Council of Foreign Ministers. Acheson supported the British, feeling that "something should be done at once to bolster Austrian morale and strengthen its ties with the western states." By August the State Department gave "all possible support" to Whitehall's demand that a four-power commission investigate the denazification program in Austria—especially in the Soviet zone.[15]

At the same time there was an increasing amount of strategic and military cooperation. Well before the Japanese attack on Pearl Harbor there had been Anglo-American strategy discussions, and in April 1941 a British military mission had been established in Washington. Staff meetings took place regularly until the United States entered the war, and at the Arcadia conference the allies established the Combined Chiefs of Staff. After V-E Day Britain hoped to continue these relations, and at Potsdam the British Chiefs of Staff sent a memorandum to the Americans urging "continuation of machinery for combined United States/British collaboration in the military sphere after the defeat of Japan." They reasoned that in the future both nations could best solve military problems through the formal continuation of the combined chiefs. Canny as usual, Churchill appealed to American self-interest during a discussion with Truman at Potsdam: "Why should an American battleship calling at Gibraltar not find the torpedoes to fit her tubes, and the shells to fit her guns deposited there? Why should we not share facilities for defense all over the world? We could add 50 per cent to the mobility of the American Fleet." The offer was premature:

the Truman administration was still attempting to mediate between the Allies and did not see a Soviet threat or care to raise suspicion by signing an agreement with the British.[16]

Six months later, however, American military officials became more interested in ties with the British. By February 1946 the Joint Chiefs of Staff (JCS) had arrived at two conclusions. They endorsed a firm and friendly attitude toward Russia, "with the emphasis upon 'firmness,'" and they conceded that "from a military point of view the cohesion of the Western European countries into a bloc would be not only desirable but also advantageous." This plan meant more coordination with the British. A month earlier General Eisenhower, newly appointed Army Chief of Staff, had informed the director of the British military mission in Washington, Field Marshal Sir Henry Maitland Wilson, that the JCS now felt that the two nations should begin informal discussions concerning military collaboration. In early March Wilson met with Leahy; they discussed continuing the standardization of arms and the Combined Chiefs of Staff, both established during the war, and American desires to maintain sovereignty over British islands in the Pacific containing bases. Byrnes had asked Bevin if Britain would cede the islands, and on 8 March the Labour government authorized representatives in Washington to begin discussion. Although Bevin would have made the concession, the Dominion and Colonial offices rejected the scheme, and eventually the two governments compromised on a joint sovereignty.[17]

During the last two weeks in May Leahy met with British Chiefs of Staff in London and discussed other strategic and military issues. Earlier in the month the JCS had supported a British proposal for the U.S. Air Force to exchange strategic plans and information with the RAF. Now leaders of M.I.-5, Britain's secret service, wanted to continue the wartime policy of exchanging secret information with the FBI. British military men were interested in the status of the Pacific islands that the United States had captured from Japan. The administration considered giving them to the United Nations, but the British objected, preferring joint utilization by Anglo-American forces. On the evening of 21 May Leahy dined with

Churchill, who informed him that he remained completely devoted to the principles enunciated at Fulton and proclaimed that British and American military installations, "wherever situated, should be available for common use."[18] The islands remained under American control, and by the end of 1946, Churchill's suggestion had become policy.

There were other examples of rising Anglo-American cooperation. As a trading nation Britain was concerned about free passage for shipping in the Baltic Sea for after the war Russian soldiers had retained an outpost on an island in the Danish straits. Bevin felt that the best way to ensure free passage and bring about the withdrawal of Soviet troops was by adopting a joint policy with the United States and presenting it to the Kremlin. He urged this to Byrnes in January 1946, but in vain. Although the Red Army evacuated the island without incident in the spring, Bevin still sought an Anglo-American protocol on free shipping and in June sent a draft to Washington that he hoped both democracies would submit to Moscow. By now the State Department had decided to pursue a "common line with the British Government in any future discussions of this subject." Both nations also collaborated in the maintenance of air and naval bases in the Azores. An Anglo-American-Portuguese agreement granting continued use of the bases was signed in May.[19]

While showing more interest in discussing strategic issues with the British, the United States naturally became more concerned about hemispheric defense and negotiated with its southern neighbors for the mutual defense treaty proposed the preceding year by the Act of Chapultepec. Washington also improved military collaboration with Ottawa, a move that had worldwide implications since Canada was a member of the British Commonwealth and had traditionally joined Great Britain as soon as war broke out in Europe. In 1940 the United States and Canada had created a Permanent Joint Board on Defense and they continued this liaison after V-J Day. In February 1946 they established a cooperation committee to coordinate defense, military, and foreign policy. The two governments exchanged military information and participated in such exercises as MUSKOX, the movement of a mechanized force some three thousand miles through the Arctic. By June the Permanent Joint Board on Defense recommended that both nations construct an air defense system, begin surveillance to stop infiltration, institute antisubmarine patrols, and establish a combined command structure.[20]

The press noticed the rise of this Anglo-American partnership. As early as 10 March, the *New York Times* noted an identical policy toward Iran and Bulgaria, and it declared that the British and American protest about Russian actions in Manchuria demonstrated "a similar, if not joint, policy toward the Soviet Union." During the Council of Foreign Ministers meeting in early May the *Manchester Guardian* noted a more forceful and coordinated approach of the two countries, and after interviewing officials in the administration, James Reston concluded that there was "no future in trying to break up the Anglo-American bloc or denying that it exists."[21]

IV

During the summer there were two significant examples of the new partnership. The United States realized that Britain would need a postwar loan. In 1944 Roosevelt told Hull that the "real hub of the situation is to keep Britain from going into complete bankruptcy at the end of the war." The British hoped that lend-lease would be continued during the transition to a peacetime economy, but just days after Japan surrendered Truman abruptly terminated the wartime aid. The president's action caused hard feelings in Britain, and the noted economist, Lord John Maynard Keynes, called it "a financial Dunkirk." Now it was urgent that the British government secure assistance from the United States, and talks commenced in Washington on 11 September 1945. Britain's negotiator, Lord Keynes, originally asked for a gift of $5 or $6 billion, but he soon landed on earth and recognized that the most he could hope for was a $3.75 billion loan at 2 percent interest.[22] The agreement was signed on 6 December and sent to Congress.

There was much opposition to the loan. Many Americans thought the Labourites would use the money to support their socialistic program or to prop up the tottering empire. Zionists felt that it would finance Britain's restrictive Jewish policy in Palestine, and some conservatives feared it would be an expensive precedent if other nations, especially Russia, asked for assistance. The loan application rekindled Anglophobia. Sen. Kenneth McKellar of Tennessee was suspicious, writing the president and asking if Britain was "going to use money borrowed from us to build a stronger navy than we will have." Remembering the loan defaults after the First World War, the public was against aiding Britan. Opinion polls during the winter of 1945–1946 found that about 30 percent of those asked supported the loan, and only one in eight believed it would be fully repaid.[23]

Regardless of opposition, the administration demonstrated new support for Britain by making the loan one of its primary objectives. Early in March 1946, Truman began the campaign by declaring that the loan would rebuild commerce, end trade barriers, and be the cornerstone of world peace. The loan would be good business for American industries, workers, and farmers. These themes were restated throughout the spring by Acheson, Clayton, Henry A. Wallace, and other administration officials.

The Kremlin helped the British cause. As the Soviets became more unmanageable, Americans perceived the importance of a financially healthy junior partner to form a democratic-capitalistic front against Communist expansion. A former assistant secretary of commerce, Ernest G. Draper, felt that with the growing Soviet threat Americans must help the British because they would "powerfully aid us in sustaining a free enterprise world." Senator Vandenberg led the fight in Congress, even working to break opposition within his own party. After Soviet obstinacy at the Paris conference, supporters became more vociferous. The Speaker of the House, Sam Rayburn, feared that without assistance Britain would be forced toward communism, leaving the United States with no ally across the Atlantic. The *New York Times* went even further, insisting that the congressional vote on the bill would decide whether the entire world "shall look to the American or to the Russian system for salvation."[24]

Truman signed the loan agreement on 15 July 1946. The administration's campaign had been decisive. No longer attempting to ascertain opinion and then formulate policy, officials in Washington were now acting to build a consensus that supported their international goals. The administration's vigorous support for the loan also signaled the future path of America's relations with its former allies. In August 1945 the Soviet Union had requested a $1 billion loan, and while the administration feverishly campaigned for the British, the State Department mysteriously "lost" the Russian application. The Soviet government tried again in May 1946, now apparently willing to discuss American trade in Eastern Europe. But by then American officials had little intention of negotiating a loan to Russia.[25] The administration had made its choice, and it was in favor of the "junior partner."

Three days before the president signed the loan agreement Britain and the United States agreed to merge their zones in Germany. This step had obvious political and military gains for Britain, but its economic advantages were even more important. The British zone included the industrial areas of Hamburg and the Ruhr, where about 60 percent of the houses and 90 percent of the transportation had been damaged or destroyed by Allied bombs. The English had to provide for about two million displaced persons, many of whom had fled the advancing Red Army, and for some two-and-a-half million former German soldiers. Food and housing were scarce. A year after V-E Day the normal ration still consisted of a thousand calories per day, and ten people lived in a dwelling that had housed four in 1939. Reconstruction was slow, and in July 1946 the volume of industrial production was only a third of what it had been in 1936. A year later it had risen 1 percent. Financing the zone placed a heavy burden on British taxpayers—about $320 million for 1946. The Labour government could not afford this expense, and Bevin sought to alleviate the burden by urging the Allies to treat Germany as an economic unit in which resources would be equitably distributed. The Soviets opposed, and the British approached the American military governor in Germany, Gen. Lucius D. Clay. According to Clay's political adviser, Robert D. Murphy, the "British decided very soon after

Potsdam that Germany was permanently divided between East and West, and they proposed then that the United States and France cooperate with them in the three Western zones."[26]

Confronted with similar but less severe economic problems in their southern, agricultural zone, the Americans desired interzonal cooperation, but in 1945 they were not yet interested in joining the British. In November Assistant Secretary of War John J. McCloy told Michael R. Wright that Clay was a firm believer in four-power collaboration and like many other Americans felt that any appearance of joint efforts against the Soviets would make Allied cooperation difficult or impossible. As a result, McCloy continued, the general would occasionally "go through the motions of aligning himself with the Russians" as a matter of tactics. During the first half of 1946 the situation degenerated in Germany. While the Soviets accused the British of maintaining the Wehrmacht for possible use against the eastern zone, their own inhumane transfers of people, their brutal denazification program, their restriction of interzonal travel and trade, their control of the press and political parties, and their reparations policy all repelled the Anglo-Americans.[27]

Clay became pessimistic about cooperating with Russia, and as German economic conditions deteriorated he drew closer to the British. By early 1946 Western officials were working for common goals, and they urged German leaders to meet and discuss interzonal cooperation, especially concerning economic matters. At a conference of German officials on 16 February, one spokesman revealed that Americans "dangle before us the combination of the zones. Coordination between the British and American zones is the purpose of our meeting." In April Clay urged Byrnes to support his plan for central administrative agencies, common financial policy, and a provisional government, and a month later he submitted a full proposal to the War Department. He complained that integration was becoming more difficult every day because of Russian (and French) obstinacy and recommended that if Moscow refused to cooperate the Americans should approach the British.[28]

The Americans took the initiative in Germany, and Bevin

vigorously promoted Brynes's proposal for a twenty-five-year, four-power treaty to keep Germany disarmed. This proposal implied that the United States was prepared to remain involved in European affairs. Bevin announced to Parliament that the proposed treaty was the "greatest possible hope for the removal of misunderstanding and the creation of confidence" and that the United States had accepted the obligations of peace. Little was accomplished in April, and at the 11 July session of the Council of Foreign Ministers Byrnes placed before the Allies what he called his "last resort—the merger of the zones of occupation, with or without the Soviet Union."[29]

A day after Byrnes's proposal, on 12 July, Bevin accepted in principle. His acceptance was expected, for Clay had predicted that response in May, and the merger had been discussed privately by Bevin and Byrnes. The foreign secretary reported to the cabinet on 15 July that the secretary of state suggested immediate arrangements for "co-operation between the British and American Zones to the exclusion of the Russian Zone." After France and the Soviet Union rejected the proposal, the British cabinet accepted it. Interzonal differences were overcome. In August and September officials in Germany negotiated agreements creating common agencies of economics, transport, agriculture, finance, food, and communication, and in November financial discussions took place in Washington. On 2 December Byrnes and Bevin signed the Bizonal Fusion Agreement, and on 1 January 1947 the two zones became one. If the Russians refused to cooperate, Truman told Davies in September, "Britain and the United States would have to go alone without them."[30]

V

During the long summer of 1946, Russian behavior became increasingly alarming which, of course, encouraged closer Anglo-American relations.

Behind the expected strong language and tenacious negotiation Western observers had the uneasy feeling that the Soviet Union was initiating an offensive aimed at provoking the United States. For the first time America supplanted Britain as the Kremlin's primary propaganda target. In June, Washington's new ambassador to Moscow, Walter Bedell Smith, informed the State Department about the rise of criticism. The Soviet press was claiming that Byrnes had repudiated Roosevelt's foreign policy and that Truman had initiated "anti-worker" domestic programs. The *Red Star* charged on 24 June that American intervention was responsible for the civil war in China. A month later *Pravda* noted that an "orgy of war profiteering continues in the U.S. despite the curtailing of war orders," and papers detailed acts of violence such as the lynchings of blacks in the South.[31]

There was also indication of a Soviet military buildup. During the spring Leahy received a message from observers in Vladivostok who noticed arrival of large amounts of military supplies. The admiral underlined the concluding remark— *"There certainly must be a war going on somewhere"*—and sent the message to the president. Leahy wrote in his diary that many experts in Washington held the opinion that Russia was "so intoxicated with power as to be capable of starting another war." Such thoughts lingered during June when he received warnings that Moscow might be planning a surprise attack either in Germany or, more likely, in the Balkans. The naval attaché in Odessa sent information that Marshal Zhukov had arrived there to mobilize Russian, Rumanian, and Bulgarian forces for a "major campaign." According to gossip in the city, Russia would be at war within two months. In July observers reported from Belgrade that all the Kremlin's energies were directed toward rebuilding the military and from Albania that the little country was going to give an island to Russia for a naval base. Next month the Swedish spotted "ghost rockets" in their skies, apparently launched from the Soviet zone of Germany. The State Department received startling news a few months later from Poland: the Russians had moved eight divisions through that country to Eastern Germany in October. Slogans appeared on the sides of tanks and railroad cars: "We destroyed Germany, we shall now destroy England and America," and "Death to Anglo-Saxons."[32]

Events of August added to Western suspicions. During the

war Russia had advocated changes in the Montreux Convention, which regulated transit through the Dardanelles. Moscow officials desired a naval base and joint power with Turkey to regulate transit through the straits, but Britain and the United States preferred a free international waterway guaranteed by the great powers. In 1946 the Kremlin adopted a threatening tone toward Turkey, which resisted with Anglo-American support. Apparently attempting to unnerve the Turks, on 7 August Moscow demanded that the Dardanelles be placed under control of the Black Sea nations with joint Russian-Turkish defense. This scheme seemed little more than a bid for domination since, with exception of Turkey, all Black Sea countries were occupied by the Red Army. Two days later an unarmed American transport plane flying supplies from Austria to Italy was shot down by Yugoslav fighters. The C-47 had veered off course during a storm and was some two miles inside Yugoslav airspace. American officials protested, demanding to see the crew members held in prison. Tito refused. On 19 August a Yugoslav fighter shot down another C-47, this time killing five crew members. On the same day the partisan leader rejected the American version of the first incident and protested the "constant and systematic flights of Americans over Yugoslav territory." Tito said he wanted peace "but not at any price."[33]

Americans were outraged. The *Cleveland Plain Dealer* felt that the United States should "fight fire with fire," and the *New York Daily News* suggested dropping an "atomic bomb on some uninhabited Yugoslav country district." The *San Francisco Chronicle* pugnaciously demanded that the Truman administration give Tito a "backhand in the teeth." There was no doubt in the United States or Britain that the Yugoslavs were acting on orders from the Kremlin. *Newsweek* declared that "All Roads Lead to Moscow." Forrestal felt, as he earlier told the secretaries of state and war, that "Tito is, in fact, 'Russia' and that if any move was made it would be by Russian instigation."[34]

To the satisfaction of the British, the American response was quick and forceful. One day after the second C-47 was shot down, Byrnes met with the Yugoslavian vice-premier at the Paris peace conference and demanded an explanation. In Washington Acheson drafted a cable for the American ambassador in Belgrade. It was an ultimatum, insisting that the Yugoslavs renounce "outrageous acts" and free the crew of the C-47. If Yugoslavia did not comply within forty-eight hours, the United States would "call upon the Security Council of the United Nations to take appropriate action." Britain protested Yugoslav behavior, and both democracies made public their earlier notes warning Tito that any attempt to enter Venezia Giulia would be considered an act of war. The aviators were released before the deadline. Tito later announced that his air force would not fire on foreign planes. The Americans took no more chances—the next flight from Austria to Italy was made not by an unarmed C-47 but by a B-29 bomber.[35]

Britain and America reacted forcefully to Soviet demands on Turkey. Loy W. Henderson of the State Department later recalled that he, Acheson, the secretaries of war and navy, and the Joint Chiefs of Staff drew up a statement opposing Russian designs and delivered it to the White House. The president studied the memorandum, reading it over many times, and then leaned back in his chair and said, "Yes, this is a serious decision. The Soviet Union, Turkey, and the other powers, however, should know where we stand. I agree with the policy suggested, and it should be carried out with the minimum of threat and without provocation." British officials had come to the same conclusion and on 19 and 21 August, respectively, Washington and London supported Turkey and rejected the Kremlin's demands on the straits.[36]

Cooperation was becoming a habit. At the second session of the Council of Foreign Ministers in June and July the Big Four agreed to convene a general conference to consider the peace-treaty drafts that they had written for Italy, Finland, Rumania, Bulgaria, and Hungary. Twenty-one nations were represented during the session, which met in Paris from August to October. Bevin and Byrnes had many conversations about the treaties and other issues such as the straits, German and Austrian affairs, Palestine, and tactics before the United Nations and Council of Foreign Ministers meetings. Parallel representations were common, and it soon was obvious that the most salient characteristic of the conference was the appearance of blocs. Votes on controversial clauses in the treaties resulted in divisions between Eastern Europe and the West. During autumn the State Department instructed representatives to "coordinate US and UK programs," informing them that from now on there would be "periodic consultations" between the United States and Britain. By December Washington proclaimed that to counter Communist propaganda they would begin Russian-language broadcasts to the Soviet Union; London had made a similar announcement the previous April.[37]

Meanwhile Byrnes had become irritated at what he called the "Soviet campaign of misrepresentation" in Germany, and after Molotov's policy statement of 11 July he decided to clarify America's position by delivering an address at Stuttgart. On 6 September, after mentioning that security forces would remain in Germany for a long time, he came to the point: "I want no misunderstanding. We will not shirk our duty. We are not withdrawing. As long as an occupation force is required in Germany the Army of the United States will be part of that occupation force."[38]

Byrnes's speech received support on both sides of the Atlantic. *Newsweek* felt it was a sign that the administration was "Starting a Policy" and redefining relations with the wartime Allies. During a cabinet meeting of 6 September Forrestal and Patterson praised the speech, and Byrnes received congratulations from senators and congressmen. In Britain, the *Manchester Guardian* and London *Times* welcomed the address. It pledged American involvement in Europe, something Britain had desired since 1918. As soon as Byrnes returned to Paris he received applause from Bevin, who later added in Parliament: "It cannot be too often repeated that the continuance of American interest in Europe is vital to the peace of Europe and particularly to the future of Germany." From Switzerland, Churchill sent congratulations and asked if he could visit Byrnes on his return to London. The secretary of state, who had shunned the former prime minister after the Fulton speech six months earlier, was now eager for a meeting. The two men discussed the world situation, and Churchill heartily approved Byrnes's remarks.[39]

Yugoslav and Soviet behavior also stimulated an urgent desire for a combined show of force to meet the apparent threat to Europe. On 22 August ten thousand Anglo-American troops paraded along the Venezia Giulia border, and the British ordered three thousand reinforcements. During the previous March the Russians had told Greece that they wanted a naval base in the Aegean or guarantees that Greek isles would not become an obstacle to the Red Navy. Greece rejected the demands with support from London and Washington. To demonstrate support for the Greek plebiscite in September, the United States dispatched seven ships to the Aegean. The British government announced on 1 September that ships of the Royal Navy were steaming for Greek waters, and next day the largest American aircraft carrier, U.S.S. *Franklin D. Roosevelt,* anchored off Piraeus. Three weeks later twenty British warships arrived at Nauplia. Forrestal told reporters that the navy would protect the interests and support the diplomacy of the United States. He established the Sixth Fleet, which consisted of nine vessels by the end of the year and participated in naval exercises with the twenty-two ships of the Mediterranean fleet of the Royal Navy. At the same time, planners of the two nations were collaborating in Washington. The Joint Chiefs of Staff inquired about the capabilities of the British forces in Europe and invited British representatives to attend JCS meetings. At the 30 August conference Leahy called for contingency plans for Anglo-American forces in case of Russian attack. The British concurred, and arrangements were made to begin the necessary deliberations.[40]

In September, Field Marshal Montgomery, now chief of the imperial general staff, crossed the Atlantic. He felt that "the time had come for Britain, Canada, and the U.S.A. to cooperate closely in all defense matters," and while touring the Canadian Rocky Mountains received permission to begin discussions in Ottawa and Washington. Arriving in America, Montgomery told his plans to Eisenhower, and on 11 September he met Truman at the White House. The field marshal stated that defense talks should begin, and the president replied without hesitation: "That's O.K. by me, go right ahead." The first meeting convened five days later aboard the *Sequoia,* camouflaged as a social cruise down the Potomac to Mount Vernon. All the American chiefs were present and Admiral Leahy recorded in his diary: "Discussion was devoted to parallel action that may be possible for the British and American forces in Europe in the event of a sudden attack by Soviet or Yugoslav armies." The men agreed that talks were to begin concerning the concept of the West in a third world war.[41]

The democracies worked to increase military cooperation after Montgomery's visit. While attending the Paris peace conference, Byrnes and Bevin agreed on joint use of air and naval facilities, and by the end of the year, the Royal and American air forces began exchanging officers to study each other's research, equipment, and tactics. On 3 October JCS planners concluded that "it appears to be in the best interest of the United States to enter into discussions with the British" concerning the adoption of common designs and standards in arms, equipment, organization, training methods, and plans for research and development. That same month the JCS recommended an agreement with Britain for a full exchange of technical information, especially concerning electronic equipment and systems, and decided to continue joint research in bacteriological warfare. Canada collaborated; Prime Minister King met Truman on 31 October and agreed that the "closest cooperation was necessary." On 20 November the Permanent Joint Board on Defense recommended exchange of personnel, adoption of standard equipment, reciprocal use of facilities, and joint construction and maintenance of military projects. Both nations agreed to inform Great Britain, and on 29 November the JCS approved a British proposal for Anglo-American-Canadian long-term military planning. The plan called for combined communication and cryptographic systems and exchange of technical information. In case of war, the three countries would fight as one.[42]

Thus, the alliance built to crush Nazi Germany survived in the West. During the third week of November, American

British, and Canadian military experts conducted secret conversations in Washington and discussed arms standardization,
weapon research, and common tactical doctrines. Reversing
an earlier plan, Britain and the United States decided not to
disband the Combined Chiefs of Staff. More important, the
service missions of the two nations continued to communicate
on all levels; the British maintained offices at the Pentagon,
minutes away from the Joint Chiefs of Staff. By 1947 the
officer-exchange program was started, officials from the
British air ministry visited Maxwell Field and discussed
weapon development, and American B-29s began testing
British-made bombs.[43] Britain and America were constructing
an alliance that would eventually become the North Atlantic
Treaty Organization.

VI

In October 1946 Churchill remarked: "What I said at Fulton has been outpaced and overpassed by movements of
events, and by the movement of American opinion. If I were
to make that speech at the present time and in the same place,
it would attract no particular attention." That was true, for six
months after the former prime minister called for a military
alliance, the British and American chiefs of staff were busy
creating it. Less than a year after the war the Big Three were
divided, and the United States had discarded its desire to
mediate between the Allies in favor of an Anglo-American
parallel policy. *Newsweek* declared in September that "cooperation is becoming so close that the foreign policies of
Washington and London are practically identical, although
the fiction of independence is still maintained."[44]

American policy had changed considerably during the first
nine months of the crucial year, 1946. Officials were aban-
doning the dream of universalism, no longer pondering the
idea of a community of nations working together within a
world organization to resolve global issues. The United Nations would not be able to solve problems between the former
Allies, for those differences were too fundamental. Wilsonian
hopes evaporated, and instead Americans initiated another

approach, one that the British had hoped for and had expected. At Whitehall, Francis B. A. Rundall had predicted an American shift "away from compromise and toward the establishment of adequate safeguards against Russian expansion," and after this shift appeared in August he noted with a touch of irony that Washington was "adopting the balance-of-power foreign policy that she so roundly condemned in us for so many years."[45]

Indeed, the Truman administration had accepted old-world tactics for the new atomic age and now was supporting a balance of power between East and West. In both diplomatic and military strategy the United States was cooperating with Great Britain to form a policy that would later be labeled containment.

What produced this partnership? Britain had taken the initiative—challenging Russian aims in Europe, warning the State Department of Soviet intentions, emphasizing common democratic goals, proposing Anglo-American stratagems, reinforcing the administration's stand, and cooperating with Washington in such programs as Bizonia in Germany. In all these actions, the government sought to convince the United States that Britain was a valuable junior partner.

But the most important factor was Soviet behavior. Russian intransigency at the conference table, rising anti-American propaganda, and provocations in August baffled and then frustrated administration officials. By the second half of 1946 they could agree with Churchill's epigram that the Kremlin was a riddle wrapped in a mystery inside an enigma. Byrnes publicly confessed his bewilderment over Molotov's charges that the United States sought to enslave Europe economically, and no doubt he was thinking of negotiating with the Soviets when he ruefully remarked, "Any man who would want to be Secretary of State would go to hell for pleasure." By the Yugoslav crisis in August the administration was convinced, as Inverchapel reported to Whitehall: the Soviet Union was the "ubiquitous trouble maker."[46]

This conviction was significant for future Anglo-American relations. As criticism of Russia increased, Truman and the State Department no longer blamed Britain for the deterioration in Allied relations. Instead, the administration sought closer cooperation with a nation that had similar aims in Europe and throughout the world. Inverchapel said it best: the average American feels that "when troubles are brewing it is nice to have a friend."[47]

Chapter 6

Shifting the Burden

The Anglo-American partnership became apparent during the crisis in Greece, a nation torn apart by a brutal civil war. As relations between Moscow and Washington deteriorated in 1946, the Truman administration increased cooperation with Great Britain and soon became concerned about upholding the shaky regime in Athens. Domestic problems and the election of a Republican Congress in November 1946, however, discouraged the administration from assuming responsibilities proportionate to American wealth and power in the eastern Mediterranean. Britain, plagued with economic and political difficulties, continued as benefactor of Greece until the disastrous winter of 1947. Then the British government shifted the burden to the United States.

I

The war had left Greece in a shambles. During the Nazi occupation over a thousand villages had been burned, nearly all livestock slaughtered, and when the Wehrmacht withdrew in October 1944, they left behind only a few railroad tracks, six locomotives, and a hundred freight cars. Over four-fifths of the merchant marine had been sunk, often while in Allied service, and food and equipment shortages hampered reconstruction. By May 1946 industrial production had not reached half of the 1939 level.

Inflation was rampant. The government confronted the crisis by seeking foreign aid and attempted to stabilize the currency by introducing a new drachma in November 1944, but the inflation continued. The regime spent twice what it collected in taxes and financed the deficit by printing more money. In late 1944 about 150 new drachmas equaled one dollar, a figure that reached 500 by June 1945, and 5,000 by the beginning of

1946. Britain's first postwar ambassador, Sir Reginald S. Leeper, reported that after liberation the price of a newspaper reached ten billion drachmas and that notes of high denominations lay in the streets because no one would take the trouble to bend over and pick them up. Wages and salaries lagged, resulting in worker resentment, the black market, tax evasion, and bribery of officials.

Even the weather was uncooperative; a drought in 1945 reduced farm production to half the prewar level, keeping the war-weary Greeks on the edge of starvation.[1]

The political situation naturally deteriorated. Civil war erupted in December 1944, lasting six weeks and ending with an agreement at Varkiza in February 1945 that provided for the immediate return of hostages, amnesty for political crimes, restoration of most civil liberties, demobilization of the Communist (ELAS) forces, and the formation of a new army. But reestablishing stable conditions seemed impossible, for few politicians honored the Varkiza agreement. Bitter accusations from both sides resulted in a shaky caretaker regime during the spring and summer, and by October the situation reached crisis proportions. The cabinet resigned, and with some forty-six political parties—every newspaper editor and his delivery boy—a search for a successor failed to find a workable coalition. After nine days the British induced the king of Greece to accept the responsibility temporarily. A premier was found on 1 November, but he resigned three weeks later. For five days Greece had no government.

Foreign Secretary Bevin sent his undersecretary, Hector McNeil, who miraculously assembled a coalition and pledged to devise a reconstruction program. But workers in utilities and industries went on strike, and shortly thereafter guerrilla war broke out in Macedonia. By early 1946 Greece was poised on the brink of chaos.[2]

During this postwar turmoil Britain had remained Greece's primary benefactor. Two divisions of the British army maintained internal security throughout 1945, and in December the War Office agreed to continue supplying and rebuilding the Hellenic army. The British military mission in Athens deliberated with the Greek Supreme Council of National Defense, commented on laws or decrees before they were issued by the regime, and discussed all matters considered by the cabinet and general staff. British experts implemented fiscal programs and influenced trade-union and employment policy. Economic assistance, begun in 1940, was reinstituted after liberation, and both governments established an economic-and-supply committee in November 1944; thereafter British military notes circulated as a second Greek currency.[3]

Officials desired American aid, but the Truman administration continued its wartime policy of treating Greece as primarily a British responsibility. When the Greek ambassador requested credits of $25 million in July 1944, American officials stalled, explaining that the Johnson Act of 1934 prohibited such credits until the currency stabilized. In May 1945 the Greeks tried another angle, approaching the U.S. Foreign Economic Administration (FEA) with the argument that since their government-in-exile in London had signed the lend-lease agreement in 1942, they were entitled to assistance. But before the FEA could act, the European war ended. The Greeks were then referred to the new Export–Import Bank and began laborious negotiations with hesitant bank officers. Neither American military nor State Department officials wanted to become involved in Greece. A Joint Chiefs of Staff memorandum in April 1945 stated that the British should maintain the Hellenic army, and members of the department who remembered the popular outcry over British policy in December 1944 hoped to avoid another confrontation. The resulting noninvolvement was barely distinguishable from a complete lack of policy.[4]

Unlike British Conservatives who willingly maintained responsibility, the Labour government in 1945 sought more American involvement in Greece, and Truman reported that Labour officials began asking for assistance soon after the Potsdam conference. Bevin had outlined his policy in a cabinet meeting on 14 August, obtaining approval for a plan to secure full support of the Dominions in world affairs and to "lose no opportunity of associating the United States Government with us." Thereafter the campaign mounted. The British embassy in Washington informed the State Department that it hoped the Truman administration could offer technical advisers, and on 4 December it requested cooperation in restoring the shattered Greek economy. Bevin inquired whether the administration would agree to an Anglo-American advisory team, and when the Americans refused in mid-December, Roger Makins of the embassy again urged a joint mission. Two weeks later, the British government asked the State Department to send a representative to the Anglo-Greek economic discussions taking place in London and to join a currency control board. Ambassador Halifax reported to Bevin early in the new year that he had urged the State Department at the highest level to consider Britain's proposals regarding Greece. In a message to both Bevin and Byrnes, Leeper wrote that if the Western democracies "fail to deal with the Greek problem with imagination and understanding at this moment ... the present Democratic Government will certainly fall."[5]

The American ambassador in Greece, Lincoln MacVeagh, agreed with his British counterpart. As early as 1944 he warned of increasing Communist influence, but officials in Washington ignored him. In a long dispatch of December 1945 he described the dismal economy, the rising Communist menace, called for financial support and later agreed with Leeper's request that Anglo-American-Greek financial talks begin immediately, reminding his superiors that Greece was the only Balkan country attempting to retain "private property and free enterprise." On 11 January 1946 MacVeagh and Leeper teamed up to express their opinion to Bevin and Byrnes. The ambassadors and their staffs felt the West was not contributing enough to keep Greece safe from the Communists and recommended that London and Washington supply more assistance. Otherwise, they warned, Greece will be "condemned to bloodshed and famine."[6]

Confronted with pleas from Athens and London, the Truman administration became more interested. To be sure, the United States had always displayed sentimental feelings for the cradle of democracy, and in November 1945 the Truman administration agreed to a British request to help observe the forthcoming Greek elections. To lead the mission, Truman appointed Henry F. Grady, who suitably reiterated American ideals: "It is for the Greek people to decide what kind of government they want." In early December the first postwar example of American naval diplomacy in the eastern Mediterranean supported Grady's statement. The ten-thousand-ton cruiser *Providence* and two destroyers anchored off Piraeus for six days. Greeks enthusiastically welcomed the ships and their crews, and the commanding officer of the cruiser held discussions with the regent and dined with the foreign minister. Americans also showed more concern for the deteriorating economy. The Truman administration had left direct postwar loans to Britain, contributing only indirectly through the U.N. Relief and Recovery Administration, whose programs prevented starvation but could not rebuild the country. In autumn 1945 the Greeks again approached Washington, this time asking for a $250 million loan from the Export–Import Bank. The request was in the stratosphere, far beyond the bank's resources, and officials said they could consider an application for only one-tenth that amount. In late September the Athens regime duly requested $25 million, and after months of urging from MacVeagh, the British, and the Greeks, the bank granted the loan in January 1946.[7]

As Soviet-American tension increased early in 1946 so did collaboration with the British. U.S. Navy ships began to appear in the Aegean, and the battleship *Missouri* anchored off Piraeus in April. Elated, MacVeagh called the visit the "most impressive demonstration of American interest in the Mediterranean since the action against the Barbary Pirates in 1805." He informed the State Department that about five thousand guests boarded the ship, and basketball games and dances created a festive mood. Romance ensued, and Athenians were amused but disappointed when police prevented a young woman, "dressed in Navy blues and with hair cut short," from boarding the battleship for the voyage to the states. The visit emphasized Anglo-American cooperation, for H.M.S. *Sirius* also participated in the ceremonies.[8]

American involvement, however, had limits. Byrnes had written Truman in November 1945 that financial assistance should be granted only after the Athens regime began a pro-

gram of economic stabilization. When Whitehall asked the
United States in early December to join in sending an economic mission, State Department officials felt that the British
"were going in anyway . . . and would be blamed if all wasn't
immediately perfect; by staying out US would not share op-
probrium" and could still retain Greek goodwill. The secretary of state agreed to send a representative to attend
Anglo-Greek currency talks in January 1946, but for the first
two weeks the envoy had no instructions. Byrnes had "serious
misgivings" about participating, and Undersecretary Acheson
informed Ambassador Winant in London that the administration would assume no responsibility for the currency
committee or for future aid to Greece. When the Greek premier, Constantine Tsaldaris, asked the Export–Import Bank
for another loan in July, officials agreed to examine the request but gave no encouragement. Meanwhile, the Grady
mission had received strict instructions to observe the elections and to report facts in Greece without becoming involved
in internal affairs. The president and the secretary of state
did not want to extend military aid, and in February 1946 the
Joint Chiefs of Staff advised avoiding commitments because
of problems of maintaining lines of communication. Indeed,
the JCS discouraged a stronger role in Greece, Turkey, the
Levant, or Iran, except through the United Nations.[9]

Great Britain continued to support Greece. Talks in London resulted in an Anglo-Hellenic convention of January
1946, again demonstrating British generosity. The Labour
government agreed to provide an interest-free loan of $40
million, to cancel repayment of the $186 million lent to
Greece in 1940–1941, to free Greek assets and balances in
Britain, to sell $2 billion worth of military and rehabilitation
equipment at cost, to supply monetary and technical experts
for eighteen to twenty-four months, and to support Greek
efforts to secure loans from other sources.[10]

But officials in the British Treasury began to balk at support for Greece. Hugh Dalton strongly contested the agreement of January 1946, remarking that the government had
no intention or ability to maintain the Greek economy indefi-
nitely. Treasury officials felt that giving the Greeks the

slightest idea that Great Britain would support them was un-wise because the Athens regime would then be less likely to take "the necessary but unpopular measures to put their own house in order." This assumption proved correct. Six months later Premier Tsaldaris again knocked at the Treasury door. In July he visited London with a formidable document—a request for a five-year reconstruction plan that called on the Attlee government to supply $6 billion!

To the British government this request meant one thing—Greece must look for future aid in Washington. The chancellor of the exchequer was emphatic: "We must bring in the Americans." Bevin advised Tsaldaris to go to the United States for assistance, adding, "If you go, I am going to help you."[11]

The Greeks needed little encouragement, and in early July Tsaldaris met Byrnes at the meeting of the Council of Foreign Ministers in Paris. The men twice discussed aid for recon-struction, and during another conversation with Harriman in London, Tsaldaris asked if he should take his case to Washington. The ambassador called that premature but said that his government would receive Greek financial experts. In August a mission headed by Sophocles Venizelos, former prime minister and son of a great republican of a generation earlier, arrived in the United States. He talked with Export–Import Bank officials, Secretary of the Treasury John W. Snyder, Acheson, and Truman, seeking $175 million in cred-its. Tsaldaris again confronted Byrnes in October, this time asking for $500 million.[12]

American policy toward the eastern Mediterranean began to shift during the autumn of 1946, partly because of sugges-tions from Athens and London, but more important, as a response to Soviet and Yugoslav provocations. After Russian demands on the straits and the shooting down of two C-47s in Yugoslavia, the Joint Chiefs of Staff became concerned about preventing the Soviet Union from dominating Turkey and thus advancing what they now called the "iron curtain"; they suggested that the administration supply technicians to the Turks and sell them military equipment. On 20 August, one day after Yugoslavian partisans shot down the second plane,

Byrnes accepted Bevin's proposal of an Anglo-American mission to observe the Greek plebiscite in September. Byrnes agreed with JCS and State Department recommendations and wrote that the world "situation had so hardened" that the time had come to "help our friends in every way and refrain from assisting those who . . . are opposing the principles for which we stand." In Paris Byrnes discussed the situation with Bevin and British Minister of Defense Albert V. Alexander and arrived at what came to be known as the Byrnes–Bevin understanding. As Byrnes told Alexander on 15 October, the West should help Turkey and Greece to maintain military readiness, and since the British already had an alliance with those nations they should continue supplying military equipment while the Americans did "everything they possibly could to help the two countries economically." The secretary of state also felt that if Britain could not supply equipment, the United States would try to assume that responsibility as well.[13]

American interest in the eastern Mediterranean became increasingly evident. MacVeagh advised the Greek king in October to strengthen the economy by initiating limited reconstruction projects. The king responded, "This is just the way Bevin talks to me." The United States granted Greece $35 million credit to purchase surplus military and maritime property in late September, and three weeks later the Export–Import Bank approved a $25 million loan for Turkey. Administration officials then announced that early in December the aircraft carrier *Randolph,* cruiser *Fargo,* and two destroyers would visit the Aegean and an economic mission would go to Greece. The new British ambassador in Washington, Lord Inverchapel, informed the Foreign Office: "The importance to the United States, no less than to Great Britain, of the Mediterranean and Middle East is now much more widely understood."[14]

II

The Truman administration had clearly become more interested, but any desire to assume more responsibility, either by sharing the burden with Britain or by supplanting the

British as the primary benefactor of the region was curtailed by domestic political events in the autumn of 1946.

Since the end of the war Americans had demanded rapid demobilization of the armed forces. Just three months after V-J Day some two hundred "Bring Back Daddy" clubs had been organized, sending congressmen thousands of baby shoes. Early in 1946 an estimated 50 percent of congressional mail urged demobilization. Homesick soldiers became restless; troops stationed in France, Germany, Guam, and China protested, and some twenty thousand demonstrated in Manila.[15]

The administration responded by discharging troops at a rapid rate, to the distress of many officials. General Marshall voiced concern in early November 1945 to a member of the British embassy, commenting that "demobilisation has become disintegration, not only of the armed forces but apparently of all conception of world responsibility." He felt that the American people were passing through an emotional crisis, adding that he intended to "lay it on thick" in order to obtain support for postwar military training. Undersecretary Acheson complained in a cabinet meeting that "Army discipline has gone to Hell," and in March 1946 Byrnes and Patterson discussed the deplorable effect of demobilization on foreign policy. During the spring Truman advocated a slowdown in reduction of the armed forces, extension of the draft, and universal military training.[16]

The public will prevailed, and by the end of 1945, the administration was discharging 35,000 troops per day. The armed forces declined from 12 million in June 1945, to 3 million a year later, to 1.5 million by June 1947. Troops in Europe dwindled from approximately 3.5 million to 200,000. By mid-1947 the American army ranked sixth in size among nations of the world.[17]

Political problems continued to badger the administration throughout 1946 and some of them had overtones of Anglophobia. British policy toward Jewish immigration to Palestine elicited sharp attacks from Americans, stiff rebuttals from the British government and press, and scarred Anglo-American relations throughout the early postwar years. Palestine was a political headache for President Truman, who naturally desired to maintain Jewish support for the Democratic party in the November 1946 elections. A more explicit example of anti-British sentiment appeared on 12 September 1946 when Secretary of Commerce Henry A. Wallace delivered a speech at Madison Square Garden. After Sen. Claude D. Pepper of Florida charged that Truman was trying to "pull the British chestnuts out of the fire," Wallace stated that he saw more danger in British imperialism than in communism: "We must not let British balance-of-power manipulations determine whether and when the United States gets into war." Soviet-American relations, he said, would improve when Kremlin leaders understood that America's primary objectives did not include saving the British Empire or controlling Middle Eastern oil, and he called for a more cooperative attitude from the president, proclaiming that the United States had no more business in Eastern Europe than Russia had in Latin America and Western Europe. The "tougher we get, the tougher the Russians will get."[18]

The speech confused Americans and irritated the British, since it conflicted with the tough policy initiated by Byrnes at the Paris peace conference. Naturally Republicans seized the opportunity to score political points. Senator Vandenberg said his party could only cooperate with one secretary of state at a time, and Sen. Robert A. Taft of Ohio claimed that the futile and contradictory Democratic policy made the United States the "laughingstock of the world." Because Britain was in the midst of withdrawing troops from the Middle East and devising a plan of independence for India, the charges of imperialism seemed incredible. In London, the *Daily Herald* asked, "Where is the Evidence?" and the *News Chronicle* declared that Wallace had resuscitated a bogeyman who could no longer stand up. The *Manchester Guardian* regretted that some Americans still have "a naive mixture of forward-looking ideas and gross historical ignorance." Some Labourites began to wonder if the United States were a dependable partner, and a Foreign Office official, Francis B. A. Rundall, felt that the speech created a "sorry mess"; Truman had "staggering disregard of the implications. . . . Such ineptitude is hard to visualise." From Washington, Inverchapel wrote that the president's reputation had been "seriously, and perhaps fatally, injured" and that from now on he will "tend to be regarded less as a national leader than as a little man struggling to do his best in a post which is too big for him."[19]

Truman, who had thumbed through the Wallace speech and approved it, realized his error and resolved the episode. He wrote his aged mother, "Never was there such a mess and it is partly my making. But when I make a mistake it is a good one." The president forced Wallace to resign and reaffirmed his support for the secretary of state, demonstrating that his administration would continue the Anglo-American front against the Kremlin. Yet the Wallace affair showed that Anglophobic statements still received American applause. A public-opinion poll in December 1946 asking which was the most imperialistic nation—United States, France, England, or Russia—found that the Soviet Union led England by just four percentage points.[20]

Meanwhile, domestic problems harassed the administration. In 1946 strikes crippled the nation. In a single year Truman had irritated labor by seizing railroads, coal mines, oil refineries, meat-packing plants, and even tugboats. By the end of the year prices had soared 30 percent above what they had been on V-J Day, and food-and-housing shortages remained acute. The president's popularity declined correspondingly; in October 1946 only 32 percent of those asked were satisfied with his performance in office.[21] During the congressional elections of 1946, few Democratic candidates sought their party leader's support.

Desiring a better life after the sacrifices of war, Americans were frustrated, and a Boston advertising man summarized the national mood in just two words: "Had Enough?" Republicans adopted the slogan for the November congressional elections, campaigned vigorously, and dealt a crushing defeat to the Democrats. The GOP elected governors in twenty-five states and for the first time since the bull-market days of 1928 won control of Congress, gaining fifty-six seats in the House and thirteen in the Senate. The majorities were substantial: 51 to 45 in the Senate, and 245 to 188 in the House. Moreover, the "class of '46" included some of the most conservative members of the Republican party, such as William Jenner of Indiana, William Knowland and Richard M. Nixon of California, John W. Bricker of Ohio, and Joseph R. McCarthy of Wisconsin.

The Republicans won on a platform of raising tariffs and reducing taxes, expenditures, the national debt, and foreign aid. When the Eightieth Congress convened on 3 January 1947 they attempted to carry out their pledges. Speaker of the House Joseph Martin of Massachusetts called for a 20 percent reduction in income taxes and government spending, and his colleagues took the offensive, demanding maximum expenditures for fiscal 1948 of $34 billion. A week later Truman submitted his budget, estimating expenditures of $37.5 billion and receipts of $37.7 billion—figures that he said were the lowest possible without jeopardizing domestic and foreign policies. He had cut military expenditures $3.4 billion from the previous year, making the total bill for national defense $11.2 billion. As expected, the class of '46 rejected the plan, clamoring to slice from $4 to $8 billion off the proposed budget by reducing operating expenditures of the army and navy by about $1.75 billion and by cutting in half the $1 billion overseas-relief program to prevent starvation and unrest in Japan and Germany. On 14 February a joint congressional committee recommended a ceiling of $31.5 billion, which the House accepted six days later. Mostly because of Vandenberg's concern for foreign affairs the Senate sought higher expenditures, and both houses compromised on $34.7 billion. Sen. Henry Cabot Lodge, Jr., a Massachusetts Republican, commented that his party approached the budget "like a man wielding a meat ax in a dark room" who "might cut off his own head."[22]

Such cuts were in accord with previous GOP designs to restrict foreign aid and raise tariffs, policies opposed by two Democratic administrations faced with growing responsibilities in the world. In 1934 only two Republicans had voted for the three-year Reciprocal Trade Act (only thirty-three did in 1946), and in the Seventy-ninth Congress they had opposed the Export–Import Bank Act of 1945, the British loan, and the Bretton Woods agreement establishing the International Bank and International Monetary Fund. After the Eightieth Congress convened, Republicans in the House introduced a resolution to prevent the administration from reducing tariffs or sending representatives to world-trade conferences until studies detailed American industry's need for protection. In February 1947 House Republicans summoned the chairman of the board of directors of the Export–Import Bank and Undersecretary of State Acheson and told them to restrict lending.[23]

By early 1947 the message was unmistakable. Popular cries for demobilization, Anglophobic speeches, and the Republican victory meant that if Truman wanted to assume some of Britain's responsibilities in the eastern Mediterranean, it would be no easy task to convince the people and Congress.

That was unfortunate, for the partner across the Atlantic faced serious economic difficulties. The $3.75 billion loan had purchased far fewer goods than anticipated. Truman's removal of wartime price controls encouraged inflation, increasing by 40 percent prices that Britain paid for imports from the United States. By June 1947 Dalton complained to Undersecretary of State William L. Clayton that American inflation had reduced the value of the loan by a billion dollars. Serious housing and food shortages continued; an estimated twenty thousand squatters lived in deserted military camps and in vacant apartment buildings in London. In April 1946 Bevin told Byrnes the "British people were getting pretty weary of the severe rationing which has existed for nearly seven years." The government allotted each person about one pound of meat and two pints of milk per week. In November the minister of food announced that bread rationing would continue and further reduced spirits by maintaining the ban on distilling whisky.[24]

Industrial production recovered slowly after the war, reaching only 92 percent of the depression rate of 1938 by the end of 1946. Total exports barely surpassed depression levels by the third quarter of 1946, and it was estimated that exports would have to increase by 75 percent before the British could live at prewar standards. Reconstruction demanded large imports, resulting in an enormous deficit of payments—in 1946 almost £300 million, and in 1947 a postwar nadir of £443 million, seven times larger than the average for 1936–1938. A white paper divulged the fragile nature of the economy: the Labourites gingerly predicted a favorable balance of trade by 1950 only "if all goes extremely well, if no unforeseen contingencies arise, and if the uncertain factors mostly turn out on the favourable side."[25]

Uncertain factors turned out unfavorably. Disraeli's nineteenth-century epigram—those wretched colonies are the millstone around our necks—seemed more relevant to the postwar years. Nationalism flared in India, Malaya, Burma, Nepal, Borneo, Afghanistan, Thailand, and Ceylon. Other areas controlled by Britain likewise demanded independence —Palestine, Egypt, Syria, Lebanon, Saudi Arabia, Yemen, and Jordan. While the civil war continued in Greece, fighting erupted between Arabs and Jews in Palestine; conflict in the empire became so commonplace that Bevin quipped to one of his companions, "if peace breaks out anywhere, I'll let you know." The government had to station troops in the colonies and mandates and fulfill postwar obligations by occupying Japan, Germany, Austria, Venezia Giulia, and Greece. By December 1946 Britain had to support almost 400,000 more troops than expected and could only maintain a military establishment of almost 1,500,000 by an expensive peacetime draft.[26]

Bevin's foreign policy also caused problems for the government. During the 1945 election campaign the Labourites had condemned Churchill's anti-Soviet pronouncements and support for conservative elements in Spain and Greece. The party chairman, Harold Laski, had promised that the Labourites would support liberation of the Spanish people from their "Fascist prison" and would help the Greeks to obtain democracy. Many people thought that only a Labour government could prevent the Allies from drifting apart after the war by forming a bridge between capitalistic America and Communist Russia. Others hoped for closer Anglo-Soviet relations; Laski told the party conference of 1946 that, while capitalistic nations mistrusted each other, governments like the British and Russian were the "surest hope of peace."[27]

By the last half of 1946 the leftists within the Labour party felt betrayed and were charging that the government initiated socialist policies at home and Tory plans abroad. They noted Conservative applause for Bevin's restoration of the Greek king and protection of the Franco regime and claimed that his hostility to communism had alienated progressive forces in Europe. They said that Washington and Wall Street controlled Whitehall and that the government was collaborating in an Anglo-American bloc against the Communist ally. Richard Crossman and others complained that when Britain had clashed with the Truman administration on the loan and atomic energy, America had won on both occasions, for Keynes received stiff terms for the loan, and Congress established domestic control of the bomb, ending any hope for sharing atomic secrets. In late October 1946 Bevin received a letter demanding "a genuine middle way" between East and West and abandonment of the "anti-red" policy. Twenty-two Labour party members signed the letter, including Crossman, Michael Foot, and a man destined years later to be prime minister, James Callaghan. Dissatisfaction emerged publicly on 18 November when Crossman presented a motion in Parliament for a more socialistic and independent posture. In the so-called foreign-policy revolt, forty-four Labour M.P.s criticized the leadership, and about sixty back-benchers signed a statement rebuking present policy. They denounced Anglo-American conversations begun after Montgomery's visit to Washington, and one dissenter carped in the *Daily Telegram* that Britain soon would become a mere American aircraft carrier off the coast of Europe.[28]

The leftists were vocal but not strong enough to force a showdown. During parliamentary debate, as Gallman informed the State Department, Attlee defended the government's position and "paid clear and unmistakable tribute" to American policy.[29] The Commons upheld current policy by 353 to 1, the leftists abstaining.

The revolt had little effect on Bevin's foreign policy. Whitehall officials saw no chance for the "British Henry Wallaces," and Bevin, who considered the mutiny by Labour M.P.s as a stab in the back, later told Parliament that he would not permit a wedge to be driven between America and Britain. A State Department memorandum was revealing: "It is hard to believe that Bevin will at this time significantly change his attitude toward *Russia* and the *United States*. He has been letting us take the lead with respect to Russia in recent months, and he will undoubtedly continue to do that."[30]

Burdened with domestic and international commitments, British officials had become more subdued as America replaced Great Britain as the primary protagonist against the Soviet Union. The Truman administration's policy had so stiffened that Bevin no longer had to make anti-Soviet statements that might cause discord within his party. He now worked behind the scenes, maintaining close relations with Washington, involving America in Greece, and remaining a reliable junior partner.[31]

III

During the remaining months of 1946 and throughout 1947 the situation in Greece continued to deteriorate. Three years after liberation only a third as many locomotives and ships were in use as in 1939 and industrial production had reached only two-thirds of the prewar level. Inflation continued; the government's policy of printing more money and fixing prices had failed miserably. By October 1947 the regime had to fix the minimum wage for unskilled work at 11,000 drachmas per day, 183 times more than the prewar rate. Living standards deteriorated, as wages did not keep up with increased prices. In Athens the cost of living rose from an index of 1 during the second half of 1938 to 145.5 in December 1946 and 185 by October 1947. The military situation darkened as the third round of the civil war erupted in spring 1946, with street fighting and political assassinations in the cities and guerrilla warfare in Macedonia. By September the rebel attacks had forced the government to put twenty-seven of fifty-one national regions under martial law, including all northern Greece. Whitehall admitted that the situation was serious, and Tsaldaris labeled it a half-war. Markos Vafiadis, known as General Markos, announced creation of the "democratic army" in October. His support grew to approximately seven thousand followers by the end of 1946, and in January 1947 he claimed control of over a hundred villages, enforcing his rule, collecting taxes, and drafting men and women into his army. His strength grew quickly in 1947, from thirteen thousand in March to twenty-three thousand by July.[32]

The Greek government again approached the British, this time seeking more military aid. Great Britain had agreed to maintain the armed forces until the end of its fiscal year, 31 March 1947. Between February 1945 and August 1946 Britain had supported increases in troop strength from about 30,000 to 92,000. The Royal Navy steamed about the Aegean, a few squadrons of the Royal Air Force patrolled the skies, and Greek soldiers wore Tommy uniforms and used Enfield rifles. Yet to deal with the civil war, Athens demanded more support and on 15 September 1946 requested arms, clothing, and equipment for an additional 30,000 soldiers. The Labour government studied the proposal, and in mid-November the chief of the Greek general staff and the head of the British military mission arrived in London. The defense ministry now hesitated, forcing the Greeks to reduce their demands to 12,000 troops. On 28 November the imperial chiefs agreed to support a total army of 100,000 with an additional 4,000 in a special antiguerrilla unit but stated that further increases would need Treasury approval. To evaluate the situation Field Marshal Montgomery went to Athens in early December and advised converting the army into a force for fighting rebels, "infantry with mounted guns and mules," and attacking in the spring. If that were not done, he informed Ambassador MacVeagh, Greece would be lost. Montgomery continued with a truism: "If the bands come across the border, kill them. Kill them all. People don't like to be killed and they'll stop coming over if they know this will happen to them." More pleas for aid followed Montgomery's visit. On 18 December Greece asked for arms, ammunition, vehicles, draft animals, and uniforms to equip an army of 128,000, and after that request was denied, sought the necessary support in February to increase the army by 15,000 troops.[33]

Faced with its own chronic economic problems, Great Britain was unable to increase its commitment to Greece and had been attempting to reduce expenditures while urging the United States to share responsibilities. In September 1946 British officials announced withdrawal of an army division from Greece, decreasing troops from 28,500 to 16,000 by the end of the year. The British told Greek generals in November that, though they had been sponsors of the Hellenic armed forces for over two years, they no longer objected if the Greeks requested aid and advisers from the Pentagon. In Athens, the British ambassador, Sir Clifford Norton, urged Tsaldaris to leave immediately for Washington and ask for aid. Sharing financial responsibilities for Greece appears to have been one topic of conversation on 25 November between Bevin and Byrnes. The parliamentary undersecretary for foreign affairs, Hector McNeil, later complained to Orme Sargent that Byrnes's position was too vague and that Britain must have a more precise idea of America's plans before committing·itself for another year. At Whitehall, officials discussed the United States' role in Greece. Sir William Eady of the Treasury advocated getting Americans "working on a three year basis like ourselves" and Warner of the Foreign Office declared that the government should "go to the Americans, tell them what we were prepared to do and say to them that that was all we could do and that . . . they must be prepared to do the rest." The tactic seems to have been accepted by Bevin, who met Byrnes during the second week of December in New York and said that Britain would continue to help with military equipment but hoped the United States would provide economic assistance. He urged immediate dispatch of the promised economic mission, admitted that Britain wanted to withdraw troops, but did not say when forces would be reduced.[34]

Meanwhile the Greeks had accepted British advice and approached the Americans. In late November, on instructions from Tsaldaris, the Greek ambassador in Washington requested that the United States arm, supply, and maintain an additional eighty thousand troops for the Greek army. A week later the Greek premier met Byrnes and tearfully described the desperate situation in his homeland; he later told Clayton that Greece would need $14 million per month for the first quarter of 1947. The third week of December, the premier began a four-day official visit to Washington, meeting separately with officials of the Export–Import Bank, Clayton, and Byrnes and requesting both short-term credits for consumer goods and help in attracting American firms to reconstruction projects. After discussions with Byrnes, Acheson, Vandenberg, and Henderson, Tsaldaris addressed a long letter to the secretary of state, citing a United Nations report that declared that Greece would obtain economic self-sufficiency only after securing $708 million in reconstruction aid and an additional $538 million in development funds.[35] The premier requested the Truman administration to grant Greece the astronomical sum of $1,246,000,000—more than twice the amount Britain had given that nation from 1944 to 1947!

The administration stalled. According to law the Export–Import Bank could not lend funds unless it had reasonable assurance of repayment. Given the Greek situation, Byrnes had little hope for a loan and realized that aid could only be provided by congressional action. The possibility of legislation declined after the November election; the budget-slashing class of '46 was in no mood to increase foreign assistance. The election seemed to sober officials who in September and October had called for a radical change in policy toward the eastern Mediterranean. Now they devised plans more in line with the economizing tenets of the Eightieth Congress. Many Americans objected because the Greeks had shown little ability to govern their country and manage the economy. Instability was chronic; Tsaldaris, leader of the twelfth cabinet in the two years since liberation, resigned in January 1947. Cabinets had employed unsound fiscal policy; Clayton commented that if Greece did not take steps to improve its economic administration, giving the regime money would amount to "pouring funds down a rat hole." Byrnes had been "unfavorably impressed by Tsaldaris's lack of precision and by a complete lack of any well-prepared data to substantiate exaggerated demands." Such negative thoughts reappeared a few weeks later among members of the American economic mission, one of whom decided that Greek politicians were "so preoccupied with their own struggle for power that they have no time, even assuming capacity, to develop economic policy." He reported corruption and deterioration of services and labeled the civil service a "depressing farce."[36]

Pleas for assistance thus yielded few immediate returns. Only a few days after the November 1946 elections Acheson asked MacVeagh to "discourage the Greeks from asking us for arms and military equipment" and to refer them instead to the British government. Acheson dispatched an almost identical message to Amb. Edwin G. Wilson in Ankara, who, incidentally, refused to inform the regime because the "completely negative attitude would discourage Turks" and lead them to think that American support was a "mere matter of words." Later that month Acheson gave a disappointing answer to Greek hopes for aid to purchase commodities: "Difficulties may be insurmountable and no optimistic report can be given at present." The Export–Import Bank gave no encouragement to Tsaldaris's loan proposal in December, refused to help him get in touch with American firms that might be interested in reconstruction projects, and in mid-January 1947 turned down the request. The premier returned to Athens empty-handed but, for political reasons, informed the populace that the United States soon would grant aid. When Inverchapel questioned Byrnes about this statement, the secretary of state reaffirmed his policy, adding that "there was no commitment at all," and that Tsaldaris had been told not to "make any statement which would lead his people to be optimistic and then later cause them disappointment."[37]

But the U.S. government did not lose interest in Greece during the winter of 1946–1947. In December the administration approved a British request to supply Greece with eight C-47s; asked Britain for a list of supplies needed by the Hellenic army; supported the Athens regime in the United Nations against attacks by Albania, Bulgaria, and Yugoslavia; and named Paul A. Porter as director of a new economic mission. In January 1947 the Porter mission arrived in Greece. Porter and his associate, Mark F. Ethridge, agreed with the alarming prediction of Ambassador MacVeagh; Ethridge reported in mid-February that the Soviets considered Greece a "ripe plum ready to fall into their hands in a few weeks." This assessment startled the State Department. The chief of the Near East and African desk, Henderson, wrote a memorandum on 20 February calling for cooperation with the British to establish a coalition regime, to initiate administrative and financial reforms, and to supply economic and military aid. Henderson recommended and Acheson approved a special proposal to Congress "on an urgent basis for a direct loan to Greece."[38]

Policy was evolving, but for the most powerful nation in the world, these were meager and at times insincere gestures. The economic mission had been promised in October; it took Truman two months to name a director. Porter later admitted that he, along with the president and State Department, knew that the mission was "first of all a delaying tactic, not a prelude to significant new American aid." After arriving in Athens, Porter announced to a hopeful audience that Greece must depend on its own resources, not on outside aid, and that he had not come with his pockets full of checks. A month later his concern mounted, but his report of 17 February recapitulated the same old themes of American policy—criticizing inept Greek leadership, hoping for continued British subsidies, and suggesting the possibility of aid only after the Greek government carried out economic reforms. Even as late as March, Porter told a British colleague that if the United States assumed responsibility in Greece it would receive a "packet of trouble." Acheson had informed MacVeagh in late December 1946 that it would take Congress two or three months to consider appropriations for Greece, but in February 1947 the State Department had not yet drafted a proposal that could be submitted to the legislators. Henderson's call for a congressional loan (not a grant) was only a preliminary proposal and did not mention an amount. Although MacVeagh had first called for such a plan over fourteen months earlier, in December 1945, the administration had not yet acted.[39]

Greece needed large-scale financial and military aid. During the winter of 1946–1947 the Truman administration became more concerned but still remained unwilling to assume a significant share of the burden. Writing to the Foreign Office at the end of the war in Europe, Lord Halifax had stated a theme relevant to early 1947: the United States preferred to stay clear of involvements "so long as His Majesty's Government continues to be willing to keep the initiative."[40]

IV

At dawn on 6 January 1947 snow began to fall in London. Scotland and the Midlands reported heavy drifting, clogged roads, and disrupted train service. The accompanying cold used up fuels—Birmingham reduced gas consumption by 25 percent, officials in Leeds announced the possibility of a coal shortage, and because of delivery problems the government reduced coal allocations to all industries by half. By 21 January a white paper on economic recovery labeled the situation extremely serious. On Saturday, 25 January, a blizzard began. By Monday morning a town in Kent reported nine inches of snow, and the rest of the nation was covered with four inches. Temperatures dipped to fifteen degrees in London, the coldest in six years. Roads became impassable as stalled cars and trucks littered the shoulders. Villages relied on supplies carried by sleigh or dropped by the RAF. The snow continued in February. Transportation was at a standstill—some forty thousand railroad cars loaded with coal were stuck in northeast England. The government announced on 7 February that electricity would be cut off to industrial consumers in London, southeast and northeast England, and the Midlands. Domestic electricity would be turned off between 9:00 A.M. and noon, and between 2:00 and 4:00 P.M. Next day the minister of fuel and power, Emanuel Shinwell, declared that if the country did not conserve coal and electricity "we shall find ourselves in the next ten days in a condition of complete disaster." On Monday, 10 February, the electricity went off, forcing thousands of factories to shut down and throwing two million people out of work. Unemployment soared to 15.5 percent of the labor force, and the prime minister told the nation: "We face an emergency of the utmost gravity."

In February the Labourites issued another white paper, described by the *Times* as the most disturbing statement ever made by a British government. The trade deficit was not the projected $1.3 billion, but $1.8 billion. Exports from Britain's frozen ports were alarmingly low. On 19 February the government announced it had used $800 million of the American loan. Five days later Britain drew $100 million, and this amount was consumed weekly for the remainder of 1947, virtually eliminating vital dollar reserves.[41]

The winter of 1947 caused a showdown in the cabinet. Against the opposition of the defense ministry and the Foreign Office, Dalton had long advocated cutting Britain's foreign commitments. In January 1946 he had opposed the Anglo-Hellenic convention, and in October he informed the cabinet that supporting Germany was "a scandalous state of things," an intolerable drain on resources. During Anglo-American negotiations establishing Bizonia he demanded that Whitehall ask the United States to pay three-fourths of the bill, and on other occasions that autumn he urged Attlee to reduce overseas expenditures. No surprise that the snowstorms early in 1947 were followed by acrimonious debate. On 16 January the committee on economic planning reported "an increasing gap between our requirements and our productive resources." This report was followed by what Dalton described as "a first-class row" over the number of men required for defense. Three days later he sent a note to Attlee giving his displeasure that the cabinet had rejected his plan to cut the foreign budget, adding that the huge expenditures of manpower and money on defense made nonsense of Labour's economic program. The same day the chancellor told the cabinet that if they swept aside all his arguments he would have to reconsider his position in the government. On

5 February he recorded, "There is a strange uncertainty about the personal future of many Ministers."[42]

There was no recourse. As the nation faced disaster, Bevin and Alexander were unable to defend overseas expenditures. Britain had spent $330 million on Palestine over the last two years, and feeding Germans cost $320 million in 1946. From 1944 to spring 1947 aid to Greece reached $540 million, and Turkey received $375 million between 1938 and 1947. During fiscal year 1946 almost one man in five between the ages of eighteen and twenty-four was serving in the armed forces and defense expenditures equaled 19 percent of Britain's national income (compared to about 10 percent in the United States). A white paper summarized the situation: "The central fact is that we have not enough resources to do all that we want to do. We have barely enough to do what we *must* do."[43]

The power and influence of the British Empire receded. During the last week of January Dalton demanded a 10 percent reduction in defense expenditures, saving $320 million for the forthcoming year, and obtained a 5 percent compromise. Decisions were eventually made to reduce the armed forces from 1,427,000 to less than 1,100,000 during fiscal 1948, while slashing defense and supply budgets to $3.6 billion, a savings of over $3 billion from the previous year. On 28 January the government announced the future independence of Burma, and a white paper on 14 February pledged a balance of foreign and domestic commitments. On the same day the government handed the Palestine issue to the United Nations, and Attlee informed Parliament a week later that Britain would quit India by June 1948.[44]

Britain's position in Greece, of course, was affected. Throughout January Bevin had continued the policy of the previous year, urging his government to aid Greece while seeking a sharing arrangement with the United States. At a cabinet meeting on 30 January, he supported a request by the chiefs of staff to increase the Greek army to 150,000 troops, which would allow the British to cut their forces in half, to 8,000, and the Greeks to begin an offensive against the Communists. Bevin wanted to leave British soldiers in Greece until the Russians evacuated Bulgaria. Concerning commitments after 31 March, he proposed that the Foreign Office discuss the situation with American officials to ascertain "what part of the burden they would be willing to bear." He hoped to devise an Anglo-American aid package that would last three years. Bevin admitted a week later that the Americans would have to contribute "the lion's share of the financial burden," but as late as 10 February he still wanted a "joint Anglo-U.S. policy of economic and military support." He also advocated reequipping the Greek army "free of charge," believing that such selfless behavior during the winter crisis would stimulate Washington officials to act generously.[45]

But during the middle of February Bevin changed his mind; a sharing arrangement with the United States was no longer possible. When Dalton sent a memorandum to Attlee on 11 February calling for the termination of aid for Greece, Bevin scribbled in the margin: "I think Mr. Dalton is justified. We get no help from the Greeks. The whole area must be reviewed." The two cabinet ministers directed their subordinates to discuss future policy toward Athens and Washington, and a minute on 14 February by Warner of the Foreign Office defined the issue between the two departments: "The crux is that the Chancellor wants to tell the Americans and Greeks at once that we will cease *all* financial help to Greece. We propose to discuss with the Americans first, leaving the possibility open that we might make a small contribution if U.S.A. will do the rest." Whitehall officials continued their search for a way to salvage the situation, some proposing that the Dominions be asked for donations, but by the time he met with Dalton on 18 February, Bevin had reversed his earlier position. The only alternative was to send "a strong telegram to the United States asking them what they were going to do and on the other hand telling the Greeks that we could not continue." This move, Bevin concluded, was for "the sole purpose of bringing matters to a head."[46]

On Friday, 21 February 1947, the British embassy in Washington telephoned the State Department requesting an immediate appointment with the new secretary of state, George C. Marshall. He had already left the office to prepare for a speaking engagement, and Acheson arranged a conference between the embassy's first secretary, H. M. Sichel, and the director of the office of Near Eastern and African affairs, Henderson. Sichel gave Henderson copies of two messages. The first described earlier discussions between Bevin and Byrnes concerning aid to Greece and stated that outside help would be necessary to prevent starvation and political disturbance. It noted the strategic importance of keeping Greece from falling into Soviet hands and suggested that the Anglo-American chiefs of staff urgently consider the situation in the eastern Mediterranean. The British estimated that in 1947 Greece would need from $240 to $280 million. They had promised $160 million up to the end of March, and since this sum had strained their resources to the utmost, they found it impossible to grant further assistance. The note announced that aid would end 31 March and continued: "His Majesty's Government trust that the United States Government may find it possible to afford financial assistance to Greece on a scale sufficient to meet her minimum needs, both civil and military."

The second note concerned Turkey, and the message was similar; Britain awaited America's response.[47]

V

State Department officials began working immediately, formulating a policy proposal over the weekend before Secretary Marshall returned to Washington. After seeing Inverchapel on Monday, 24 February, Marshall talked at some length with the president and the secretaries of war and navy. The idea of a Communist Greece revolted Truman, and a few days later he told the cabinet: "The decision is to ask Congress for 250 million [dollars for Greece] and to say this is only the beginning. It means U.S. going into European politics. It means the greatest selling job ever."[48]

Congress and the public were unaware of the crisis. The State Department speech writer, Joseph M. Jones, urged "bold action at the top . . . a grave, frank statesmanlike appeal to the people." On 27 February Truman, Marshall, and Acheson met congressional leaders at the White House. After statements by Truman and Marshall, Acheson took the floor, summarizing the British notes and describing the turmoil. In the last eighteen months, he said, the Soviets had increased pressure on the straits and in the Balkans, while domestic Communists agitated in Italy and France. Greece might succumb, and then like "apples in a barrel infected by one rotten one, the corruption of Greece would infect Iran and all to the east." Communism would sweep Asia Minor, Africa, and Europe. No time remained for appraisal; only action could stop the Communist infection. Senator Vandenberg responded solemnly: "Mr. President, if you will say that to the Congress and the country, I will support you and I believe that most of its members will do the same."[49]

Less than two weeks later, on 12 March, Truman proclaimed to a joint session of Congress: "The very existence of the Greek state is today threatened by the terrorist activities of several thousand armed men, led by Communists. . . . Greece must have assistance if it is to become a self-supporting and self-respecting democracy." Turkey also deserved attention, and the United States was the only country able to help. Truman warned that if Greece fell under control of an armed minority the effect on Turkey would be serious. "Confusion and disorder might well spread throughout the entire Middle East." He asked Congress for $400 million—the United States must support "free peoples who are resisting attempted subjugation by armed minorities or by outside pressures."[50]

Congress acted immediately. On 13 March Acheson, Patterson, Forrestal, and advisers explained the situation to the Senate Foreign Relations Committee. The House introduced a bill on 18 March, the Senate a day later. Hearings were held later that month. Ambassador MacVeagh described the Greek situation as "exceedingly grave and critical, actually critical." Delay would push the country into the Soviet orbit. Ambassador Wilson proclaimed that the Russians desired to expand. If Turkey succumbed, nothing remained between the Soviets and "the Persian Gulf, Suez Canal, on out to the East—Afghanistan, India, and China."[51]

Some congressmen objected to the proposed aid because of its cost, provocation to Russia, and the need to stop communism at home. Senator Pepper advocated presenting the issue to the United Nations, while others feared that the United States would find itself underwriting the whole British Empire. State Department officials soothed Anglophobic concerns, carefully informing senators that the proposed legislation was "not based in any way upon the idea that the United States should assume the obligations or take over the position which Great Britain may have ... in either Greece or Turkey." Rather the bill enabled the administration to pursue American interests.[52]

As Congress held more hearings and debates, the administration privately pledged aid to Greece, and on 18 March the navy announced that the carrier *Leyte,* three light cruisers, and six destroyers would visit Crete and Istanbul. The Senate passed the aid bill on 22 April by a vote of 67 to 23; the House on 9 May by 287 to 107. On 22 May the president signed Public Law 75, assistance to Greece and Turkey, and thus gave America's response—the Truman Doctrine.[53]

VI

Some British observers have contended that the Truman Doctrine, which promised an enlarged American involvement in Europe, proved that Bevin's diplomacy from 1945 to 1947 had been a striking success. Francis Williams maintained in the early 1950s that Bevin had shrewdly calculated a grand design, waited with "grim patience for the right moment and the right issue," and then in February 1947 sent the note that forced the United States to accept its new responsibilities. Prime Minister Attlee encouraged such ideas some years later, during interviews in 1959: "We were holding the line in far too many places and the Americans in far too few." By giving "notice at the right moment ... we made the Americans face up to the facts in the eastern Mediterranean. As a result we got the Truman Doctrine, a big step." The former chancellor of the exchequer, Roy Jenkins, has written that withdrawal from Greece and Turkey meant risks "but President Truman accepted the baby which Bevin with excellent timing had placed in his lap." Describing this diplomacy as brilliantly successful, he concluded that Bevin's "role was pivotal."[54]

American commentators have emphasized other themes, neglecting British diplomacy and considering the Truman Doctrine a logical action for a superpower developing a policy of containment. Early accounts by such traditional historians as Norman A. Graebner, John W. Spanier, and Louis J. Halle emphasized that as British power waned the United States naturally assumed responsibility for the eastern Mediterranean. Herbert Feis saw an even less complicated situation in which the Truman administration simply "felt impelled" to relieve Great Britain of the chore of maintaining Greece. William A. Williams and other revisionist historians dismissed the Truman Doctrine as another example of open-door expansionism and American imperialism. More recent accounts by John L. Gaddis and the biographer of Dean Acheson, David S. McLellan, continue to neglect British diplomacy while emphasizing the Truman administration's rising role in world affairs. McLellan stated that Acheson anticipated the British "capitulation" many months before it became official, was preparing for his country to assume the burden, and then simply accepted the responsibility.[55]

Problems exist with both interpretations. British writers have overestimated their country's power to change American policy and have underestimated America's postwar commitment to the Continent. They fail to emphasize the primary reasons for an evolving American policy—Soviet behavior and the Roosevelt and Truman administrations' desire to remain involved in postwar affairs. Although domestic pressure forced curtailing some responsibilities after the war, the U.S. government obviously expanded its commitments in 1946; it extended some credits to Greece and Turkey, granted Italy $100 million in December, and as snowstorms swept from the Thames to the Vistula early in 1947, Truman asked the Eightieth Congress for $350 million in relief for Austria, Hungary, Italy, Poland, and Greece.

The contention that Bevin formulated a grand design to prompt America into accepting responsibility for Greece deserves attention. As late as 11 February he advocated a sharing arrangement with the United States, and along with Defense Minister Alexander, he urged the cabinet to continue assistance. Whitehall officials supported this stand, for many of them feared what would happen to Greece if aid were terminated; M. S. Williams wrote that it "seems very doubtful whether assistance of the magnitude required will be found in the United States." In his opinion, also held by many British officials, Greece would soon fall to the Communists, hardly the goal the government had been striving to achieve for two-and-a-half years. Also, it seems doubtful that Bevin would have devised a scheme that conflicted with the advice of his most trusted subordinates. Sargent urged the government to "avoid irritating the Americans and throwing the Greeks into despair by finally shutting the door on all possibility of further help from us." And if sending the February note had been planned, then it is strange that the Foreign Office allowed their ambassador in Athens to reassure the Greek king as late as 19 February that Britain intended to continue assisting the regime and even would pay for an additional fifteen thousand troops for the Greek army. Finally, the idea that Bevin calculated the right issue at the right time is convenient—especially considering America's response—but it has not yet been substantiated by a single document. Neither public statements nor cabinet and Foreign Office records support the assumption.[56]

The American interpretation also has shortcomings. The supposition that the Truman administration would have acted decisively without Britain's abrupt withdrawal is questionable. No document has been found demonstrating that at the beginning of 1947 Truman was preparing to accept more responsibility for the eastern Mediterranean. Acheson admitted before the Foreign Relations Committee in March 1947 that the U.S. government had known of Britain's problems for four or five months; yet during this time the administration had not substantially enlarged its commitment, and it certainly had not implemented the sharing arrangement that Byrnes and Bevin devised in September 1946. The president had made no statements supporting new burdens—with the exception of winter relief—and in fact seemed content to let the British Treasury continue to pay for Greek and Turkish security. Even if it had wanted to, the administration probably could not have persuaded Congress to vote appropriations without a powerful stimulus. The mood on Capitol Hill was illustrated on 26 February 1947 when the Senate reduced the president's proposed budget by $4.5 billion—a budget Truman had described as the "rock bottom" amount necessary to maintain domestic and foreign commitments. Finally, Washington officials reacted with surprise—not anticipation —upon receiving the British notes. Acheson labeled the notes "shockers," and a presidential aide, Clark M. Clifford, revealed the hesitant and somber mood at the White House in the margin of a rough draft of the speech Truman would deliver on 12 March: "This is a grim task we are accepting. Nothing to recommend it except *alternative* is *grimmer. Tough!*"[57]

By neglecting British diplomacy, American commentators have distorted postwar relations. The basic conflict during the postwar years, of course, lay between the United States and Soviet Russia. But the superpowers did not live in a vacuum. Concerned with Washington's plans for the Continent, the British—and Europeans—continually attempted to influence American policy. Desperately fearing the extension of Russian rule, the governments of Western Europe echoed British calls for an American presence to contain the Soviets and to bolster democracy. They advocated a financial commitment, urging both immediate relief and long-term reconstruction. The Truman administration's decision in 1947 to address these problems represented neither chance nor completely independent action.

What was Britain's special role in bringing about an enlarged American commitment to the eastern Mediterranean? The Labour government had urged the United States to accept more responsibility in Greece and in 1946 encouraged Tsaldaris to seek assistance from Washington. Ambassador MacVeagh joined his British colleague in Athens and called for more involvement, but this effort had little effect until the Russian demands and Yugoslav action in August 1946. Then Byrnes accepted a sharing arrangement with Bevin, but domestic political events—the Wallace episode and the congressional elections of November 1946—forced reevaluation; as a result, the administration stalled and would not assume a larger share of the burden during the winter of 1946-1947.

The British notes of 21 February 1947 stimulated action and directly caused the United States to accept new responsibilities. In an executive session of the Foreign Relations Committee a few weeks later Sen. Walter F. George of Georgia put the question to Acheson: "Now, Mr. Secretary, what brought on the immediate emergency calling for action by this Government in the form proposed here in this legislation? What was it? Was it the British note?" "Yes, sir," Acheson replied. But unlike Bevin's earlier attempts to influence policy and to get the United States involved in Europe, the notes were not a shrewd tactic or a calculated maneuver. Nor were they a coup de main following years of diplomacy. Whitehall officials did not want to renege on their responsibilities; they wanted to share them. In March 1947, Sargent explained Bevin's action when writing to a Treasury official: "I must . . . point out that the Foreign Secretary has never agreed that what you call the Greek pit is either bottomless or profitless. In view of our financial difficulties Mr. Bevin agreed that our policy towards Greece must be so conducted as to eliminate the burden which it has hitherto imposed on the British taxpayer."[58] The notes thus developed out of pressing domestic factors: Labour's unfulfilled promises, postwar economic problems, burdening international commitments, and the hard winter of 1947. As snow swept across the British Isles, bringing the country to a standstill and confronting cabinet members with national survival, insurgency in the hills of Macedonia no longer seemed so important. The Treasury prevailed; the Foreign Office sent the notes.

Chapter 7

The United States, Great Britain, and the Cold War 1944-1947

The British and the American governments had a special relationship during the crusade against Nazi Germany. A great personal friendship existed between Churchill and Roosevelt that allowed the nations to work more closely than perhaps any two countries in recent history. Churchill's eulogy after Roosevelt's death accurately described the feelings of the British people: "For us it remains only to say that in Franklin Roosevelt there died the greatest American friend we have ever known." Sentiment between the diplomats was on the same level; in Washington, London, and Moscow these men usually worked easily together over difficult issues and after hours often shared thoughts and ideas.[1]

But behind this friendship were two nations with different policies for achieving similar goals for Europe, which became apparent in 1944 as officials began to consider the postwar settlement. In Washington planners wanted to forestall peacemaking until after victory, while adopting the role of mediator between Russia and Britain. The British advocated joint tactics to contain Soviet expansion.

Lacking the power necessary to secure their aims against the Russians, the British sought to influence American relations with the Kremlin during and after the war. On three occasions this tactic apparently succeeded. After Yalta, in March 1945, Churchill began a cable campaign to induce President Roosevelt to abandon an independent, mediating approach and to join the British in joint representations to Stalin. Roosevelt accepted this course just before he died and stiffened policy toward Russia. Truman continued this approach in April, but in late May he revived the mediating policy and Secretary of State Byrnes used it until early in

176

1946. In January and February the Red Army's continued occupation of northern Iran created a new problem, and in the first meeting of the U.N. Security Council Foreign Secretary Bevin forcefully defended Iran against Soviet pressure. Bevin's stand received much support in the American press, raised questions about Truman's position, and prompted Senator Vandenberg of the American delegation to return to Washington calling for a tougher policy and more involvement in world affairs. A few weeks later Churchill provoked the American people at Fulton, Missouri, declaring that an iron curtain existed in Eastern Europe, burying the Grand Alliance, and advocating an Anglo-American partnership. After an initial outburst of Anglophobia, Churchill's speech positively influenced opinion—Americans in May 1946 overwhelmingly favored closer relations with Great Britain, and by autumn the two nations were forming a partnership.

To be sure, the British could not have changed American policy without the assistance of the Kremlin. The campaign against Nazi Germany had marked the height of Russian-American friendship, encouraging an optimistic, independent policy and decreasing British influence. But Soviet actions in Eastern Europe, Korea, Iran, and the eastern Mediterranean offended Americans and frustrated first Roosevelt and then Truman. As it became apparent that the independent, mediating policy was not succeeding and as doubts increased about Russian designs, the two presidents and their advisers began to look for alternatives. At that point British proposals became attractive. During those periods of declining Soviet-American relations—March 1945 and the early months of 1946—British diplomacy was able to influence American policy.

In the spring of 1946 the U.S. government began to confront the Soviet Union, making strong statements about Russian behavior and showing increased leadership at the Paris meeting of the Council of Foreign Ministers. After the Kremlin issued its demands concerning the straits and Yugoslavia shot down two C-47s in August, the United States clearly replaced Britain as the major antagonist of the Soviet Union and assumed leadership of the West. Yet because of domestic political reasons, the dominant member of the rising Anglo-American partnership balked at accepting financial and military responsibilities proportionate with its wealth and power. The British notes of February 1947 left no viable alternative, and America responded by giving $400 million to Turkey and Greece.

This assistance, and the doctrine that Truman enunciated on 12 March 1947, signaled a profound change in American foreign relations. Aid to Greece and Turkey broke the tradition of isolation after a world conflict, of leaving European problems for Europeans. No longer could Americans enjoy the luxury of retreating behind their seacoasts and regarding themselves only as guardians of the Western Hemisphere. The administration and Congress now realized a continuing need to support nations with similar beliefs. As the *New York Times* declared, "The epoch of isolation and occasional intervention is ended. It is being replaced by an epoch of American responsibility."[2]

The desire to cooperate with Russia or to mediate between London and Moscow at last had come to an end. Americans had long detested British tactics in international affairs—the balances of power and spheres of influence—and favored a universalist system of collaboration within the United Nations. The limits of the world organization had become apparent in 1946 as the conflict arose between Washington and Moscow: the system worked only as long as the Allies had common goals. Perhaps for domestic political reasons the Truman administration continued to speak of resolving issues in the United Nations, but by early 1947 the congressional debate over aid to Greece and Turkey shattered the facade. Senator Connally asked in executive session of the Foreign Relations Committee, "Why kid the American people? Why try to make it appear that the United Nations can handle the crisis in the Eastern Mediterranean? We know it cannot. Why not be frank with them?"[3] American officials publicly accepted the need for a balance of power between East and West.

Truman's speech unveiled the new enemies—communism

and the Soviet Union. "The President did not name 'Russia' or the Soviets at any point," Eben Ayers recorded in his diary, "but his words were clear. They marked the end of appeasement of Russia." All free peoples must be protected; the United States would become a bulwark against what it perceived as Soviet aggrandizement. The administration presented a simplistic choice: Communist totalitarianism or free-enterprise democracy. The president later wrote that he wanted no hedging on the address, describing it as America's answer to the "surge of expansion of Communist tyranny."[4]

It was no coincidence that nine days after the speech Truman issued executive order 9835 initiating a loyalty program aimed at finding Communists in the federal civil service. At home, a campaign was beginning that in a few years would become an hysterical Red Scare. Abroad, the United States soon would be boosting a Greek regime that fought subversives by stifling civil liberties and executing political prisoners.[5]

Thus the Truman Doctrine set forth a policy advanced by Great Britain. The United States adopted an approach in Greece that the British had employed since 1944. The administration also accepted Churchill's conviction, first expressed in 1943, that the postwar menace was Russia. American officials finally abandoned their desire for an independent diplomacy; they gave up mediating between the Allies and working for Soviet cooperation and joined the British against the Kremlin. The United States had accepted responsibility for the eastern Mediterranean and made a commitment to European security—it had assumed leadership of the West. As Jones wrote in a memorandum, Truman's speech marked America's "passing into adulthood in the conduct of foreign affairs."[6]

The British, partly by design and partly default, had prompted the United States to adopt a policy of containment in the eastern Mediterranean, and thus one must ask what responsibility Britain must bear for the decline of East–West relations and the rise of the cold war. Some revisionist historians have argued that Churchill was the "first cold warrior," and it is true that he—and later Bevin—advocated that the

United States abandon its conciliatory approach and join them in a tough policy against the Kremlin. To some extent the British must assume responsibility, for their diplomacy accelerated the evolution of America's firm approach. Yet the British were urging Washington to accept the same policy that American diplomats in Eastern Europe were advocating, and thus the British were no more responsible than Harriman, Kennan, MacVeagh, and other American representatives throughout Soviet-dominated Europe. Washington officials finally accepted London's evaluation because it seemed accurate—Soviet behavior was incompatible with the aims of the West. Russian leaders' continual rejection of American designs supported the abandonment of a conciliatory approach and the adoption of a firm policy. In other words, British aims toward America were boosted by Soviet actions. If the Kremlin would have accepted Roosevelt's and Truman's desires in Eastern Europe, then both presidents would have continued to dismiss British plans. In May 1946 James Reston accurately noted that Britain and America were forming a parallel policy, but he added that, if Russia began to compromise, then the United States probably would "flirt again with the role of mediator."[7]

What responsibility must Britain assume for the policy enunciated in the Truman Doctrine? Whitehall officials were constantly prompting the Western giant to grant more aid to Greece, and the note of 21 February 1947 resulted in a $400 million appropriation. Attending the foreign ministers' conference in Moscow, Bevin received the news of the speech from Frank K. Roberts, who translated the story in *Pravda*. The British were delighted, and thankful that Truman made the "bold and statesmanlike speech." But the ideological tone and worldwide implications of the doctrine startled some officials. Rundall wrote that it was too anti-Russian, even dangerous, and Dalton later noted his "little push for a small economy in Whitehall had released world forces far more powerful than I ever guessed." At no time had Treasury or Whitehall officials advocated support for "all freedom loving peoples" or a crusade against communism. The British urged a consistent Anglo-American posture against the Soviets and an American financial commitment to Greece. They cannot be blamed for the rhetoric of the Truman Doctrine or what followed—an expansive U.S. foreign policy.[8]

The declaration of a new policy in 1947 revealed that Washington officials had misunderstood both wartime allies. Americans had been unduly suspicious of Britain; too often they had discounted London's proposals as imperialistic, or wondered whether the wily English were using American power to bolster the faltering empire. Feeling that friendly relations with Moscow were paramount, American officials often neglected London, took the British for granted, and too seldom analyzed Anglo-American relations. Before the war was over awkward situations resulted, first in such liberated areas as Greece and Italy, later in 1945 at the conferences with the Russians. The mediating approach might have solved a few difficulties with Stalin but it alienated the British, since it denied similar Anglo-American goals for Eastern Europe. Only as the Grand Alliance crumbled and American officials concluded that alone they were incapable of making the Russians accept a Western peace did they realize the importance of Britain—a valuable junior partner in the rising confrontation with the Kremlin.

Washington officials, and especially President Roosevelt, either misunderstood or failed to face up to Russian designs in Europe. During the crusade against the Nazis optimism for postwar cooperation had soared. Allied collaboration had resulted in the defeat of a common enemy, and Americans hoped it would prevent future conflict and establish a lasting peace. The United States tried to ignore ideological differences, prewar relations, the Katyn Forest massacre, the Warsaw uprising, the constant warnings from American and British diplomats and looked forward to a universal organization that would maintain one world—an impossibility.

The Soviets were different—a fact too often ignored in Washington. They did not fight a war that devastated their homeland and slaughtered 20 million of their citizens to establish capitalistic democracies in areas liberated by the Red Army. Personal, economic, or atomic diplomacy would not pry the Russians out of Eastern Europe.

Also, American policy reflected more knowledge of democratic procedure than of international relations. How could one capitalistic democracy mediate between another and a Communist nation? American officials pretended that their aims were somehow between those of the European allies—an illusion, not a policy. It took many months of disagreement with the Soviets and agreement with the British before the Truman administration abandoned hope and accepted reality.

The British had suffered from few illusions about the Soviet Union. After centuries of involvement in Europe they had established traditional aims that guided their relations with other nations, promoted consistency in negotiation, and discouraged optimism about international cooperation. The Congress of Vienna and the Paris peace conference a century later had shown that alliances disintegrated as victors divided the spoils. Whitehall officials believed that the Russians—whether ruled by tsars or commissars—would try to spread their influence throughout Europe. Given such aims, the sacrifices of the war, and the vacuum of power in Central Europe, Stalin would try to secure Russia's borders, if necessary by permanent occupation of the liberated territories. For the sake of their own security, the British had to contain Soviet influence as far east as possible, so their officials called for negotiation before the Red Army crossed the Vistula and urged campaigns in the Balkans. When they were unable to construct an Anglo-American front, they attempted to secure support from the Dominions and to strengthen their ties with Western Europe.

The British understood America's universalist aims, but they saw no reason to expect success from an independent attempt to build friendship with Stalin. To them peace was not a question of trust but of national interest. Unable to persuade the Americans during the war and realizing their declining power within the Big Three, the British became querulous and complained that policymakers in Washington were naive, amateurish, and inconsistent, and that American policy represented a repudiation of European diplomacy, personal whims, and blind idealism—the same factors that had produced much talk after the First World War but few lasting results. They feared that the United States would turn its back on Europe in 1945 as it had in 1919. At times this apprehension led to unfortunate unilateral actions that confirmed American suspicions, stimulated Anglophobia, and decreased British influence. Churchill's Balkan deal with Stalin and interference in Italy and Greece were the worst examples.

Yet the British had one advantage over the Soviet Union in dealing with the United States—a common heritage. It allowed them to understand American aims for Europe and to use the power of the press and personal influence to guide the Western giant. Churchill's messages to Roosevelt and Truman detailed Soviet misdeeds and raised agonizing questions such as, how should West respond to the Communist domination of Poland? When personal diplomacy failed, British officials presented the issues directly to the American people. In early 1945 Michael R. Wright virtually demanded more American participation in European affairs, and during the first three months of 1946 Bevin and Churchill provoked the American public, bringing pressure for change.

The adoption of a joint policy had meaning mainly for Anglo-American relations. Anglophobia, rampant in 1944, had practically disappeared by 1947, superseded by fear of communism. By then, few Americans complained about British imperialism, and in fact Inverchapel informed his superiors that it was strange to read in American newspapers that Britain was proceeding too fast in weakening the empire. Proposals to work with the British now found support instead of suspicion. As the Truman administration assumed the burdens of a great power, British officials gained more respect for the nation they once called the "lumbering giant." In September 1947, Churchill thanked Truman from the bottom of his heart for keeping the world safe from tyranny and war, and in 1949 Bevin wrote the president: "It is difficult to find words to express to you not only the thanks of myself but of my Government and of my country for your great efforts on behalf of Europe."[9]

For the United States the postwar commitment to British security that had begun with the $3.75 billion loan in 1946 was only the beginning. While the president spoke out on Greece and Turkey the State Department asked the British if they would be interested in discussing policy toward Austria, Hungary, Italy, Iran, and China.[10] In June the administration announced the Marshall Plan, in 1948 they stationed B-29 bombers in Great Britain and opposed the Russians in Berlin, in 1949 they joined the North Atlantic Treaty Organization. By 1961, Pres. John F. Kennedy had expanded the Truman Doctrine, proclaiming in his inaugural address: "Let every nation know, whether it wishes us well or ill, that we shall pay any price, bear any burden, meet any hardship, support any friend, oppose any foes, in order to assure the survival and success of liberty. This much we pledge—and more." By 1970 the British could peer across the Atlantic and point to the new empire, for while London had relinquished most of its colonies the United States had assumed military commitments to forty-seven nations, occupied 375 major bases and 300 minor facilities on foreign soil, and stationed a million troops overseas.

Indeed, the British had advocated a larger American role in world affairs, but they had gained more than they had bargained for.

Notes

Notes to the Preface

1. Perhaps the first traditionalists were the contemporary American policymakers; for example, see James F. Byrnes, *Speaking Frankly* (New York, 1947); W. B. Smith, *My Three Years in Moscow* (Philadelphia, 1950); Joseph M. Jones, *The Fifteen Weeks* (New York, 1955); and the two-volume memoirs by Harry S. Truman, *Year of Decisions* and *Years of Trial and Hope* (Garden City, N.Y., 1955 and 1956). A brief survey of traditional historians includes T. A. Bailey, *America Faces Russia* (New York, 1950); Herbert Feis, *Churchill, Roosevelt, Stalin: The War They Waged and the Peace They Sought* (Princeton, 1957); John L. Snell, *Wartime Origins of the East-West Dilemma over Germany* (New Orleans, 1959); and Norman A. Graebner, *Cold War Diplomacy, 1945–1960* (New York, 1962). Some years later traditionalists began responding to attacks from the revisionists; consult Arthur M. Schlesinger, Jr., "Origins of the Cold War," *Foreign Affairs* 46 (October 1967); Robert W. Tucker, *The Radical Left and American Foreign Policy* (Baltimore, 1971); and Robert H. Ferrell, "Truman Foreign Policy: A Traditional View," in *The Truman Period as a Research Field: A Reappraisal, 1972*, ed. Richard S. Kirkendall (Columbia, Mo., 1974).

2. An introduction to the cold war debate is Joseph M. Siracusa, *New Left Diplomatic Histories and Historians: The Revisionists* (New York, 1973). The most influential revisionist interpretations can be found in William A. Williams, *The Tragedy of American Diplomacy* (Cleveland, 1959; New York, 1962); D. F. Fleming, *The Cold War and Its Origins: 1917–1960*, 2 vols. (New York, 1961); Gar Alperovitz, *Atomic Diplomacy: Hiroshima and Potsdam* (New York, 1965); Gabriel Kolko, *The Politics of War: The World and United States Foreign Policy, 1943–1945* (New York, 1968); Lloyd C. Gardner, *Architects of Illusions: Men and Ideas in American Foreign Policy, 1941–1949* (Chicago, 1970); and Thomas G. Paterson, *Soviet-American Confrontation: Postwar Reconstruction and the Origins of the Cold War* (Baltimore, 1973).

3. Major postrevisionist books include John L. Gaddis, *The United States and the Origins of the Cold War, 1941–1947* (New York, 1972); Lynn E. Davis, *The Cold War Begins: Soviet-American Conflict over Eastern Europe* (Princeton, 1974); and Daniel Yergin, *Shattered Peace: The Origins of the Cold War and the National Security State* (Boston, 1977).

4. Peter G. Boyle, "The British Foreign Office View of Soviet-American Relations, 1945–46," *Diplomatic History* 3 (Summer 1979);

Wilson D. Miscamble, "Anthony Eden and the Truman–Molotov Conversations, April 1945," *Diplomatic History* 2 (Spring 1978); Lawrence S. Wittner, "American Policy toward Greece during World War II," *Diplomatic History* 3 (Spring 1979); William Roger Louis, *Imperialism at Bay, 1941–1945: The United States and the Decolonization of the British Empire* (Oxford, 1977); Robert M. Hathaway, Jr., "The Paradoxes of Partnership: Britain and America, 1944–1947" (Ph.D. diss., University of North Carolina, 1976).

Notes to Chapter 1
Britain and the "Great Unwieldy Barge"

1. Harold Macmillan, *The Blast of War, 1939–1945* (London, 1967), p. 521.

2. Roosevelt to Churchill, 30 November 1944, in Elliott Roosevelt and Joseph Lash, eds., *F.D.R.: His Personal Letters, 1928–1945* (New York, 1950), 2:1558. Churchill to Roosevelt, 3 December 1944, *Wartime Correspondence,* pp. 614–15. This volume by Loewenheim, Langley, and Jonas contains 548 messages between the president and the prime minister. Warren Kimball is preparing a series that will include the complete text of all 1,700 messages, including important prior drafts and unsent cables available in American and British archives.

3. For a survey of the combined boards, see William H. McNeil, *America, Britain, and Russia, 1941–1946* (London, 1953), pp. 129–37.

4. Waldemar J. Gallman, oral biography, Indiana University Oral History Project, pp. 31–32. Also see Gallman's unpublished manuscript, "Some Thoughts on Foreign Affairs: From the Sidelines," chap. 10, Mugar Memorial Library, Boston University, Boston. H. Freeman Matthews, oral-history interview, HST Library, p. 23. The comments of British diplomats on the Anglo-American relationship were common in late 1943 and early 1944; see FO records, A33/6/G45 and AN34/6/G45.

5. Benjamin D. Rhodes, "Anglophobia in Chicago: Mayor William Hale Thompson's 1927 Campaign against King George V," *Illinois Quarterly* 39 (Summer 1977):5–14.

6. Earl of Birkenhead, *Halifax: The Life of Lord Halifax* (Boston, 1966), pp. 494–95. *Life*'s editorial of 12 October 1942, Willkie's pronouncements, and other such statements appear in William Roger Louis, *Imperialism at Bay, 1941–1945: The United States and the Decolonization of the British Empire* (London, 1977), pp. 198ff. Roosevelt's comments to Churchill were related by Hull and Stettinius. Cordell Hull, *The Memoirs of Cordell Hull* (New York, 1948), 2:1151, 1477–78;

and Julius W. Pratt, *Cordell Hull* in *The American Secretaries of State and Their Diplomacy,* ed. Robert H. Ferrell and Samuel Flagg Bemis (New York, 1964), 13:738–41. Edward R. Stettinius, Jr., *Roosevelt and the Russians: The Yalta Conference,* ed. Walter Johnson (Garden City, N.Y., 1949), p. 237; and Thomas M. Campbell and George C. Herring, *The Diaries of Edward R. Stettinius, Jr., 1943–1946* (New York, 1975), p. 40. Hadley Cantril and Mildred Strunks, eds., *Public Opinion, 1935–1946* (Princeton, 1951), pp. 274, 327–28. For an extreme British view of Roosevelt's "assault" on the British Empire, see Chester Wilmot, *The Struggle for Europe* (London, 1952), pp. 632ff; also consult J. F. C. Fuller, *The Second World War, 1939–1945* (New York, 1949). (Wilmot was actually an Australian; Fuller was British.)

7. Hickerson to Acheson, 28 March 1947, SD records, record group 59, John Hickerson Files.

8. Popular feelings toward each nation are in H. C. Allen, *Great Britain and the United States: A History of Anglo-American Relations, 1783–1952* (London, 1954); see also Macmillan, *Blast of War,* pp. 158–59. Eden's statement, made to Hull on 29 March 1943, was recorded by Hopkins; Robert E. Sherwood, *Roosevelt and Hopkins: An Intimate History* (New York, 1948), p. 719.

9. Leahy recorded Churchill's comment at Yalta; Adm. William D. Leahy Papers, diary entry, 9 February 1945, Library of Congress, Washington, D.C.

10. Oliver Harvey Papers, diary entry, 6 March 1944, Student Room, British Museum, London. Anthony Eden, *The Reckoning* (Boston, 1965), p. 593. Ambassador Halifax wrote Churchill on 27 January 1945: "The trouble with these people [Americans] is that they are so much the victims of labels: 'Power Politics, Spheres of Influence, Balance of Power, etc.' As if there was ever such a sphere of influence agreement as the Monroe Doctrine! And, as I can only tell them when they talk about being outsmarted . . . they evidently outsmarted somebody when they made the Louisiana Purchase!" From the Halifax Papers and quoted in Daniel Yergin, *Shattered Peace: The Origins of the Cold War and the National Security State* (Boston, 1977), p. 61.

11. Harvey Papers, diary entry, 23 September 1943. Not all British leaders agreed with Harvey. First Sea Lord and chief of naval staff, Adm. Sir Andrew B. Cunningham had a high regard for American military leaders; Andrew B. Cunningham Papers, diary entries, 30 August and 2 November 1944, Student Room, British Museum, London. Eden to Halifax, 28 January 1944, FO records, A447/6/G45; and minutes, 2 February 1945, AN350/22/45.

12. Quoted in Robert Garson, "The Atlantic Alliance, Eastern Europe and the Origins of the Cold War: From Pearl Harbor to Yalta," in *Contrast and Connection: Bicentennial Essays in Anglo-American History,* ed. H. C. Allen and Roger Thompson (Athens,

Ohio, 1976), pp. 298–99. Concerning the Roosevelt administration's failure to define its goals in Eastern Europe, see Lynn E. Davis, *The Cold War Begins: Soviet-American Conflict over Eastern Europe* (Princeton, 1974), pp. 160ff.

13. Roosevelt to Churchill, 18 March 1942, *Wartime Correspondence*, p. 196.

14. Leahy's 16 May 1944 letter and the State Department's September comments appear in *FR*, 1944, *The Conference at Quebec*, pp. 190–93; also consult Stettinius's memorandum of 8 November 1944, *FR*, 1944, 4:1025. The January 1945 briefing paper is in *FR*, 1945, *The Conference at Malta and Yalta*, pp. 230, 243.

15. Having had a long involvement in European affairs, the British felt that the Americans were amateurs in Continental diplomacy. Harvey noted in his diary on 4 August 1943: "These Americans! They are so excitable and they oversimplify so. They are incapable of sitting quietly and thinking out the implication of a proposal. They rush off at once, in a high state of excitement, and commit themselves." Also see diary entries on 25 August and 12 September. On 3 October 1943 he noted: "The Americans are so dense and the Russians so suspicious." Harvey Papers. Wilmot certainly agreed with such statements. In 1952 he discussed America's "immaturity" in European diplomacy, "the cause for so much of Europe's present suffering"; *Struggle for Europe*, pp. 640, 714–17. The feelings of British diplomats were clarified by Lord Gore-Booth during a 21 March 1977 interview. He said that State Department officials that he had worked with, such as Theodore Achilles and John D. Hickerson, were very professional, but that the actual decisions were made by amateurs in the White House. Sir Frank K. Roberts related similar thoughts about American foreign-service officers stationed in Moscow during an interview on 22 March 1977. Also consult Paul Gore-Booth, *With Great Truth and Respect* (London, 1974), pp. 123–24; Eden, *Reckoning*, pp. 375, 395; Lord Moran (Sir Charles Wilson), *Winston Churchill: The Struggle for Survival, 1940–1965* (London, 1968), pp. 154, 212; and David Dilks, ed., *The Diaries of Sir Alexander Cadogan, 1938–1945* (New York, 1971), pp. 577–78, 582, 587.

16. Quoted in John W. Wheeler-Bennett and Anthony Nicholls, *The Semblance of Peace: The Political Settlement after the Second World War* (New York, 1972), p. 290.

17. Churchill's comments to the Spanish ambassador are quoted in Wheeler-Bennett and Nicholls, *Semblance of Peace*, p. 295. See also Winston S. Churchill, *The Grand Alliance* (Boston, 1950), p. 370.

18. Churchill's concern about the Soviet threat is described in Wilmot, *Struggle for Europe*, p. 636; and Moran, *Churchill*, pp. 161, 181, 193. Sargent reported his complaint about the British military leaders to Eden on 18 August 1944, FO records, N5126.

19. Harvey Papers, diary entry, 6 October 1943. Harvey forecasted the Labour party's electoral victory in June 1945 when he noted on 6 October 1943: "On the future his [Churchill's] attitude is disastrous. If he tries to swing the peace against Russia, there will be a revolution here." See also Sargent to Eden, 18 August 1944, FO records, N5126.

20. Military figures appear in Forrest C. Pogue, *The Supreme Command, U.S. Army in World War II: European Theater of Operations* (Washington, D.C., 1954), app. E, pp. 542–43; and Lisle A. Rose, *Dubious Victory: The United States and the End of World War II* (Kent, Ohio, 1973), 1:6–7.

21. John W. Wheeler-Bennett, ed., *Action This Day: Working with Churchill* (London, 1968), p. 96, n. 1. "The Essentials of an American Policy," 21 March 1944, FO records, AN1538/16/45. Eden, *Reckoning*, p. 395.

22. Diary entry, 23 November 1943, Joseph Stilwell, *The Stilwell Papers* (New York, 1948), p. 245. Sholto Douglas, *Years of Command* (London, 1966), pp. 227–30. Churchill's demand to capture Rhodes is related in Samuel Eliot Morison, *Strategy and Compromise* (Boston, 1958), p. 51. Forrest C. Pogue, *George C. Marshall: Organizer of Victory* (New York, 1973), pp. 415, 573. Eisenhower discussed Churchill's strategy a generation later in James Nelson, ed., *General Eisenhower on the Military Churchill: A Conversation with Alistair Cooke* (New York, 1970). Sir Arthur Bryant presents a British view of America's difficulty in grasping the Mediterranean strategy in *Triumph in the West, 1943–1946* (London, 1959), chap. 1. Also consult Bryant's *The Turn of the Tide: A History of the War Years Based on the Diaries of Field Marshal Lord Alanbrooke, Chief of the Imperial General Staff* (New York, 1957). Wilmot discusses General Marshall's "simple and rigid" ideas in *Struggle for Europe*, p. 454.

23. Moran records Churchill's feelings in *Churchill*, p. 181. For the prime minister's pleas for the Italian campaign and against Operation Anvil, see his 25 and 28 June 1944 messages to Roosevelt, *Wartime Correspondence*, pp. 542–45; Winston S. Churchill, *Triumph and Tragedy* (Boston, 1953), pp. 716ff; and Pogue, *Organizer of Victory*, pp. 410ff. After Roosevelt supported Eisenhower's plan, the American ambassador in London, John G. Winant, wrote the president on 3 July 1944: "I wanted you to know how deeply the Prime Minister felt . . . in his accepting your decision. I have never seen him as badly shaken. He believed completely in the program he was supporting." FDR Library, Map Room File, Box 33, Folder "Anvil." Eisenhower's firm stand was reported by Harry C. Butcher, *My Three Years with Eisenhower* (New York, 1946), p. 634. For the American decision to invade southern France, consult Maurice Matloff, "The Anvil Decision: Crossroads to Strategy," in *Command Decisions*, ed. Kent Roberts Greenfield (Washington, D.C., 1960), chap. 16.

24. Lord Tedder, *With Prejudice: The War Memoirs of Marshal of the Royal Air Force* (London, 1966), p. 587; and Montgomery of Alamein, *Memoirs* (Cleveland, 1958), p. 297. Martin Blumenson, ed., *The Patton Papers, 1940–1945* (Boston, 1974), pp. 550, 608, 628. Bryant contends that Montgomery's plan would have ended the war by the end of 1944; see *Triumph in the West,* pp. 283ff.

25. Minute by V. Cavendish Bentinck, 10 October 1944, concerning a report by the British director of military information, S.H.A.E.F., FO records, AN4648/6/G45. Marshall interview with Pogue, 29 October 1956, Forrest C. Pogue, *George C. Marshall: Ordeal and Hope, 1939–1942* (New York, 1966), p. 264.

26. The Foreign Office's and Churchill's views toward a West European bloc can be found in the official history by Llewellyn Woodward, *British Foreign Policy in the Second World War* (London, 1976), 5:chap. 64. The Public Record Office has changed the title of some papers since Woodward did his research. For example, those he cites as "Churchill papers" are now labeled PREM (premier's papers). Paul-Henri Spaak, *The Continuing Battle: Memoirs of a European, 1936–1966* (Boston, 1971), chap. 11. Eden to Cooper, circulated to the cabinet on 25 July 1944, Cab w.p. (44) 409. Memorandum, 23 September 1944, FO records, N5793.

27. Churchill to Eden, 4 May 1944, PREM 3/66/7; see also M497/5. Memorandum by Eden, "Soviet Policy in the Balkans," 7 June 1944, Cab (66/51) w.p. (44) 304. The prime minister's anxieties are recorded in Moran, *Churchill,* pp. 212–13, 229. The Roosevelt administration's antipathy toward spheres of influence is examined in Hull, *Memoirs,* 2:1452–53; Davis, *Cold War Begins,* chap. 5; *FR,* 1944, 5:112–15; and *FR, 1945, The Conference at Malta and Yalta,* pp. 103–5. Charles E. Bohlen, *Witness to History, 1929–1969* (New York, 1973), pp. 161–64. Bohlen memorandum to Hopkins, 3 October 1944, SD records, record group 59, records of the Office of European Affairs, Box 12.

28. Harriman to Roosevelt, 10 and 11 October 1944, *FR,* 1944, 4:1005–10. British minutes of the Moscow talks are in PREM 3/434/2 and 3/434/4. For American documents on the meeting, see FDR Library, Map Room Files, Box 32, Folder "Churchill–Stalin Conference, 9–16 October 1944." W. Averell Harriman and Elie Abel, *Special Envoy to Churchill and Stalin, 1941–1946* (New York, 1975), pp. 356–58. Harriman's statement that he did not attend any meetings with Stalin and the prime minister contradicts British documents; see PREM 3/434/2. For more detail and analysis of the meeting and the percentage deal, consult Albert Resis, "The Churchill–Stalin Secret 'Percentages' Agreement on the Balkans, Moscow, October, 1944," *American Historical Review* 83 (April 1978); Joseph M. Siracusa, "The Meaning of TOLSTOY: Churchill, Stalin, and the Balkans, Moscow, October 1944," *Diplomatic History* 3 (Fall 1979); and

Bruce R. Kuniholm, *The Origins of the Cold War in the Near East: Great Power Conflict and Diplomacy in Iran, Turkey, and Greece* (Princeton, 1980), pp. 100–129.

29. Bohlen felt that Churchill's meeting was cynical; *Witness to History,* p. 163. Churchill to Stalin, 11 October 1944, PREM 3/66/7. The prime minister explained to his cabinet that the percentages were "not intended to be more than a guide" and did not "set up a rigid system of spheres of influence. It may however help the United States to see how their two principal Allies feel about these regions when the picture is presented as a whole." In the same file, see Eden to Sargent, 12 October 1944. After more reflection on the value of the talks with Stalin, the prime minister became more interested in establishing a Western European organization. He wrote to Eden on 25 November 1944 that a bloc is a "political and strategic interest of this country, since a weak and divided Europe would not only be a political storm centre but also be exploited by the *Machtpolitik* of the Soviet Union." PREM 4/30/8.

30. Minutes by V. Cavendish Bentinck, 10 October 1944, and by Eden, 26 November 1944, FO records, AN4648/6/G45.

31. Pogue, *Supreme Command,* pp. 329–33; L. F. Ellis and A. E. Warhurst, *Victory in the West* (London, 1968), 2:413–15; *New York Times,* 3, 4, and 20 December 1944. Eden explains Britain's policy toward Belgium in a memorandum to the war cabinet, 19 December 1944, Cab (66/59) w.p. (44) 750.

32. Macmillan, *Blast of War,* p. 478. British-Greek relations are examined in Woodward, *British Foreign Policy,* 3:chap. 43; the situation in Greece is described in John O. Iatrides, *Revolt in Athens: The Greek Communist "Second Round," 1944–1945* (Princeton, 1972); and C. M. Woodhouse, *The Struggle for Greece, 1941–1949* (London, 1976), chap. 5. A thoughtful interpretation of "American Policy toward Greece during World War II" is Lawrence S. Wittner in *Diplomatic History* 3 (Spring 1979); and see Kuniholm, *Origins of the Cold War in the Near East,* chap. 2. Prime Minister to Athens embassy, 5 December 1944, FO records, R19933; also see PREM 3/212/4 which contains most of Churchill's messages to General Scobie and Ambassador Leeper.

33. Woodward, *British Foreign Policy,* 3:440, 442, 453–68. Charles to Foreign Office, 22 November 1944, FO records, R19030/15/22. Prime Minister's note to Eden, 23 November 1944, FO records, M1136/4. Foreign Office to Charles, 28 November 1944, FO records, R19153/15/22. Prime Minister to Halifax, 2 December 1944, PREM 3/243/5.

34. MacVeagh to State Department, 5 December 1944, *FR,* 1944, 5:142–43; and MacVeagh to Roosevelt, 8 December 1944 and 15 January 1945, FDR Library, PSF, Box 54, Folder "MacVeagh (Greece)." Kirk to State Department, 28 November 1944, *FR,* 1944,

3:1158–59. Stettinius to Winant, 30 November 1944, ibid., pp. 1159–61. Also consult *FR, 1945, The Conference at Malta and Yalta,* pp. 271, 430. The State Department's view of British actions in Italy was written by H. Freeman Matthews to Stettinius: "This is a further example of British practice of demanding prior consultation before any action which we propose but in callously refusing to consult us when it doesn't suit their purpose"; 1 December 1944, Edward R. Stettinius, Jr., Papers, Box 222, University of Virginia Library, Manuscripts Department, Charlottesville, Va.; also see Box 245.

35. Department of State *Bulletin* 11 (10 December 1944):722.

36. Churchill to Roosevelt, 6 December 1944, *Wartime Correspondence,* pp. 619–21. Woodward, *British Foreign Policy,* 3:461. Eden to Halifax, 6 December 1944, FO records, R20027/15/22. *Manchester Guardian,* 6 December 1944. *Economist,* 9 December 1944. *Daily Herald,* 6, 7, and 8 December 1944. *New York Times,* 10 December 1944. *Time* (18 December 1944): 17, wrote that the press release was a "bare-knuckle blow to Britain," and Sherwood felt that the prime minister's 6 December message to Roosevelt might have been the "most violent outburst of rage in all of their historic correspondence." *Roosevelt and Hopkins,* p. 839. It was calm, however, compared to the first draft that Churchill did not send: "I have as you must realize been struck a very blow from a quarter when I least expected it. . . . [M]y task in Greece has been rendered far more difficult by the encouragement given in Mr. Stettinius' last sentence to the ferocious bands who are descending upon the capital and had already seized the bulk of the police stations at the time our troops were ordered to intervene, and preserve order. We have only to stand aside to provoke a massacre in Athens on a hideous scale followed by a Communist terror. If it is the wish of the American Government that we should stand aside and let things take their course, that should surely be represented to us through official channels." PREM 3/243/5.

37. The Wright–Stettinius meeting is described in Halifax to Foreign Office, 7 December 1944, FO records, R20235/15/22, and briefly mentioned in Campbell and Herring, *Stettinius Diaries,* p. 191. The secretary of state apologized to Eden on 8 December 1944, FO records, R20235/15/22. British feelings were emphasized in a minute by Sargent on 9 December 1944, FO records, R20319/15/22: "It is satisfactory that the State Department should be embarrassed by being asked to make a decision and accept responsibility in the case of Badoglio. They no doubt would much prefer us to take action and then to have criticised us again from the sidelines. For this reason I think it is essential that we should make them shoulder their share of responsibility." Anglo-American policy is described in Department of State to British Embassy, 8 December 1944, *FR, 1944,* 3:1162–63; Halifax to Foreign Office, 8 December 1944, FO records, R20370/

15/22; and Woodward, *British Foreign Policy*, 3:462–66. Differences in dealing with liberated countries, however, still remained. See Stettinius to Winant, 11 December 1944, *FR*, 1944, 3:1164–65.

38. Wittner has written, "In reality, America's policy toward Greece bolstered Britain's at key points." True, if Wittner means Roosevelt's secret actions and not the response of the American public and press; "American Policy toward Greece during World War II," p. 149. Stettinius to Roosevelt, 13 December 1944, *FR*, 1944, 5:149–50. Roosevelt to Churchill, 13 December 1944, ibid., pp. 150–51. Churchill to Roosevelt, 28 December 1944, ibid., pp. 173–75. Roosevelt to George II, 28 December 1944, ibid., p. 177. The messages also can be found in *Wartime Correspondence*, pp. 619–42.

39. *Congressional Record*, vol. 90, pp. 9308–9. Stettinius diary entry, 18 December 1944, in Campbell and Herring, *Stettinius Diaries*, pp. 200–201. *New York Times*, 10 December 1944. *Chicago Daily Tribune*, 30 November 1944. *Nation*, 16 December 1944.

40. Halifax to Foreign Office, 2 December 1944, FO records, AN4528/20/45, and 10 December 1944, AN4618/20/45. Halifax to Eden, 19 February 1945, FO records, AN763/763/45.

41. "Noble Negatives," *Economist*, 30 December 1944; for statements in the *Yorkshire Post* and other British papers, see *Time* (15 January 1945): 34; *Life* (15 January 1945): 22; and *United States News* (12 January 1945): 13–14, 32. The poll of June 1943 and Roosevelt's response appear in William D. Hassett, *Off the Record with F.D.R.* (New Brunswick, N.J., 1958), p. 173.

42. Conciliatory letters from both Britons and Americans appear in *New York Times*, 27 January and 6, 9, and 18 February 1945.

43. The Department of State survey is recorded in John L. Gaddis, *The United States and the Origins of the Cold War, 1941–1947* (New York, 1972), pp. 154–55, and n. 39. Cantril and Strunks, eds., *Public Opinion*, p. 777. To the American public, Britain would still be the primary rascal as late as February 1945. By May, however, because of Soviet behavior in Eastern Europe and at the San Francisco conference, Russia would supersede Britain, remaining in first place for the remainder of the cold war. Gaddis feels that "Americans distrusted Britain more than they did Russia"; *Origins of the Cold War*, p. 155. Gaddis Smith states that "one of the most significant aspects" of Roosevelt's thinking was that "Britain, rather than Russia, might be the principal disruptive force in the postwar world"; *American Diplomacy during the Second World War, 1941–1945* (New York, 1965), pp. 63, 81, 143. A similar theme is expressed by Gabriel Kolko, *The Politics of War: The World and United States Foreign Policy, 1943–1945* (New York, 1968). No doubt, Anglo-American relations sank to their nadir in the winter of 1944–1945. But while the press and public jeered, feelings between British and American diplomats remained cordial; interviews in April 1978 with Waldemar J. Gallman and

Samuel Berger of the U.S. embassy in London and Theodore Achilles, director of the State Department's British Commonwealth desk. It is doubtful that the Churchill–Roosevelt friendship suffered. After Congress enacted a joint resolution in December 1944 honoring the late director of the British military mission in Washington, Sir John Dill, the president wrote the prime minister on 10 January 1945 that it was "evidence of a very wholesome state of mind in the midst of the bickerings that are inevitable at this stage of the war." FDR Library, PSF, Box 52, Folder "Great Britain, Winston Churchill, 1944–1945."

44. Halifax to Foreign Office, 24 December 1944, FO records, AN4730/20/45. In an undated minute found in the same file, J. C. Donnelly wrote that "American opinion is an ocean particularly prone to hurricanes of this kind. It would be foolish to pretend that they do not do great damage but, like other natural phenomena, they must be endured with fortitude and understanding."

Notes to Chapter 2
Churchill and Roosevelt

1. Eden to Churchill, 10 January 1945, PREM 3/51/1; and minute, 12 January 1945, FO records, N390/165/G. Also consult Winston S. Churchill, *Triumph and Tragedy* (Boston, 1953), pp. 338, 341.

2. Churchill, *Triumph and Tragedy*, p. 344. Stettinius did meet Eden but not to form a joint policy; *FR*, 1945, *The Conference at Malta and Yalta*, pp. 508–9. W. Averell Harriman and Elie Abel, *Special Envoy to Churchill and Stalin, 1941–1946* (New York, 1975), p. 390.

3. Cordell Hull, *The Memoirs of Cordell Hull* (New York, 1948), 2:1436, 1471. For Russian losses, see Lisle A. Rose, *Dubious Victory: The United States and the End of World War II* (Kent, Ohio, 1973), pp. 44–47; and John L. Gaddis, *Russia, the Soviet Union, and the United States: An Interpretive History* (New York, 1978), p. 154. The suppression of White's book appears in Thomas M. Campbell and George C. Herring, *The Diaries of Edward R. Stettinius, Jr., 1943–1946* (New York, 1975), pp. 177–78. For Snow's article of 14 December 1942 in the *Saturday Evening Post, Collier's* essay of 7 August 1943, and many other examples, see Paul Willen, "Who 'Collaborated' with Russia?" *Antioch Review* 14 (September 1954): 259–83; and consult Robert A. Divine, *Second Chance: The Triumph of Internationalism in America during World War II* (New York, 1967), pp. 52–68.

4. Roosevelt informed his speech writer of his mediating role; Samuel I. Rosenman, *Working with Roosevelt* (New York, 1952), p. 526. For a British interpretation, consult Chester Wilmot, *The Strug-*

Notes

gle for Europe (London, 1952), p. 632. Anthony Eden, *The Reckoning* (Boston, 1965), pp. 591–93.

5. Robert E. Sherwood, *Roosevelt and Hopkins: An Intimate History* (New York, 1948), p. 870. Department of State survey, 13 February 1945, reported in John L. Gaddis, *The United States and the Origins of the Cold War, 1941–1947* (New York, 1972), p. 165; and see Hadley Cantril and Mildred Strunks, eds., *Public Opinion, 1935–1946* (Princeton, 1951), p. 368. Churchill's comment to Dalton, and other confessions of British optimism, appear in David Dilks, ed., *The Diaries of Sir Alexander Cadogan, 1938–1945* (New York, 1971), pp. 716–17.

6. Sherwood, *Roosevelt and Hopkins,* p. 871.

7. Adm. William D. Leahy Papers, diary entry, 14 February 1945, Library of Congress, Washington, D.C. Stettinius's comment appears in Walter Millis, ed., *The Forrestal Diaries* (New York, 1951), p. 35.

8. Henry Maitland Wilson, *Eight Years Overseas, 1939–1947* (London, n.d. [1949?]), pp. 252–53. Halifax reported the McCloy conversation to Eden, 2 January 1944, FO records, AN447/6/G45. Foreign Office proposals for close coordination with the United States are prevalent during the early months of 1944; FO records, American File No. 6. Earl of Halifax (Edward L.), *Fullness of Days* (London, 1957), and *The American Speeches of the Earl of Halifax* (Oxford, 1947), which includes sixty-five addresses from March 1941 to May 1946; and consult FO records, File "Speeches by Halifax," 1944.

9. Minutes by J. C. Donnelly, 29 December 1944 and 16 February 1945, FO records, AN4614/34/45 and AN505/22/45, respectively.

10. Wright to Philip Broadmead, 26 January 1945, FO records, AN505/22/45; and Wright to Neville Butler, 12 March 1945, FO records, AN929/22/45.

11. Wright to Broadmead, 26 February 1945, FO records, AN929/22/45; *Jackson Citizen Patriot,* 11 January 1945; and *Detroit News,* 14 January 1945.

12. Presidential aide Steve Early wrote a memorandum informing Roosevelt on 4 January 1945 of Halifax's talks with newsmen. Stephen T. Early Papers, Box 24, Folder "President Roosevelt—Memos 1945," FDR Library. The ambassador's addresses of 23 and 26 February 1945 appear in Halifax, *American Speeches,* pp. 383, 392.

13. Michael R. Wright, "British Foreign Policy in Europe," *Annals of American Academy of Political and Social Science* 240–42 (1945):73–78.

14. Stettinius to Roosevelt, 6 January 1945, FDR Library, PSF, Box 91, Folder "State Department, 1945." Three days earlier the secretary of state sent this accurate analysis of the British outcry and the *Economist* article to the president: "The difficulty is more emotional than substantive but the British feel that we are unwilling to accept responsibilities commensurate with our strength, our desire for influence in world affairs, and our tendency to comment freely

and critically upon them." FDR Library, PSF, Box 95, Folder "State Department—Stettinius, 1945." Halifax to Foreign Office, 7 January 1945, FO records, AN117/4/45.

15. *Christian Science Monitor,* 26 January 1945. Murrow supported Churchill's anti-Franco statement during an 11 February 1945 broadcast on WABC. Lindley wrote in the *Washington Post,* 9 February 1945. *Life* (5 February 1945):28. *Knoxville News-Sentinel,* 5 March 1945. These commentaries were reported by Wright in his 26 February and 12 March letters to Broadmead and Butler, FO records, AN929/22/45 and AN1165/22/45, respectively. U.S. liberals, of course, also urged more American participation in world affairs, but for different reasons. See a summary of their protest in *Time* (8 January 1945):13.

16. Minute, 23 March 1945, FO records, AN929/22/45. Donnelly had written in January (undated): "This is much more encouraging. It shows again that when American journalists have had a chance to know the facts, they are not necessarily unintelligent." FO records, AN117/4/45.

17. A detailed account of America's relations with Poland is Richard C. Lukas, *The Strange Allies: The United States and Poland, 1941-1945* (Knoxville, Tenn., 1978).

18. Clark Kerr's background is traced in *Current Biography,* December 1942, pp. 455–56. For Molotov, see *Time* (19 August 1946):28; Charles L. Mee, Jr., *Meeting at Potsdam* (New York, 1975), p. 122; and *Current Biography,* January–February 1940, pp. 590–91.

19. Llewellyn Woodward, *British Foreign Policy in the Second World War* (London, 1976), 3:276–77. Churchill informed Clark Kerr on 2 March 1945: "What we should aim at is that there should be parallel British and American Missions." PREM 3/356/9.

20. Harriman and Abel, *Special Envoy,* p. x. Woodward, *British Foreign Policy,* 3:490ff. Clark Kerr to Foreign Office, 24 February and 10 March 1945, PREM 3/356/9. The British ambassador informed his superiors on 10 March that Harriman promised not to act on the State Department's instructions "without fullest consultations with me. He is keeping in very close touch with me." Also see Halifax to Foreign Office, 21 March 1945, FO records, N3098/6/G55.

21. Clark Kerr to Foreign Office, 24 August 1944, FO records, N5152, mentioned the hope for a honeymoon during the Normandy invasion but noted that it never materialized. Eden to war cabinet, 9 August 1944, FO records, N4957. Memorandum by V. Cavendish Bentinck, 18 December 1944, FO records, N678/20/G. Memorandum by O. Sargent, 13 March 1945, FO records, R7333/G. Oliver Harvey Papers, diary entry, 31 March 1945, Student Room, British Museum, London. Memorandum by Sir R. H. Bruce Lockhart, 11 April 1945, FO records, N4102/20/G38.

22. Churchill to Roosevelt, 28 February 1945, *Wartime Correspondence,* pp. 657–59.

23. Lynn E. Davis argues in *The Cold War Begins: Soviet-American Conflict over Eastern Europe* (Princeton, 1974), pp. 212–15, that when American officials realized in March 1945 that Soviet actions had violated the Yalta agreement and the Atlantic Charter, they "concluded that the United States had no choice but to oppose Soviet attempts to establish complete political domination of Poland." True, the British did not have to convince Americans to work for a democratic Poland. The issue between the Western allies was the type of policy and plan of action that would most likely achieve that goal. Churchill urged an Anglo-American approach, while Roosevelt feared accusations of "ganging up" and favored his independent policy.

24. Grew memorandum to Roosevelt, 3 March 1945, SD records, 860c.01/3-245. Grew was still optimistic about Soviet-American relations over Poland until the third week in March. Grew to Harriman, 6 March 1945, SD records, 860c.01/3-645. The Polish negotiations are described in Woodward, *British Foreign Policy,* 3:chap. 45; and Davis, *Cold War Begins,* chap. 7.

25. 26th conclusions, minute 5, 6 March 1945, Cab (65/51) w.m. (45); and see Woodward, *British Foreign Policy,* 3:497. Roosevelt responded eleven times.

26. Churchill to Roosevelt, 8 March 1945, *Wartime Correspondence,* pp. 660–65.

27. Grew to Harriman, 8 March 1945, *FR, 1945,* 5:150–52. Davis, *Cold War Begins,* pp. 205-6.

28. Churchill to Roosevelt, 10 March 1945, *Wartime Correspondence,* pp. 669–70; and Woodward, *British Foreign Policy,* 3:501. "Summary of the More Important Information Sent from Poland in the Period 17th January to 1st March," PREM 3/356/9. The British had been attempting to arouse the State Department for a month by giving them startling reports of the situation in Soviet-dominated Poland. Durbrow memorandum to Hickerson, 7 February 1945, SD records, 860c.00/2-745.

29. Roosevelt to Churchill, 11 and 12 March 1945, *Wartime Correspondence,* pp. 666–70.

30. Roosevelt to Churchill, 12 March 1945, *Wartime Correspondence,* pp. 669–70.

31. Churchill to Roosevelt, 13 March 1945, *Wartime Correspondence,* pp. 670–72. On 14 March Halifax met the president and that same day informed the Foreign Office that Roosevelt "was reluctant to weigh in just yet with main shot from locker in shape of message from the Prime Minister and himself. But he had in mind if Ambassadors could not make progress, possible desirability of his sending what he described as a very personal message to Stalin in

three or four days." The president, Halifax continued, was now "very conscious" of possible domestic political effects of the Polish situation. FO records, N2895/6/G55.

32. Churchill, *Triumph and Tragedy,* pp. 426, 429. Churchill told Admiral Cunningham on 1 April that "the President was in a pretty bad way and only the last day or two had been writing his own telegrams." Andrew B. Cunningham Papers, diary entry, 1 April 1945, Student Room, British Museum, London. Charles E. Bohlen, *Witness to History, 1929–1969* (New York, 1973), p. 207. Bohlen memorandum to Secretary of State, 15 March 1945, SD records, record group 45, Box 6.

33. Roosevelt to Churchill, 15 March 1945, *Wartime Correspondence,* pp. 674–75. Churchill to Roosevelt, 16 March 1945, is partly published in *Wartime Correspondence,* pp. 675–76, and Churchill, *Triumph and Tragedy,* pp. 428–29. The full text appears in SD records, record group 45, Box 6.

34. Halifax to Foreign Office, 11 and 17 March 1945, FO records, AN875/4/45 and AN935/4/45, respectively. Memorandum of conversation, 17 March 1945, SD records, 860c.00/3-1745. Leahy Papers, diary entry, 18 March 1945. Acheson to Harriman, 19 March 1945, *FR,* 1945, 5:172–76.

35. Eden to Halifax and to Clark Kerr, 19 March 1945, PREM 3/356/9.

36. Churchill to Eden, 24 March 1945, PREM 3/356/9. Churchill to Roosevelt, 27 March 1945, *Wartime Correspondence,* pp. 684–87.

37. Churchill to Roosevelt, 27 March 1945, *Wartime Correspondence,* pp. 687–88.

38. Harriman and Abel, *Special Envoy,* pp. 422–23, 470. George F. Kennan, *Memoirs, 1925–1950* (Boston, 1967), p. 212. The head of the American military mission in Moscow, Gen. John R. Deane, agreed with his colleagues; *The Strange Alliance: The Story of Our Efforts at Wartime Co-operation with Russia* (New York, 1946), pp. 84–86. Harriman to State Department, 4 March 1945, *FR,* 1945, 5:141–42. Harriman to State Department, 25 March 1945, ibid., pp. 180–81. Harriman wrote the president again on 3 April 1945 and enumerated Russian violations of the Yalta agreement. He urged a firm stand—the "only way we can hope to come to a reasonable basis of give and take with these people." FDR Library, Map Room File, Folder "President–Harriman, 1945."

39. The Bern incident is described in Gaddis, *Origins of the Cold War,* pp. 92–94; and Allen Dulles, *The Secret Surrender* (New York, 1966). Bohlen was present during Roosevelt's outburst; *Witness to History,* pp. 208–9.

40. Roosevelt to Churchill, 29 March 1945, *Wartime Correspondence,* pp. 689–90. Churchill to Roosevelt, 30 March 1945, ibid.,

pp. 691, 696 n. 6. The joint message of 1 April appears in *FR,* 1945, 5:194–96.

41. Montgomery of Alamein, *Memoirs* (Cleveland, 1958), pp. 296–97. In 1957, the field marshal wrote that the "Americans could not understand that it was of little avail to win the war strategically if we lost it politically; because of this curious viewpoint we suffered accordingly from VE-Day onwards, and are still so suffering." Churchill to Roosevelt, 1 April 1945, *Wartime Correspondence,* pp. 696–99.

42. Churchill, *Triumph and Tragedy,* pp. 400, 460–61. Roosevelt to Churchill, 4 April 1945, *Wartime Correspondence,* pp. 701–3. James Nelson, ed., *General Eisenhower on the Military Churchill: A Conversation with Alistair Cooke* (New York, 1970), p. 55; and Forrest C. Pogue, *The Supreme Command, U.S. Army in World War II: European Theater of Operations* (Washington, D.C., 1954), pp. 441–47. Alfred D. Chandler, ed., *Papers of Dwight David Eisenhower* (Baltimore, 1970), 4:2549ff.

43. Roosevelt to Churchill, 6 April 1945, *Wartime Correspondence,* pp. 704–5.

44. Roosevelt to Churchill, 21 March 1945, *Wartime Correspondence,* pp. 680–81. Churchill to Roosevelt, 3 April 1945, ibid., p. 699. Roosevelt to Churchill, 8 April 1945, ibid., p. 706.

45. State Department to President, 10 April 1945, SD records, record group 45, Box 6. Halifax to Foreign Office, 31 March 1945, FO records, AN1075/4/45.

46. Harriman and Abel, *Special Envoy,* p. 429.

47. Harriman's report of Roosevelt's comment, ibid., p. 444.

48. Bohlen describes Roosevelt's physical condition in *Witness to History,* pp. 206–7. Morgenthau was "terribly shocked" when he saw the president on the day before his death; Henry Morgenthau, Jr., Papers, presidential diary, vol. 6, 11 April 1945, FDR Library. Also consult William D. Hassett Papers, diary entries, 30 and 31 March 1945, FDR Library. Churchill to Roosevelt, 11 April 1945, *Wartime Correspondence,* p. 708. Roosevelt to Churchill, 11 April 1945, ibid., p. 709. Rosenman, *Working with Roosevelt,* p. 538.

49. Traditional historians and some revisionists have supported the contentions that Roosevelt's attitude toward Russia hardened, especially concerning the Polish issue, and that therefore Truman did not change his predecessor's policy. Davis, *Cold War Begins,* pp. 212ff; Herbert Feis, *Churchill, Roosevelt, Stalin: The War They Waged and the Peace They Sought* (Princeton, 1957), pp. 596–600; Gabriel Kolko, *The Politics of War: The World and United States Foreign Policy, 1943–1945* (New York, 1968), pp. 315, 382; Robert Maddox, *The New Left and the Origins of the Cold War* (Princeton, 1973), p. 78; Arthur M. Schlesinger, Jr., "The Origins of the Cold War," *Foreign Affairs* 46 (October 1967):24; Diane Shaver Clemens, *Yalta* (New

York, 1970), p. 279. More recently, Robert Dallek states in his award-winning book, *Franklin D. Roosevelt and American Foreign Policy, 1932–1945* (New York, 1979), p. 534: "had he lived, Roosevelt would probably have moved more quickly than Truman to confront the Russians. His greater prestige and reputation as an advocate of Soviet-American friendship would have made it easier for him than for Truman to muster public support for a hard line."

Notes to Chapter 3
Truman and Churchill

1. Many revisionist historians will disagree with the interpretation stated in this chapter. Although they are not united on the issue, some of them have contended that Truman reversed Roosevelt's policy of cooperation for one of confrontation. I do not feel that American or British documents support their contention. For the New Left's interpretation, see D. F. Fleming, *The Cold War and Its Origins, 1917–1960* (New York, 1961), 1:265–69; Gar Alperovitz, *Atomic Diplomacy: Hiroshima and Potsdam* (New York, 1965), pp. 12–13; Walter LaFeber, *America, Russia, and the Cold War, 1945–1967* (New York, 1967), pp. 2, 21–22; Barton J. Bernstein, ed., *Politics and Policies of the Truman Administration* (Chicago, 1970), pp. 15–40; David Horowitz, *The Free World Colossus* (New York, 1965), chap. 1; Bert Cochran, *Harry Truman and the Crisis Presidency* (New York, 1973), chap. 8; and for a postrevisionist study stating the same theme, consult Daniel Yergin, *Shattered Peace: The Origins of the Cold War and the National Security State* (Boston, 1977), pp. 68, 73, 83, 86.

2. The farmer-boy quote is in *Life* (21 August 1944): 75, and Lisle A. Rose, *Dubious Victory: The United States and the End of World War II* (Kent, Ohio, 1973), p. 85. "Show me" appears in Eben Ayers Papers, diary entry, 17 October 1945, HST Library. Truman once said that "you can understand the Russian situation if you understand Jackson County"; for this and other such statements, see Jonathan Daniels, *Man of Independence* (Philadelphia, 1950), pp. 276–86. Memorandum by Stimson, 21 July 1945, *FR, 1945, The Conference of Berlin (Potsdam)*, 2:1156–57. Truman's thoughts on totalitarian governments, Communists, and "parlor pinks" are revealed in William Hillman, *Mr. President: The First Publication from the Personal Diaries, Private Letters, Papers and Revealing Interviews of Harry S. Truman* (New York, 1952), pp. 116, 121. *The Public Papers of the President of the United States: Harry S. Truman* (Washington, D.C., 1947), p. 238.

3. Richard S. Kirkendall, "Truman and the Cold War," in *Studies in Mediaevalia and Americana: Essays in Honor of William Lyle Davis,*

S. J., ed. Gerard G. Steckler and Leo Donald Davis (Gonzaga, 1973), pp. 151–71; and Wilson D. Miscamble, "The Evolution of an Internationalist: Harry S. Truman and American Foreign Policy," *Australian Journal of Politics and History* 23 (August 1977): 268–83.

4. Daniels, *Man of Independence*, p. 259. Merle Miller, *Plain Speaking: An Oral Biography of Harry S. Truman* (New York, 1973), pp. 36–37. Paul-Henri Spaak, *The Continuing Battle: Memoirs of a European, 1936–1966* (Boston, 1971), p. 99. Joseph E. Davies Papers, journal entry, 13 May 1945, Library of Congress, Washington, D.C. Similar apprehensions appear in Robert H. Ferrell, ed., *Off the Record: The Private Papers of Harry S. Truman* (New York, 1980), pp. 14–16.

5. Samuel I. Rosenman, oral-history interview, HST Library, pp. 21–22.

6. Harriman's statements appear in Walter Millis, ed., *The Forrestal Diaries* (New York, 1951), pp. 38–40, 57; Harriman to Secretary of State, 4 and 6 April 1945, *FR*, 1945, 5:817–20; W. Averell Harriman and Elie Abel, *Special Envoy to Churchill and Stalin, 1941–1946* (New York, 1975), chap. 19. John R. Deane, *The Strange Alliance: The Story of Our Efforts at Wartime Co-operation with Russia* (New York, 1946), pp. 84–86, 262–65. Grew to Moscow Embassy, 9 May 1945, SD records, 711.61/5-945; and see Adm. William D. Leahy Papers, diary entry, 6 March 1945, Library of Congress, Washington, D.C., in which Grew informed the admiral that the president should "act slowly on a Russian request for Naval vessels with the purpose of obtaining Russian cooperation in some of our European political problems, such as Roumania."

7. Davies Papers, diary entry, 17 May 1945. Stimson diary entry, 3 April 1945, in Henry L. Stimson and McGeorge Bundy, *On Active Service in Peace and War* (New York, 1947), p. 611. Forrest C. Pogue, *George C. Marshall: Organizer of Victory* (New York, 1973), pp. 579–81.

8. Winston S. Churchill, *Triumph and Tragedy* (Boston, 1953), pp. 513–14, Anthony Eden, *The Reckoning* (Boston, 1965), pp. 611, 621. Halifax to Foreign Office, 14 April 1945, FO records, AN1198/4/45; and Earl of Birkenhead, *Halifax: The Life of Lord Halifax* (Boston, 1966), p. 551. David Dilks, ed., *The Diaries of Sir Alexander Cadogan, 1938–1945* (New York, 1971), p. 746.

9. Roberts to Warner, 25 April 1945, FO records, N4919/165/G; and Llewellyn Woodward, *British Foreign Policy in the Second World War* (London, 1976), 3:563. Memorandum by Sargent, 19 April 1945, FO records, N4281/165/G; and see 7 April 1945, N3745/165/G.

10. Clark Kerr's notes of Prime Minister's discussion with Gousev, 18 May 1945, PREM 3/396/12. Churchill ordered Clark Kerr to either destroy his notes of the heated encounter or to return them to the prime minister's office. Churchill's plans to use the RAF against Russia, in Churchill, *Triumph and Tragedy*, p. 758.

11. Gallman letter to Matthews, 2 May 1945, SD records, 711.61/5-245. Gallman agreed that it was time to get tough with the Russians and to cooperate with the British, and so did other members of the American embassy in London such as labor attaché Samuel Berger; interviews with Gallman and Berger during April 1978, now donated to the Indiana University Oral History Research Project.

12. Churchill to Truman, 13 April 1945, in Churchill, *Triumph and Tragedy*, pp. 471-79. Truman to Churchill, 13 April 1945, *FR*, 1945, 5:211.

13. Truman to Churchill, 13 April 1945, *FR*, 1945, 5:211-12; the joint message of 15 April to Stalin appears on p. 219. For a detailed account of Anglo-American cooperation over the Polish issue, see Woodward, *British Foreign Policy*, 3:523ff.

14. Eden to Prime Minister, 14 April 1945, FO records, N4092/77/G. Eden to Prime Minister, 23 April 1945, FO records, N4549/6/G55; also consult Wilson D. Miscamble, "Anthony Eden and the Truman–Molotov Conversations, April 1945," *Diplomatic History* 2 (Spring 1978). Dilks, ed., *Cadogan Diaries*, p. 730. Memoranda of 22 and 23 April foreign ministers' conversations appear in *FR*, 1945, 5:237ff; and see Woodward, *British Foreign Policy*, 3:528ff.

15. Memorandum of conversation, 22 April 1945, *FR*, 1945, 5:235-36. Miscamble, "Truman–Molotov Conversations," p. 173, contends that the 22 April meeting "probably would have been Truman's only meeting with Molotov, and such dramatically tempting hypotheses as 'sudden reversal' and 'immediate showdown' would never have entered the historiographical arena, if it had not been for Eden, who on 21 April made sure the Polish question would be discussed in Washington before the departure of the three foreign secretaries to San Francisco for the opening of the United Nations conference."

16. The confrontation with Molotov is in Harry S. Truman, *Year of Decisions* (Garden City, N.Y., 1955), pp. 79-82; and see memorandum of conversation, 23 April 1945, *FR*, 1945, 5:256-58.

17. Truman admitted to his staff that he had talked strongly; Ayers Papers, diary entry, 24 April 1945. Truman to Stalin, 23 April 1945, *FR*, 1945, 5:258-59. For an opposing view, see Yergin, *Shattered Peace*, pp. 73-83, who contends that "what was said in that meeting on April 23 signified a major shift in American attitudes towards the Russians."

18. William Hillman memorandum of press conference to Thomas H. Beck, 29 April 1945, in Harry Hopkins Papers, Box 338, Folder "San Francisco Conference," FDR Library. Eden also told reporters: "We are completely puzzled by Russian tactics. We don't know why the Russians keep sliding out of agreements or delaying them." "Naturally, you Americans are in a strong position to bring

great pressure on the Russians because of Russia's economic necessities—greater pressure than we British can exert—and I personally intend to stand close with the United States and back up America." On 4 May 1945 Ambassador Halifax wrote Hopkins from the San Francisco conference: "Ed [Stettinius] and Anthony [Eden] are working very closely in with each other and, as far as I can judge, your people and ours are getting on well." Hopkins Papers, Box 338, Folder "San Francisco Conference."

19. Stalin to Truman, 24 April 1945, *FR*, 5:264; for Stalin's ideas on democracy and other topics, consult Milovan Djilas, *Conversations with Stalin* (New York, 1962).

20. On 24 April, after hearing of Truman's 23 April meeting with Molotov, Churchill informed the war cabinet that the Americans "should take the lead in the representations made to the Soviet Government . . . our policy should be kept closely in line with that of the United States." Cab (65/52) w.m. (45) 50th conclusion. The prime minister's statement about Truman is in Churchill, *Triumph and Tragedy*, p. 492. Churchill to Truman, 24 April 1945, *FR*, 1945, 5:262. Churchill wrote Truman on 28 April 1945, SD records, record group 45, Box 7, "I naturally would be very glad if you could support me by sending Stalin a message on similar lines." Truman to Stalin, 4 May 1945, *FR*, 1945, 5:280–81.

21. Cadogan's 15 April meeting with Winant is reported in Dilks, ed., *Cadogan Diaries*, p. 728. Churchill to Truman, 18 April 1945, is in Churchill, *Triumph and Tragedy*, pp. 514–15. Churchill to Truman, 27 April 1945, SD records, 740.00119 EW/4-2845, and partly reproduced in *Triumph and Tragedy*, p. 552. Not all British commanders agreed with the prime minister; see Arthur Bryant, *Triumph in the West, 1943–1946* (London, 1959), p. 469, which states Brooke's opposition.

22. Eden to Stettinius, 28 April 1945, *FR*, 1945, 4:444–45. Patterson to Secretary of State, 9 April 1945, *FR*, 1945, 5:1218. Churchill to Truman, 30 April 1945, SD records, record group 45, Box 7.

23. Truman, *Year of Decisions*, pp. 211, 214, 217. Truman's distrust of the British is also revealed in Ferrell, ed., *Off the Record*, p. 45. Omar N. Bradley, *A Soldier's Story* (New York, 1951), pp. 535–36; and see Pogue, *Organizer of Victory*, pp. 573–74 for Marshall's views on capturing Prague. Robert D. Murphy, *Diplomat among Warriors* (Garden City, N.Y., 1964), p. 256. King made the remark during a meeting attended by Davies and Marshall; Davies Papers, diary entry, 23 May 1945.

24. Russian behavior and Churchill's 5 May memorandum to Eden are presented in Woodward, *British Foreign Policy*, 3:530ff, 573–74. Churchill to Truman, 6 May 1945, *FR*, 1945, *Potsdam*, 1:3–4.

25. Truman, *Year of Decisions*, pp. 15, 246. Dilks, ed., *Cadogan*

Diaries, pp. 727–28, called the State Department's assessment accurate. Lauchlin Currie, "Report on Conversations with British Officials, March 1945," 24 April 1945, Folder "Commercial Policy Clayton-Thorp," office files of the assistant secretary of state, HST Library. William D. Leahy, *I Was There* (New York, 1950), p. 380. Henry L. Stimson Papers, diary entry, 30 April 1945, Yale University Library, New Haven, Conn.

26. Halifax to Foreign Office, 14 May 1945, PREM 3/430/1. Hadley Cantril and Mildred Strunks, eds., *Public Opinion, 1935–1946* (Princeton, 1951), pp. 370–71, poll of 15 May 1945.

27. On 11 May 1945 the president significantly reduced lend-lease aid to Russia, but the intent of his action remains unclear. By early June, however, Thomas G. Paterson concludes, "President Truman himself endorsed the basic premise that economic power was a valuable weapon in the growing confrontation with the Soviet Union." For an examination of this issue and the historical debate, consult Paterson, *Soviet-American Confrontation: Postwar Reconstruction and the Origins of the Cold War* (Baltimore, 1973), chap. 2; and more recently, John H. Backer, *The Decision to Divide Germany: American Foreign Policy in Transition* (Durham, 1978), chap. 6.

28. Stimson's comments and the "atomic diplomacy" debate appear in Martin J. Sherwin, *A World Destroyed: The Atomic Bomb and the Grand Alliance* (New York, 1975), chaps. 7 and 8, and see apps. I and J, pp. 291–94. Davies Papers, diary entry, 21 May 1945.

29. Davies Papers, diary entry, 21 May 1945. American diplomats in the Far East and Middle East also reported that local British authorities were deliberately obstructing American policy. In mid-July Truman allegedly told some former Senate colleagues that he was more afraid of Britain and France than he was of the Soviet Union. Consult Robert M. Hathaway, Jr., "The Paradoxes of Partnership: Britain and America, 1944–1947" (Ph.D. diss., University of North Carolina, 1976), pp. 287–88. Truman's comment to his staff appears in Ayers Papers, diary entry, 26 May 1945. The main difference between Roosevelt's wartime policy and the approach Truman adopted during late May 1945 reflected personality differences; Truman wanted to cooperate and increase friendship with Stalin, but he would not act conciliatory like his predecessor.

30. Churchill to Truman, 11 May 1945, *FR, 1945, Potsdam,* 1:6–7. Truman to Churchill, 11 May 1945, ibid., p. 8; and see memorandum of the Truman–Grew–Harriman–Bohlen conversation, ibid., pp. 12–14. Churchill to Truman, 12 May 1945, ibid., pp. 8–9. John W. Wheeler-Bennett and Anthony Nicholls, *The Semblance of Peace: The Political Settlement after the Second World War* (New York, 1972), pp. 294–95, relate the Goebbels story and Churchill's comment about the 12 May message. Truman to Churchill, 14 May 1945, *FR, 1945, Potsdam,* 1:11.

31. Truman told these ideas about obtaining peace to Davies; they appear in *FR*, 1945, *Potsdam*, 1:65. Margaret Truman, *Harry S. Truman* (New York, 1973), p. 252. Also see Keith M. Heim, "Hope without Power: Truman and the Russians, 1945" (Ph.D. diss., University of North Carolina, 1974), p. 151, who believes that the Hopkins and Davies missions served "notice on both allies, but on Britain in particular, that the United States would not be manipulated by either power to serve its own interest."

32. The documents for the Hopkins mission appear in *FR*, 1945, *Potsdam*, 1:21–62. Memorandum of conversation, 1 June 1945, ibid., pp. 57–59. Hopkins to Truman, 30 May 1945, Military records, Leahy File No. 93, "Hopkins–President, 1945–Moscow." Murphy relates Hopkins's 9 June comments in Frankfurt in *Diplomat among Warriors*, p. 260. Hopkins now considered it "vital" that there should be no ganging up; see Davies Papers, diary entry, 22 May 1945.

33. Murphy informed Davies of Soviet-American cooperation in Germany; Davies Papers, journal entry, 13 July 1945. Harriman to the President, 9 June 1945, Military records, Leahy File No. 104, "High Level (Not Prime) Messages."

34. Woodward, *British Foreign Policy*, 3:546–49, 579–80. Clark Kerr to Foreign Office, 10 July 1945, FO records, N8674/165/38; and see a Whitehall minute, 4 June 1945, FO records, N6366/165/G, stating that Stalin's concession was just a "temporary manoeuver." Churchill to Truman, 4 June 1945, *FR*, 1945, *Potsdam*, 1:92.

35. Truman's comment about Churchill was written to Mrs. Roosevelt on about 10 May (undated) and is reported in M. Truman, *Harry S. Truman*, pp. 243–44. Concerning Joseph E. Davies, see his *Mission to Moscow* (New York, 1941), p. 511; Harriman and Abel, *Special Envoy*, p. 463; H. Freeman Matthews, oral-history interview, 7 June 1973, HST Library, pp. 7–8; *Current Biography*, 1942, pp. 177–80; and Elizabeth Kimball MacLean, "Joseph E. Davies and Soviet-American Relations, 1941–43," *Diplomatic History* 4 (Winter 1980). Sargent states in a minute of 31 May 1945, FO records, N6645, "According to Mr. Davies it does pay to appease them [Soviets]. . . . For his language is far too reminiscent of what I used to hear in 1938 to be altogether pleasant." Davies Papers, diary and journal entries, 21 May 1945.

36. Davies Papers, diary entries, 26 and 27 May 1945, and "Topical Notes on Conferences with Prime Minister Churchill," 3 June 1945. Also see *FR*, 1945, *Potsdam*, 1:64–81, for Davies's written report of the talks. Churchill, of course, wrote a milder note concerning the mission; PREM 3/430/1.

37. Churchill's appearance is described by Davies, 12 June 1945 report to Truman, *FR*, 1945, *Potsdam*, 1:75–76; Davies Papers, diary entry, 28 May 1945; Winant to President, 13 June 1945, Military records, Leahy File No. 104, "High Level (Not Prime) Messages";

Oliver Harvey Papers, diary entry, 28 March 1944, Student Room, British Museum, London; Lord Moran (Sir Charles Wilson), *Winston Churchill: The Struggle for Survival, 1940–1965* (London, 1968), p. 825. The psychohistorical analysis is by Anthony Storr, "The Man," in A. J. P. Taylor et al., *Churchill Revised: A Critical Assessment* (New York, 1969), pp. 231–32, 268–73.

38. Henry Morgenthau, Jr., Papers, presidential diary, vol. 7, 1 June 1945, FDR Library. After talking with the president on 29 May the secretary of commerce, Henry A. Wallace, recorded in his diary: "Truman said that by sending Harry Hopkins to Moscow he had straightened out a fundamental misconception of Stalin and that Stalin was going to come along all right now." It is obvious "that Truman now feels much more kindly toward the Russians than he did before." John Morton Blum, ed., *The Price of Vision: The Diary of Henry A. Wallace, 1942–1946* (Boston, 1973), pp. 454–55. Davies's report to Truman, 4 June 1945, *FR, 1945, Potsdam,* 1:65–67. Davies Papers, diary entry, 6 June 1945. Leahy, *I Was There,* pp. 380–81. The breakfast meeting appears in Davies Papers, journal entry, 13 June 1945.

39. Churchill, *Triumph and Tragedy,* pp. 602–3, and Churchill to Truman, 4 June 1945, *FR, 1945, Potsdam,* 1:92. Kirk to Secretary of State, 28 June 1945, ibid., pp. 195, 712. Halifax to Foreign Office, 8 July 1945, and especially minute by Butler, 12 July 1945, FO records, AN2108/4/45.

40. On 3 January 1945 Halifax wrote the Foreign Office that it "might help to induce the State Department to take a more positive line in regard to Yugoslav affairs if I could convince them that, with the exception of the genuine collaborationists, all but a few former political leaders in Yugoslavia are throwing in their lot with Tito's movement of National Liberation." FO records, R292/292/92. Grew announced the U.S. policy of noninvolvement on 23 January; see *New York Times,* 23 January 1945. For Truman–Churchill 12 May and 2 June correspondence, consult Woodward, *British Foreign Policy,* 3:371–79, and Churchill, *Triumph and Tragedy,* pp. 551–61. Memorandum of Grew–Truman conversation, 10 May 1945, SD records, 740.00119 EW/5-1045, Box c-240.

41. Churchill to Truman, 12 May 1945, SD records, record group 45, Box 7. Churchill, *Triumph and Tragedy,* pp. 601–9. Churchill to Truman, 9 June 1945, *FR, 1945,* 3:132. Truman to Churchill, 11 June 1945, ibid., pp. 133–34. Churchill to Truman, 14 June 1945, ibid., pp. 134–35. Truman to Stalin, 14 June 1945, ibid., pp. 135–36.

42. Stettinius's statement of 28 May 1945 is in the Department of State *Bulletin* 12(3 June 1945): 1007–13. Undoubtedly another reason for the troop withdrawal was to increase friendship with Stalin. Hopkins wrote Truman from Frankfurt that the decision to set a date for withdrawal was of "great importance to our future relations

with Russia." Hopkins Papers, undated (7 or 8 June 1945), Box 338, Folder "Hopkins to Moscow, 1945." The British noted American acts of independence in a minute by Warner appropriately dated 4 July 1945, and Halifax to Foreign Office, 3 July 1945, FO records, N7973/6/55.

43. American actions are described in Hathaway, "Paradoxes of Partnership," pp. 280–82; and see Woodward, *British Foreign Policy*, 3:554–56, 592. Churchill wrote about American policy: "The United States stood on the scene of victory, master of world fortunes, but without a true and coherent design"; *Triumph and Tragedy*, pp. 455–56.

44. Roberts to Warner, 25 April 1945, FO records, N4919/165/G, which is partly reproduced in Woodward, *British Foreign Policy*, 3:563–64. Alexander told Ambassador Kirk that the Anglo-Americans should "knot together immediately those pieces which can be salvaged from what is left in our way of life on continent of Europe," and he added that he included Germany; Kirk to Acting Secretary of State, 12 July 1945, *FR, 1945, Potsdam*, 1:266. Americans were aware of British plans for a West European bloc; see State Department briefing-book paper, 28 June and 4 July 1945, ibid., pp. 256ff.

45. Memorandum of Grew–Truman conversation, 10 May 1945, SD records, 740.00119 EW/5-1045, Box c-240. Harriman and Abel, *Special Envoy*, pp. 449–51, 470; and *FR, 1945*, 5:839–46.

46. Barnes to Secretary of State, 9, 10, 13, and 21 March, 3 April, and 25 May 1945, *FR, 1945*, 4:172–82, 223. Patterson to Secretary of State, 19 April and 18 May 1945, *FR, 1945*, 5:1225–30. Schoenfeld to Secretary of State, 16 May and 16 and 19 June 1945, *FR, 1945*, 4:816–17, 828–30, and see pp. 812–14. Report on "Future Policy toward Italy" by Ellery W. Stone, 23 June 1945, *FR, 1945, Potsdam*, 1:688–94. OSS paper, "Problems and Objectives of United States Policy," 2 April 1945, given to Truman on 5 May, HST Library, Conway Files, Folder "Donovan–Chronological File, April–May 1945." Donovan apparently gave parts of this strictly secret paper to Michael R. Wright, and John Balfour of the British embassy wrote the OSS director, "we find little or nothing in it which does not square with our own less extensive knowledge of the subject." Balfour to Warner, 31 May 1945, FO records, N8125/165/G.

47. Hopkins's comment was made on 20 May 1945 to Forrestal; Millis, ed., *Forrestal Diaries*, p. 58. Forrestal was excluded from Potsdam, and Stimson and Harriman had to invite themselves. Davies, who advocated a conciliatory policy toward Russia, was invited by Truman and sat in on the sessions. Ayers Papers, diary entry, 7 June 1945.

48. Halifax to Foreign Office, 8 July 1945, FO records, AN2108/4/45; and Churchill, *Triumph and Tragedy*, pp. 611–12. State

Department briefing papers, 2 and 4 July 1945, *FR, 1945, Potsdam,* 1:253–55.

49. P.M.'s note of Churchill–Truman conversation, 18 July 1945, PREM 3/430/8. Davies Papers, diary entry, 21 July 1945; and see Leahy, *I Was There,* p. 399.

50. Sherwin, *A World Destroyed,* pp. 220–28, 237–38. Even Churchill was surprised with Truman's tougher approach, lamenting "if only this had happend at Yalta." Moran, *Churchill,* p. 306; and see Hathaway, "Paradoxes of Partnership," p. 294. Paterson, *Soviet-American Confrontation,* p. 47.

51. Bryant, *Triumph in the West,* p. 478. Stimson Papers, diary entry, 22 July 1945.

52. Leahy's statement is recorded in Davies Papers, journal entry, 1 August 1945. James F. Byrnes, *Speaking Frankly* (New York, 1947), pp. 86–87. Truman's salty remark appears in Charles L. Mee, Jr., *Meeting at Potsdam* (New York, 1975), p. 312. For the president's opinion of Stalin, Attlee, and Bevin, see Ayers Papers, diary entry, 7 August 1945; also consult Eduard Mark, "'Today Has Been a Historical One': Harry S. Truman's Diary of the Potsdam Conference," *Diplomatic History* 4 (Summer 1980). Truman's opinion of Bevin increased markedly in 1946 as Soviet-American relations declined, and his thoughts of Stalin had hardened when he wrote his memoirs ten years after the conference; *Year of Decisions,* pp. 411–12. The president's letter to his mother of 28 July 1945 appears in M. Truman, *Harry S. Truman,* p. 278.

53. Minute by Donnelly, 5 June 1945, FO records, AN1722/4/45. Minute by Sargent, 31 May 1945, FO records, N6645/165/38. Clark Kerr to Foreign Office, 10 July 1945, FO records, N8674/165/38.

54. Balfour letter to Halifax, 21 May 1945, FO records, AN1641/4/45.

Notes to Chapter 4
Lepidus and the Lumbering Giant

1. *Daily Telegraph,* 9 August 1960. The American press was unduly harsh on the new prime minister. *Newsweek* (6 August 1945): 25ff, labeled him Old Sobersides, a "chilly little man who walks with a shuffle [and] talks without rhetorical tricks" and looked like Winston Churchill's butler. This was unfair; for Attlee's impressive background, see Lord Longford and Sir John Wheeler-Bennett, eds., *The History Makers* (London, 1973), pp. 295ff; R. H. Crossman, *The Charm of Politics* (New York, 1958), pp. 69ff; and *Current Biography,* 1947, pp. 17–21.

2. Walker's story appears in an essay he wrote for Longford and Wheeler-Bennett, eds., *History Makers*, p. 279. For a biography of Bevin and Attlee's views on his foreign secretary, consult Alan Bullock, *The Life and Times of Ernest Bevin* (London, 1967), 2:100–101. Also see *Current Biography*, 1949, pp. 47–50; and Dean Acheson, *Sketches from Life* (New York, 1959), pp. 1–30.

3. Bevin's quip appears in *Newsweek* (3 September 1945):46. The *Observer*'s statement is in Bullock, *Bevin*, 2:385; and see pp. 100–101. Sir Frank K. Roberts stated in a 22 March 1977 interview that the foreign secretary "got on excellently with his men. You always knew where you were with Bevin." Interview with Lord Gore-Booth, 21 March 1977, and see his *With Great Truth and Respect* (London, 1974), p. 149. Also consult William Hayter, *A Double Life* (London, 1974), pp. 76–77, and William Strang, *Home and Abroad* (London, 1956).

4. Great Britain, House of Commons, *Accounts and Papers*, vol. 21 (1 August 1945–6 November 1946), Command Paper 6707, "Statistical Material Presented during the Washington Negotiations." Also see William L. Mallalieu, *British Reconstruction and American Policy, 1945–1955* (New York, 1956), pp. 34–46; F. S. Northedge, *British Foreign Policy: The Process of Readjustment, 1945–1961* (London, 1962), p. 33; and the London *Times*, 22 September 1945. Hadley Cantril and Mildred Strunks, eds., *Public Opinion, 1935–1946* (Princeton, 1951), pp. 195–96.

5. Churchill is quoted in Lisle A. Rose, *Dubious Victory: The United States and the End of World War II* (Kent, Ohio, 1973), p. 4; and see *FR*, 1945, *Potsdam*, 2:254, 265. Halifax reported the Gallup poll to Bevin on 9 August 1945, FO records, AN2560/22/45; Sargent's minute of 1 October 1945 appears in the same file.

6. Sir Frank K. Roberts said in an interview of 22 March 1977: "Britain was very keen on getting America involved. That was the cornerstone of Bevin's policy." Minute by Gage, 4 January 1945, and Halifax to Bevin, 12 December 1945, are in FO records, AN3853/35/45. Minute by Donnelly, 5 September 1945, FO records, AN2560/22/45. Minute by Gage, 21 August 1945, FO records, AN2505/4/45. Also consult Foreign Office minutes by Gage, 25 January 1946, FO records, AN205/5/45; Donnelly, 5 December 1945, FO records, AN2851/763/45. Another minute on 20 August 1945, FO records, AN2505/4/45, states that Britain "shall have to suffer from American arrogance and suspicious inexperience as the price of their participation in world affairs. We must resist the inclination to annoyance and in the light of our greater experience try to guide them on sound lines without appearing to patronize."

7. Elaine Windrich, *British Labour's Foreign Policy* (Stanford, 1952), chaps. 11 and 12; M. A. Fitzsimons, *The Foreign Policy of the British Labour Government, 1945–1951* (Notre Dame, 1953), pp. 23ff; and see Michael R. Gordon, *Conflict and Consensus in Labour's Foreign*

Policy, 1914–1965 (Stanford, 1969), p. 148. The continuity between Conservative and Labour policy prompted some members of Parliament to suspect that "Churchill, Bevin and Prime Minister Clement Attlee had broken all precedent by consulting beforehand" and forming a united front; *Time* (19 November 1945): 36. Robert G. Kaiser, *Cold Winter, Cold War* (New York, 1974), p. 110, describes Labour's foreign-policy manifesto for the 1945 election. Hastings Ismay, *The Memoirs of General Lord Ismay* (New York, 1960), p. 403. Joseph E. Davies Papers, journal entry, 4 August 1945, Library of Congress, Washington, D.C. *Hansard's Parliamentary Debates*, Commons, 20 August 1945, clm. 291.

8. For the postwar morass, see Robert J. Donovan, *Conflict and Crisis: The Presidency of Harry S. Truman, 1945–1948* (New York, 1977), chaps. 12 and 13. Cantril and Strunks, eds., *Public Opinion*, pp. 679–80.

9. Strike figures appear in *New York Times*, 20 January 1946. Truman's comments are in Margaret Truman, *Harry S. Truman* (New York, 1973), pp. 289–90; and Donovan, *Conflict and Crisis*, p. 125.

10. Stettinius diary entry, 22 October 1945, in Thomas M. Campbell and George C. Herring, *The Diaries of Edward R. Stettinius, Jr., 1943–1946* (New York, 1975), p. 437. State–War–Navy Coordinating Committee booklet, "Foreign Policy of the United States," revised on 1 December 1945, Military records, JCS File List No. 92, United States (12-21-45).

11. Dwight D. Eisenhower, *Crusade in Europe* (Garden City, N.Y., 1948), pp. 459–68. Stalin's photograph was reported by Harriman to Truman, 20 August 1945, Military records, Leahy File No. 104, "High Level (Not Prime) Messages." During autumn 1945 American officials were confused and searching for an appropriate policy toward Russia. John J. McCloy told a group of political scientists that figuring out Soviet ambitions and discovering how to deal with the Kremlin was the "A-1 priority job for the statesmen of the world to work out," and Benjamin V. Cohen later recalled that there was "considerable conflict not only between people involved, but also within each individual"; both quted in Daniel Yergin, *Shattered Peace: The Origins of the Cold War and the National Security State* (Boston, 1977), pp. 138 and 109, respectively.

12. Memorandum on British objectives by John D. Hickerson, 31 July 1945, SD records, 841.00/7-3145. Balfour to Bevin, 20 July 1945, FO records, AN2438/35/45; and Balfour to Foreign Office 18 August 1945, FO records, AN2505/4/45. Robert M. Hathaway, Jr., "The Paradoxes of Partnership: Britain and America, 1944–1947" (Ph.D. diss., University of North Carolina, 1976), p. 404, flatly states that "the United States had no concerted policy toward the British."

13. George Curry, *James F. Byrnes*, in *The American Secretaries of*

State and Their Diplomacy, ed. Robert H. Ferrell and Samuel Flagg Bemis (New York, 1965), 14:chap. 1.

14. Walter Brown, diary entry, 20 July 1945, James F. Byrnes Papers, Folder No. 602, Clemson University Library, Clemson, S.C. W. Averell Harriman and Elie Abel, *Special Envoy to Churchill and Stalin, 1941-1946* (New York, 1975), pp. 488, 509. George F. Kennan, *Memoirs, 1925-1950* (Boston, 1967), pp. 287-88; and see Charles E. Bohlen, *Witness to History, 1929-1969* (New York, 1973), p. 248. Keith M. Heim interview with Bohlen, December 1972, in "Hope without Power: Truman and the Russians, 1945" (Ph.D. diss., University of North Carolina, 1974), pp. 76-77, n. 27. John L. Gaddis, *The United States and the Origins of the Cold War, 1941-1947* (New York, 1972), p. 347.

15. For details of the negotiations at the London and Moscow conferences, see Particia Dawson Ward, *The Threat of Peace: James F. Byrnes and the Council of Foreign Ministers, 1945-1946* (Kent, Ohio, 1979). Bevin's statements are in David Dilks, ed., *The Diaries of Sir Alexander Cadogan, 1938-1945* (New York, 1971), p. 785; and Bohlen, *Witness to History,* p. 246.

16. British Embassy to Department of State, 24 August 1945, *FR, 1945,* 2:101-4. Bevin to Byrnes, 30 September 1945, ibid., pp. 515-17.

17. Byrnes's quip was stated to Anne O'Hare McCormick and reported in Kaiser, *Cold Winter, Cold War,* p. 172. Brown diary, 17 and 21 September 1945, Byrnes Papers, Folder No. 602.

18. The British felt that "while the existence of an economic weapon in the State Department's armoury makes it more desirable to come to an agreement with them on policy towards Russia, it would be unwise in discussing it to mention the possibility of using United States loans to secure our own objectives." Record of a meeting held in Sir Orme Sargent's room, 6 October 1945, FO records, N14065/165/G.

19. Minute by R. I. Campbell, 23 September 1945, FO records, AN23801/35/45. Bevin to Byrnes, 29 September 1945; and Halifax to Foreign Office, FO records, R16611/445/92 and R17377/445/92, respectively.

20. Halifax to Foreign Office, 14 October 1945, and minutes by Donnelly, 17 October 1945, FO records, AN3159/4/45. To Donnelly's remark, undersecretary of the North American department, Neville Butler, added the next day: "Russian intransigence is being a real help to us in the U.S. . . . I would not be sorry to see that intransigence last a little longer!"

21. Bohlen, *Witness to History,* p. 247. James F. Byrnes, *Speaking Frankly* (New York, 1947), pp. 107-8. Matthew J. Connelly Files, 26 October 1945, cabinet meeting minutes, Box 1, HST Library. Gaddis, *Origins of the Cold War,* pp. 274-26.

22. Halifax to Foreign Office, 13 November 1945, FO records, N17513/165/38.

23. Roberts letter to Sargent, 23 October 1945, FO records, N14846/165/38. Halifax to Foreign Office, 7 October 1945, FO records, AN3069/4/45. Also consult John Balfour, "Analysis of the Present Attitude of the United States toward World Affairs," 28 November 1945, FO records, AN3853/35/45. Interview with Lord Gore-Booth, 21 March 1977. Leonard Miall, oral-history interview, HST Library, p. 14.

24. Sholto Douglas, *Years of Command* (London, 1966), p. 302. Winant to Secretary of State, 5 October 1945, *FR,* 1945, 2:558–59. Gallman to State Department, 18 October 1945, *FR,* 1945, 5:897. Halifax to State Department, 19 October 1945, *FR,* 1945, 2:565–66. The British memorandum on the Balkans, 9 November 1945, is in the notebook "Documents on Balkan and Miscellaneous European Problems," SD records, 740.00119 Council/12-845, Box c-226.

25. Harriman to Secretary of State, 23 October 1945, SD records, 761.00/10-2345. Barnes to Secretary of State, 13 December 1945, SD records, 740.00119 Council/12-1345, Box c-226. State Department memorandum, 27 November 1945, *FR,* 1945, 5:924. American officials were alarmed by Soviet actions throughout the world; for example, see "Conclusions Reached by the Military Intelligence Service in regard to Soviet Activities in Latin America, dated 26 September 1945," Military records, Leahy File No. 71, "Russia 1946," and see an OSS report on Russian activities in Norway, October 1945 (undated), HST Library, PSF, Folder "Donovan–Secret," Box 15.

26. Achilles, oral-history interview, HST Library, pp. 4–5, and Harriman and Abel, *Special Envoy,* p. 524. Truman's complaints are recorded in Eben Ayers Papers, diary entries, 12 December 1945 and 5 January 1946, HST Library.

27. The Truman–Attlee correspondence and the Washington conference are detailed in Richard G. Hewlett and Oscar E. Anderson, Jr., *The New World, volume One of A History of the United States Atomic Energy Commission* (University Park, Pa., 1962), chap. 13; and John W. Wheeler-Bennett, *John Anderson, Viscount Waverly* (London, 1962), pp. 327–38. Also see HST Library, PSF, Attlee Folder, Box 170; and Margaret Gowing, *Independence and Deterrence: Britain and Atomic Energy, 1945–1952* (London, 1974), 1:72–86.

28. Unfortunately, no records exist of the Attlee–Truman conversations. Both leaders agreed to conduct off-the-record talks to ensure secrecy. According to Lord Gore-Booth and Lord Sherfield (Roger Makins), then members of the British embassy in Washington, the president and the prime minister discussed a number of sensitive issues such as atomic energy, military collaboration, and Soviet behavior; interviews with Lord Gore-Booth, 27 July 1978, and Lord Sherfield, 1 August 1978. Hewlett and Anderson, *The New World,* pp. 462–69. Bush is quoted in Gaddis, *Origins of the*

Cold War, p. 272. Canadian policy is described in James Eayrs, *In Defense of Canada,* vol. 3, *Peacemaking and Deterrence* (Toronto, 1972), chap. 5.

29. Roberts to Foreign Office, 26 October 1945, FO records, N14646/165/38; for American opinions, see Yergin, *Shattered Peace,* pp. 121, 137.

30. The responses from Congress and the scientists appear in *Congressional Record,* vol. 91, part 8, pp. 10942–44; *New York Times,* 17 November 1945; and Alice K. Smith, *A Peril and a Hope: The Scientists' Movement in America, 1945–47* (Chicago, 1965), pp. 211–26. Cohen and Pasvolsky to Byrnes, 24 November 1945, cited in Hewlett and Anderson, *The New World,* p. 470.

31. For Donnelly's comments on the "shoddy thinking" responsible for Truman's Navy Day speech, see his minute of 3 November 1945, FO records, AN3301/84/45. Halifax to Foreign Office, 3 November 1945, FO records, AN3373/4/45. Minute by Donnelly, 28 November 1945 (?), FO records, AN3853/35/45. Halifax to Foreign Office, 2 and 9 December 1945, FO records, AN3657/4/45 and AN3744/4/45, respectively. *New York Times,* 23 September 1945. *Saturday Evening Post* (24 November 1945):136.

32. Winant wrote Byrnes on 11 December: "I know you will find the same friendly support and desire to cooperate with you from Bevin that you experienced at the London Conference." SD records, 740.00119 Council/12-1145, Box c-226. Winant to State Department, 27 November 1945, *FR,* 1945, 2:585; and Byrnes's reply, 29 November 1945, ibid., p. 588.

33. Winant to Secretary of State, 30 November 1945, SD records, 740.00119 Council/11-3045. Also see *FR,* 1945, 2:582–83. 588–89.

34. Byrnes to Bevin, 27 and 29 November 1945, *FR,* 1945, 2:582–83, 588–89; and see Byrnes's memoranda of conversations with Halifax, 29 November, and with Wright, 4 December, ibid., pp. 590–91, 593–95. Bohlen, *Witness to History,* pp. 247–48.

35. Record of conversation, 17 December 1945, *FR,* 1945, 2:629–31. Kennan, *Memoirs,* pp. 287–88.

36. Harriman and Abel, *Special Envoy,* pp. 276–77, 530. Kennan, *Memoirs,* pp. 287–88. Halifax informed the Foreign Office on 2 and 3 July 1945, FO records, AN2136/245/45, that Byrnes prided "himself on his capacity to act as a cautious mediator and conciliator in the most strained and tangled situations. . . . He is, in short, a born politician." Interview with Sir Frank K. Roberts, 22 March 1977. Roosevelt had apparently held similar thoughts of Byrnes. When FDR received Byrnes's resignation as director of war mobilization and reconstruction, William D. Hassett asked if it was a loss. "Yes," Roosevelt said wearily, "It's too bad some people are so prima donnaish." William D. Hassett Papers, diary entry, 31 March 1945, FDR Library. Dilks, ed., *Cadogan Diaries,* p. 786.

37. The British gave State Department officials the minutes of the

18 and 19 December conversations; SD records, 740.00119 Council/12-2645.

38. *FR*, 1945, 2:610-11; the communiqué is on pp. 815-24. Byrnes, *Speaking Frankly*, chap. 6. *New York Times*, 28 December 1945. *Isvestia* is cited in Herbert Feis, *From Trust to Terror: The Onset of the Cold War, 1945-1950* (New York, 1970), p. 54.

39. *Economist*, 5 January 1946. *Manchester Guardian*, 5 January 1946.

40. Bohlen, *Witness to History*, p. 249. Adm. William D. Leahy Papers, diary entry, 26 December 1945, Library of Congress, Washington, D.C. Harriman and Abel, *Special Envoy*, p. 530. Harry S. Truman, *Year of Decisions* (Garden City, N.Y., 1955), pp. 549-51.

41. *Newsweek* (11 March 1946):25, declared: the "soft glove policy toward the Soviet Union is being abandoned."

42. The conversation with Ross is reported in Ayers Papers, diary entry, 17 December 1945. Truman and Byrnes offer conflicting stories on the 5 January encounter. See Truman, *Year of Decisions*, pp. 550-52; James F. Byrnes, *All in One Lifetime* (New York, 1958), pp. 400-404; and Curry, *James F. Byrnes*, pp. 189-90, which explains the controversy.

43. Leahy Papers, diary entries, 21 and 22 February 1946. Ayers Papers, diary entry, 25 February 1946.

44. Kennan to Secretary of State, 10 January 1946, Military records, Leahy File No. 110, "State Department 1946." Matthews to Acheson and Byrnes, 11 February 1946, SD records, 761.00/2-1146, Box 4004. Kennan to Byrnes, 22 February 1946, *FR*, 1946, 6:696-709; and see Kennan, *Memoirs*, pp. 68-69, 292-95, 547-59.

45. Interview with Sir Frank K. Roberts, 22 March 1977. Sir Frank pointed out that "Kennan's containment policy was his own. Britain merely agreed." Gen. Lucius D. Clay felt that Kennan's long telegram, an example of the "British line," demonstrated the success of the "British technique of needling our people over a period of months"; cited in Yergin, *Shattered Peace*, p. 212. Earl Attlee, "Britain and the Communist World," *International Relations* 5-8 (April 1964):27.

46. Record of meeting of Secretaries of State, War, and Navy on 6 March 1946, SD records, 811.002/1-2446; and see Gaddis, *Origins of the Cold War*, pp. 303-4.

47. Polls on Russia appear in Cantril and Strunks, eds., *Public Opinion*, p. 371; George H. Gallup, ed., *The Gallup Poll: Public Opinion, 1935-1971* (New York, 1972), 1:492, 565, 581-82; *Public Opinion Quarterly* 10 (Summer 1946):272. *Time* (4 March 1946):24. *United States News* (8 March 1946): 11ff; and see *Newsweek* (11 February 1946): 19ff. Truman's popularity is in Gallup, ed., *Gallup Poll*, 1:512, 587. Halifax to Foreign Office, 2 February 1946, FO records, AN299/1/45.

48. Whitehall officials were pleased with Morrison's visit; consult minutes by Donnelly and Gage, 6 and 9 March 1946, FO records, AN565/7/45. Winant sent two messages to the State Department on 5 February 1946. SD records, 741.00/2-546, Box 4004. Gallman to State Department, 1 March 1946, SD records, 741.61/3-146.

49. *Current Biography,* 1944, pp. 706-9; and Acheson, *Sketches,* p. 88, describe Vishinsky. *United Nations Security Council Official Records,* 1st ser. 1 (17 January–16 February 1946): 17–18, 32–39, 56, 74–92. For more details on the Iran issue, as well as American policy in 1946 toward Turkey and Greece, see Bruce R. Kuniholm, *The Origins of the Cold War in the Near East: Great Power Conflict and Diplomacy in Iran, Turkey, and Greece* (Princeton, 1980).

50. Bevin told Harold Nicolson that he regretted that the Americans were "so feeble in the Azerbaijan [Azerbaidzhan] controversy," adding, "You can never, my dear 'arold, deal with the Russians if you lie down and let them walk over you"; 31 January 1946 entry in Nigel Nicolson, ed., *Harold Nicolson, Diaries and Letters,* vol. 3, *The Later Years, 1945–1962* (New York, 1968), p. 54. For the ideas of Whitehall officials, see minute by Gage, 25 January 1946, FO records, AN193/1/45; and minute by Donnelly, 6 February 1946, FO records, AN299/1/45.

51. *Newsweek* (11 February 1946): 30ff; and see *New York Times,* 17 February 1946, which pictures Bevin with the headline "Dominant at UNO." *New York Times,* 3 February 1946.

52. For the *Times Herald* and other responses, consult Halifax to Foreign Office, 2 February 1946, FO records, AN299/1/45. British diplomats were pleased with America's response to Bevin and had some thoughts on his success; see minutes by Donnelly, Gage, and Mason, 31 January 1946, FO records, AN257/1/45.

53. Although Dulles did not appreciate Bevin's blunt tactics, he certainly agreed with his message; *New York Times,* 23 February and 12 March 1946. Vandenberg regarded Bevin "as one of the strongest of the Western statesmen," and Bevin's statement about political murders in Poland "was blunt language which Vandenberg could understand and approve"; Arthur H. Vandenberg, Jr., ed., *The Private Papers of Senator Vandenberg* (Boston, 1952), pp. 244-51. Vandenberg's speech was recorded in the *New York Times,* 28 February 1946; and see Gaddis, *Origins of the Cold War,* pp. 294–96; and Curry, *James F. Byrnes,* pp. 195–96.

54. Press statements are cited from Vandenberg, ed., *Private Papers,* p. 250. *Newsweek* (11 March 1946): 25ff.

55. Vaughan, oral-history interview, 14 and 16 January 1963, HST Library, pp. 60–62. M. Truman, *Harry S. Truman,* pp. 310-11.

56. America's need for guidance is from John Colville's section in John W. Wheeler-Bennett, ed., *Action This Day: Working with Churchill* (London, 1968), p. 82. *Vital Speeches* 9(15 September 1943): 713–

15. Churchill to Truman, 8 November 1945, HST Library, PSF, Folder "General File: Churchill, Winston, 1945–46," italics added.

57. Churchill to Truman, 29 January 1946, and Truman to Churchill, 2 February 1946, HST Library, PSF, Folder "General File: Churchill, Winston, 1945–46." Norweb to Truman, 7 February 1946, SD records, 711.41/2-746. Leahy Papers, diary entry, 10 February 1946; and see 3 March 1946. Also consult Jeremy K. Ward, "Winston Churchill and the 'Iron Curtain' Speech," *The History Teacher* 1 (January 1968): 5ff.

58. Robert Rhodes James, ed., *Winston S. Churchill: His Complete Speeches, 1879–1963* (London, 1974), 7:7283–96.

59. *Manchester Guardian,* 6 March 1946. *Observer,* 10 March 1946. *Daily Herald,* 8 March 1946. *Daily Worker* and additional press statements appear in Ward, "Winston Churchill and the 'Iron Curtain' Speech," pp. 5ff. Rowen, Attlee's personal secretary, had informed Churchill on 2 November 1945 that the "Government would certainly favour your proposed visit to the United States of America and Mexico, and would be glad to give you suitable facilities," which meant ten pounds per day expenses; Attlee Papers, Box 4, College Library, University College, Oxford University, Oxford. In a 1959 interview the Labour prime minister gave his opinion of postwar American policy: "The Americans didn't understand the political situation in Europe, and when we advocated anything in the East of Europe they always fancied we were following some strange imperial design of our own. It took them a long while to learn the facts of life—especially the facts of European life"; Francis Williams, ed., *Twilight of Empire: Memoirs of Prime Minister Clement Attlee* (New York, 1962), p. 52. Attlee dissociated himself from the Fulton speech in *Hansard's Parliamentary Debates,* Commons, 11 March 1946, clms. 761–63.

60. Minute by Donnelly, 12 March 1946, and Halifax to Foreign Office, 10 March 1946, FO records, AN656/1/45. Minute by Mason and Gage, 11 March 1946, FO records, AN674/4/45. Gallman to State Department, 11 March 1946, SD records, 741.61/3-1146.

61. A British representative attended Harriman's talk; see British Consulate General, New York, to British Embassy, Washington, 11 March 1946, FO records, N4152/971/38. Leahy Papers, diary entry, 5 March 1946. *Time* (18 March 1946): 19. Francis Williams, *A Prime Minister Remembers: The War and Post-War Memoirs of the Rt. Hon. Earl Attlee* (London, 1961), pp. 162–63; and see Gaddis, *Origins of the Cold War,* pp. 307–8.

62. Surveys of congressional and press opinion appear in *United States News* (15 March 1946):28–29, 32–34, 39; and *Newsweek* (18 March 1946): 19. For the response of American liberals to the speech, see Alonzo L. Hamby, *Beyond the New Deal: Harry S. Truman and American Liberalism* (New York, 1973), pp. 102–5.

63. HST Library, OF, Box 237, Folder "Churchill Speech."

64. *The Public Papers of the President of the United States: Harry S. Truman* (Washington, D.C., 1946), p. 145. White House press release, as reported in the *News and Observer* (Raleigh, N.C.), 20 March 1946; also see HST Library, PSF, Box 115, Folder "Churchill, Winston, 1945–46." Acheson, *Sketches,* p. 62.

65. Jonathan Daniels, *Man of Independence* (Philadelphia, 1950), p. 312. Douglas, *Years of Command,* pp. 314–15.

66. Minute by Gage, 28 February 1946, FO records, AN504/1/45; also see his minute of 23 February 1946, FO records, AN422/1/45.

67. Donnelly wrote on 5 March 1946 that it was "precisely because at the Security Council the Secretary of State [Bevin] so clearly spoke not only as the voice of Britain but also as the defender of the principles upon which the United Nations or any moral world order would have to rest that his utterances did so much to accelerate this new and more realistic trend in the American attitude toward the problems of the world"; FO records, AN587/1/45. See his minute of 28 May 1946, AN1636/1/45. Minute by Gage, 6 March 1946, FO records, AN587/1/45. *Newsweek* (11 March 1946): 25–26. Leahy Papers, diary entry, 5 March 1946. Secretary of Commerce Wallace complained in October 1946 that ever since Churchill's speech "there has been a veritable wave of Soviet-baiting in this country"; consult J. Samuel Walker, *Henry A. Wallace and American Foreign Policy* (Westport, Conn., 1976), p. 162. Cantril and Strunks, eds., *Public Opinion,* p. 959, and Gallup, ed., *Gallup Poll,* 1:567, give March ratings. The 6 May poll is in *Public Opinion Quarterly* 10 (Summer 1946): 264–65. Both British and American historians agree on the influence of the Fulton speech; see H. G. Nicolas, *The United States and Britain* (Chicago, 1975), p. 114; and Yergin, *Shattered Peace,* pp. 177–78.

Notes to Chapter 5
The Rise of a Partnership

1. All postwar British-American issues are discussed in Robert M. Hathaway, Jr., "The Paradoxes of Partnership: Britain and America, 1944–1947" (Ph.D. diss., University of North Carolina, 1976). Concerning Palestine see John Snetsinger, *Truman, the Jewish Vote, and the Creation of Israel* (Stanford, 1974), and Herbert Feis, *The Birth of Israel* (New York, 1969).

2. Truman's words to Byrnes and about the Turkish ambassador appear in Eben Ayers Papers, diary entry, 28 February 1946, HST Library. Byrnes's speeches are in Department of State *Bulletin* 14 (10

March 1946): 355–58; and *Vital Speeches* 12 (1945–1946): 356–57. Byrnes to Molotov, 5 March 1946, *FR*, 1946, 7:340–42. George V. Allen Papers, unpublished manuscript, chap. 1, HST Library. *The Public Papers of the President of the United States: Harry S. Truman* (Washington, D.C., 1946), pp. 185–90.

3. Matthew J. Connelly Files, cabinet meeting minutes, 19 April 1946, HST Library. Department of State *Bulletin* 14 (2 June 1946): 950–54; and see George Curry, *James F. Byrnes*, in *The American Secretaries of State and Their Diplomacy*, ed. Robert H. Ferrell and Samuel Flagg Bemis (New York, 1965), 14:222.

4. *New York Times*, 30 April 1946. *Newsweek* (20 May 1946): 34. *Time* (13 May 1946): 27. London *Times*, 6 May 1946. The comments of British diplomats appear in FO records: minutes by Donnelly, 12 and 21 March 1946, AN656/1/45 and AN742/1/45, respectively; Halifax to Foreign Office, 30 March 1946, AN960/1/45; minute by Donnelly, 9 April 1946, AN1025/4/45; and see Piers Dixon, *Double Diploma: The Life of Sir Pierson Dixon, Don and Diplomat* (London, 1968), p. 212. British documents support Gaddis's contention that during spring 1946 there was a "fundamental reorientation of United States policy toward the Soviet Union"; John L. Gaddis, *The United States and the Origins of the Cold War, 1941–1947* (New York, 1972), chap. 9.

5. Roberts to Foreign Office, 4 September 1946; and 9 September 1946 minute by Brimelow, FO records, N11298/605/38. Also see N11644/605/38.

6. Minute by Gage, 26 April 1946, FO records, AN2101/1/45. The minutes by Mason, Neville Butler, and other Whitehall officials advocating British attempts to coordinate policy with the United States in Europe and the Middle East appeared in April; see FO records, AN3509/G.

7. Gallman to Secretary of State, 27 February 1946, *FR*, 1946, 5:706–7. British aide-memoire to State Department, 22 February 1946, reported but not printed in *FR*, 1946, 5:230–31. Gallman to Secretary of State, 16 March 1946, SD records, 761.00/3-1546, Box 4004. Bevin to Byrnes, 21 March 1946, *FR*, 1946, 7:368–69. British Embassy to State Department, 18 April 1946, *FR*, 1946, 5:260–61; and see memorandum of conversation, 19 April 1946, SD records, record group 59, John Hickerson Files; and Gallman to State Department, 17 April 1946, SD records, 741.61/4-1746. Bevin to Byrnes, 13 April 1946, *FR*, 1946, 2:53–55. Bevin's 29 May message to Byrnes is discussed in *FR*, 1946, 2:452, n. 12.

8. Harriman to State Department, 8 May 1946, SD records, 761.00/5-846, Box 4004. Harriman and Gallman, of course, had long agreed with such statements; interview with Gallman, 27 April 1978. Bevin to Byrnes, 6 March 1946, James F. Byrnes Papers, Folder 605 (1), Clemson University Library, Clemson, S.C. Walter Mil-

lis, ed., *The Forrestal Diaries* (New York, 1951), pp. 144–45. Concerning British response to the U.S.S. *Missouri*'s visit to Turkey, see Foreign Office memorandum, 4 March 1946, FO records, AN619/619/G; and British Ambassador to Ankara (Peterson) to Bevin, 13 April 1946, FO records, AN1214/619/45. Peterson described the visit as "the most important event in Turkey in recent months." Bevin to Byrnes, 29 May 1946, *FR*, 1946, 2:452–54; and *Hansard's Parliamentary Debates*, Commons, vol. 423, clms. 1833ff.

9. David Goldsworthy, *Colonial Issues in British Politics, 1945–1961: From "Colonial Development" to "Wind of Change"* (London, 1971), pp. 9, 37. See *New York Times,* 25 February 1946, and Mallory Browne article on 12 May 1946 in which changing American opinion is evident. Balfour to Foreign Office, 18 May 1946, FO records, AN1566/1/45; and see Halifax to Foreign Office and minutes, 23 March 1946, FO records, AN840/1/45.

10. Foreign Office ideas for promoting closer relations were listed on 12 June 1946, FO records, A1787/5/45, and in the United States File No. 4, 1946. After Ethel M. Wood of the British Information Service wrote Bevin on 24 August 1945 calling for continuing propaganda in America after the war, Donnelly and other officials supported "the indirect dissemination of information and influence through friendly relationships with journalists, broadcasters, lectures and so on"; 6 September 1945, FO records, AN2634/22/45.

11. Tom Connally, *My Name Is Tom Connally* (New York, 1954), p. 295. Byrnes reported to Truman by telephone on 2 May 1946, Ayers Papers, diary entry, 2 May 1946. Balfour to Foreign Office, 27 May 1946, FO records, AN1700/1/45.

12. "Union of Soviet Socialist Republics: Policy and Information Statement," 15 May 1946, Clark M. Clifford Papers, Folder 1, "Russia," HST Library. This booklet appears to be the predecessor of the more extensive report "American Relations with the Soviet Union" that Clifford submitted to the president on 24 September 1946; printed in Arthur Krock, *Memoirs: Sixty Years on the Firing Line* (New York, 1968), app. A. Balfour to Foreign Office, 18 May 1946, FO records, AN1566/1/45.

13. Acheson to Secretary of State, 21 June 1946, SD records, 740.00119 Council/6-2146, Box 3834. Balfour to Warner, 24 June 1946, FO records, N8694/97/38.

14. Byrnes to Molotov, 5 March 1946, *FR*, 1946, 7:340–42. Byrnes to Gallman, 8 March 1946, ibid., pp. 345–46. For the Byrnes–Bevin correspondence before the U.N.O. meeting and the Paris meeting of the Council of Foreign Ministers, consult *FR*, 1946, 2:27–36, 46, 53–55, 68–69, 82. Connelly Files, cabinet meeting minutes, 19 April 1946. Cooperation on the Danube issue is in *FR*, 1946, 5:230–31, 260–61; for Germany, see ibid., pp. 565–66; and for the Nazi-Soviet documents, ibid., pp. 200–201.

15. Cooperation against Yugoslavia is in *FR,* 1946, 6:878, 887–88, 899; and in Austria, *FR,* 1946, 5:327–28, 339–50, 358–61. Acheson's statement was made in a cable to Byrnes, 19 June 1946, SD records, 740.00119 Council/6-1946.

16. British Chiefs of Staff to American Chiefs of Staff, 15 July 1945, and U.S. Chiefs of Staff to British Chiefs of Staff, 19 July 1945, Cab (88/38). Also see the British Joint Staff Mission in Washington, "Report on the Future of British Service Mission in Washington," 31 August 1945, PREM 8/120. On the Pentagon's wartime thinking about an Anglo-American alliance, consult Michael S. Sherry, *Preparing for the Next War: American Plans for Postwar Defense, 1941–1945* (New Haven, Conn., 1977), pp. 161–66, 183. Churchill's notes of his meeting with Truman, 18 July 1945, PREM 3/430/8. The British chiefs agreed with Churchill. Ismay wrote to Eisenhower on 29 December 1945: "If your armed forces and ours had more or less the same equipment, more or less the same doctrine, more or less the same organization—AND NO SECRETS of any kind between them—they would at once constitute a hard core of resistance to any breach of the peace. Thereafter, any other nation that was worthy and willing could join 'the Club' "; quoted in Daniel Yergin, *Shattered Peace: The Origins of the Cold War and the National Security State* (Boston, 1977), p. 445, n. 36.

17. Joint Chiefs of Staff comments of 10 February 1946 on SWNCC report of 1 December 1945, Military records, JCS File List No. 92, United States (12-21-45), "Foreign Policy of the United States"; and see SWNCC report, 5 April 1946 (undated), Military records, ABC File 336, Russia (22 August 43), sec. 1-C. Wilson reported the conversation with Eisenhower to the British Chiefs of Staff, 8 January 1946, Cab (105/188) fmw 233. Adm. William D. Leahy Papers, diary entries, 8 February and 7 March 1946, Library of Congress, Washington, D.C.; and Wilson to Chiefs of Staff, 8 March 1946, Cab (105/188) fmw 244. On 13 February 1946 Admiral of the Fleet Sir James Somerville suggested a joint review of naval tactics "with a view to establishing a common doctrine for the two fleets"; reported in Hathaway, "The Paradoxes of Partnership," p. 450. Byrnes was interested in Clipperton (French possession), Christmas, Ascension, and Tarawa islands; Foreign Office memorandum, 28 September 1945, FO records, AN3121/G; and see *FR,* 1945, 6:206. Byrnes–Bevin conversation of 2 May 1946 at Paris is reported in *FR,* 1946, 5:36. Some Americans thought as early as 25 April 1946 that Australia and New Zealand should be organized into an informal defense pact, but Acheson felt such an arrangement was "premature and inadvisable"; ibid., pp. 33–34. For other examples of closer military relations, also consult Henry Maitland Wilson, *Eight Years Overseas, 1939–1947* (London, n.d. [1949?]), p. 265; and

R. N. Rosecrance, *Defense of the Realm: British Strategy in the Nuclear Epoch* (New York, 1968), pp. 48–51.

18. Leahy Papers, diary entry, 21 May 1946. British Joint Staff Mission to C.N.O., 6 February 1946, Military records, ABC File 350.5 (22 June 44), is the British request to exchange battle information with the U.S. Army Air Corps. The Americans supported it on 10 May 1946; see JCS 927/23, JCS Report, in the same file.

19. Correspondence concerning the Baltic issue appears in *FR*, 1946, 5:389–98; the Azores is in ibid., pp. 962–67; and see *New York Times*, 4 May 1946.

20. Memorandum on Canada by Acheson sent to Truman on 28 September 1945, HST Library, PSF, Folder "Foreign–Canada." James Eayrs, *In Defense of Canada*, vol. 3, *Peacemaking and Deterrence* (Toronto, 1972), pp. 336–38, 381–88; Stanley W. Dziuban, *Military Relations between the United States and Canada, 1939–1945*, in *The United States Army in World War II* (Washington, D.C., 1959), 8:336ff; C. P. Stacey, "The Canadian-American Permanent Joint Board on Defense, 1940–1945," *International Journal* (1954):107–24.

21. *New York Times*, 10 March 1946. *Manchester Guardian*, 1 May 1946; and see *Newsweek* (8 April 1946): 32. Reston's article appears in the *New York Times*, 31 May 1946.

22. Roosevelt made the comment to Byrnes; James F. Byrnes, *Speaking Frankly* (New York, 1947), p. 185. R. F. Harrod, *The Life of John Maynard Keynes* (London, 1963), pp. 605–11. The definitive study of the loan appears in Richard N. Gardner, *Sterling-Dollar Diplomacy* (New York, 1969), chaps. 10–12. Also consult Thomas G. Paterson, *Soviet-American Confrontation: Postwar Reconstruction and the Origins of the Cold War* (Baltimore, 1973), chap. 8.

23. McKellar to Truman, 6 November 1945, HST Library, OF, 48, Folder "1945–1948." Hadley Cantril and Mildred Strunks, eds., *Public Opinion, 1935–1946* (Princeton, 1951), pp. 210–13.

24. *Public Papers of the Presidents: Truman, 1946*, p. 140. Draper's comment is in the *New York Times*, 24 February 1946. Vandenberg's support of 22 April 1946 and Rayburn's statement of 13 July 1946 are in *Congressional Record*, vol. 92, part 3, pp. 4079–82, and vol. 92, part 7, p. 8915, respectively. *New York Times*, 18 and 24 April and 9 July 1946. At Whitehall Gage expressed satisfaction that "we are receiving so much help over the loan from M. Stalin"; minute, 27 March 1946, FO records, AN840/1/45.

25. For the "lost" Russian request, see George C. Herring, Jr., *Aid to Russia 1941–1946: Strategy, Diplomacy, and the Origins of the Cold War* (New York, 1973), pp. 253–57; and Paterson, *Soviet-American Confrontation*, pp. 46–56.

26. Frederick Karl Schilling, Jr., "Germany and Her Future: British Opinion and Policy, 1939–1947" (Ph.D. diss., Indiana Uni-

versity, 1954), chap. 9; and *Hansard's Parliamentary Debates*, Commons, vol. 421, clm. 1822, for German and British economic problems. Robert D. Murphy, *Diplomat among Warriors* (Garden City, N.Y., 1964), p. 303.

27. The Wright–McCloy conversation is reported in Halifax to Cadogan, 27 November 1945, FO records, C9413/24; and see Harold Zink, *The United States in Germany, 1944–1955* (Princeton, 1957), pp. 112–13.

28. Lucius D. Clay, *Decision in Germany* (New York, 1950), pp. 72–78 and chap. 9. John Gimble, *The American Occupation of Germany: Politics and the Military, 1945–1949* (Stanford, 1968), chap. 3; the meeting of the German officials is on p. 63.

29. *Hansard's Parliamentary Debates*, Commons, vol. 423 (4 June 1946), clm. 1851. Byrnes, *Speaking Frankly*, p. 195.

30. Byrnes, *Speaking Frankly*, pp. 195–96; and Clay, *Decision in Germany*, pp. 73, 164–65. Bevin's report to the cabinet is in Cab (128/6) 68(46)1. On the merger negotiations, see Gimble, *American Occupation of Germany*, chap. 5. Joseph E. Davies Papers, memorandum of conversation, 10 September 1946, Library of Congress, Washington, D.C., also cited in Gaddis, *Origins of the Cold War*, p. 331.

31. Smith to Secretary of State, 5 June 1946, SD records, 711.61/6-546, and 23 July 1946, *FR, 1946*, 6:768ff. Also see Gaddis, *Origins of the Cold War*, pp. 318–20. A survey of the Soviet press appears in *Newsweek* (8 July 1946): 34; and see *Newsweek* (5 August 1946):43. *United States News* (7 June 1946):24, accurately observed that "Russia is no longer hitting at Great Britain, with occasional blows deflected at the United States. The aim now is directly at this country, its objectives, its policies and its personalities."

32. Alusna Vladivostok representative to Leahy, 13 April 1946, Military records, Leahy File No. 71, "Russia 1946." Leahy Papers diary entry, 7 May 1946. The admiral felt that Anglo-American forces in Europe were insufficient and would be destroyed by a Russian attack; diary entry, 11 June 1946. Military attaché in Moscow to Leahy, 15 and 16 June 1946, and military attaché in Belgrade to Leahy, 12 July 1946, Military records, Leahy File No. 71, "Russia 1946." For Albania see Key to Dunn, 25 July 1946, *FR, 1946*, 3:16–17; for Greek fears of Russia, ibid., pp. 101–3. Ghost rockets are reported in Hoyt S. Vandenberg memorandum to Truman, 1 August 1946, Military records, Leahy File No. 124, "Memos to and from the President 1946"; and see *Newsweek* (26 August 1946): 32. For Soviet troop movements, see State Department to Secretary of State, 19 November 1946, SD records, 740.00119 Council/11-1946, Box c-232. The Russians, however, were actually demobilizing; according to Adam B. Ulam, *Expansion and Coexistence: The History of*

Soviet Foreign Policy (New York, 1974), p. 404, Soviet armed forces had declined from 11.3 million in April 1945 to 2.8 million by 1948.

33. For Russian demands on Turkey, see *FR*, 1946, 7:829, 836–38. Churchill desired an Anglo-American policy on the straits as early as 17 June 1945; see PREM 3/447/4a. By 3 June 1946 the Americans had agreed, and the Joint War Plans Committee requested a full-scale study to analyze the "Capabilities of Turkey to resist invasion, in the event of war with the USSR in the next three years"; Joint Intelligence Staff memorandum, 3 June 1946, Military records, JIS 253/m, CCS 400, "Turkey (5-27-46)"; and in the same file see the Joint Logistics Plans Committee reports of 10 July and 2 August 1946 that demonstrate an increasing military interest in Turkey.

34. The Tito incident was one of the most significant events leading to the cold war since it confirmed American suspicions that the Russians were aggressive. The episode has been neglected by both Gaddis and Feis; consult Curry, *James F. Byrnes*, pp. 246–47. A survey of the American press appears in *Newsweek* (2 September 1946): 35; also see p. 30. For Forrestal's comment, see the record of SWNCC meeting, 6 March 1946, SD records, 811.002/1-2446.

35. Byrnes, *Speaking Frankly*, pp. 144–46; and Robert G. Kaiser, *Cold Winter, Cold War* (New York, 1974), pp. 76–77. Department of State *Bulletin* 15 (1946): 409–11 for the 19 August press release of the 20 May 1946 message to Tito.

36. Henderson, oral-history interview, HST Library, p. 236. Acheson to Soviet chargé, 19 August 1946, *FR*, 7:847–48; and see memorandum of Inverchapel–Acheson conversation, 20 August 1946, ibid., pp. 849–50. Bevin to Soviet chargé, 21 August 1946, ibid., pp. 850–51. The American and British governments were also becoming tougher on other fronts; the Foreign Office warned on 9 August that any sudden or violent threat to Iran would be met with action so immediate that "there may not be time to consult the United Nations," and on 30 August Washington announced that American forces would remain in Korea until the establishment of a united, independent, and democratic government.

37. Curry, *James F. Byrnes*, pp. 247–48. Bertrand Fox Jarvis, "The Role of the Small Powers in the Development of the Western Bloc at the 1946 Paris Peace Conference: A Study into the Origins of the Cold War" (Ph.D. diss., University of Alabama, 1973), p. 261. The American embassy in London reported closer Anglo-American cooperation in their message of 19 September 1946 to the State Department, SD records, 741.00/9-1946, Box 3974. The State Department informed representatives in Prague on 6 November 1946 after Inverchapel–Acheson discussions: "Agreed it would be advisable [to] coordinate US and UK programs economic assistance in

Eastern Europe and henceforth there would be periodic consultation between appropriate officers [of] Dept. and Britemb"; SD records, 860F.24/10-2946.

38. *Vital Speeches* 12 (1945–1946): 706–9. Byrnes proposed the speech; Leahy and Truman reviewed it and made minor changes; Clayton to Secretary of State, 3 September 1946, SD records, 740.00119 Council/9-346. Also see Byrnes, *Speaking Frankly*, p. 186; and Curry, *James F. Byrnes*, p. 248.

39. *Newsweek* (16 September 1946): 40; and see *United States News* (13 September 1946): 22–23, 68–70. Byrnes's tougher stand against Russia increased his popularity; see Cantril and Strunks, eds., *Public Opinion*, pp. 951–52; Connelly Files, cabinet meeting minutes, 6 September 1946; and Byrnes Papers, Folders 465–67. The British response was later stated by Frank Spencer, "The United States and Germany in the Aftermath of War," *International Affairs* 44 (January 1968): 61: the speech "marked more than another nail in the isolationist coffin. It publicly proclaimed the end of the age of American diplomatic innocence in European affairs." Also see the London *Times* and *Manchester Guardian*, 7 September 1946. *Hansard's Parliamentary Debates*, Commons, 22 October 1946, clms. 1516–17; and Byrnes, *Speaking Frankly*, p. 192. From Switzerland Churchill informed Truman, 18 September 1946, that he was in "full agreement" with the Stuttgart speech; HST Library, PSF, Folder "Churchill, Winston, 1945–46."

40. Border incidents are reported in *Newsweek* (2 September 1946): 30; and see the 9 September issue, p. 46, for the size of the British and American fleets in the Mediterranean. Millis, ed., *Forrestal Diaries*, pp. 198, 211; and Robert G. Albion and Robert Howe Connery, *Forrestal and the Navy* (New York, 1962), pp. 186–88. Leahy Papers, diary entries, 23 August and 5 September 1946.

41. Montgomery of Alamein, *Memoirs* (Cleveland, 1958), pp. 392–97. Leahy Papers, diary entries, 12 and 16 September and 2 October 1946. One day after the *Sequoia* meeting, the United States ordered another aircraft carrier to the Mediterranean; consult Stephen G. Xydis, *Greece and the Great Powers, 1944–1947* (Thessaloniki, 1963), p. 348.

42. Byrnes to Hickerson, 26 September 1946, SD records, 740.00119 Council/9-2646, Box c-231. For rising Anglo-American military cooperation, see the following documents in Military records, ABC File 676.3 (12-2-42): memorandum by Joint Staff Planners, undated, (3 October 1946); JCS 1732, 29 November 1946; memorandum for the chief of staff, 13 June 1947. Also consult the memoranda from the Joint Chiefs of Staff, 29 November and 4 December 1946 and 4 March 1947, Military records, JCS File List, Folder 389, "Coordination of matters pertaining to standardization with other countries," which concerns Britain and Canada. For

Canadian-American military relations, see *FR*, 1946, 5:53–67; Dziuban, *Military Relations between the United States and Canada*, pp. 337–38; Eayrs, *In Defense of Canada*, 3:340–41; R. D. Cuff and J. L. Granatstein, *Canadian-American Relations in Wartime, from the Great War to the Cold War* (Toronto, 1975), pp. 117–19; and Acheson to Truman, 22 April 1947, HST Library, PSF, Folder "Foreign–Canada–Mackenzie King."

43. For the November 1946 discussions, see Cab (122/1474) and Cab (122/1378). The Combined Chiefs of Staff disbanded in 1949 when NATO was created. Their responsibility after the war was limited to occupied areas such as Trieste. Consult Achilles, oral-history interview, HST Library, p. 63. For the combined chiefs, see *FR*, 1948, 3:664, and *FR*, 1949, 4:107–8. For a discussion of the postwar British joint service missions, see JSM Washington to Ministry of Defense, 30 January 1947, Cab (105/188) fmw (287). Collaboration during 1947 is reported in FO records, File 61075, "Anglo-American Military Collaboration and Standardization," and see File 61000.

44. Churchill is quoted in Kaiser, *Cold Winter, Cold War*, p. 84. *Newsweek* (9 September 1946): 30. The same theme is expressed in *Time* (4 November 1946): 34–35, and *United States News* (6 September 1946): 19.

45. Minutes by Rundall, 25 and 29 July 1946, FO records, AN2218/1/45 and AN2290/1/45, respectively.

46. For Byrnes on Molotov, see Department of State *Bulletin* 15 (27 October 1946): 739–43. Byrnes made his quip about going to hell when he resigned from office early in 1947; see Curry, *James F. Byrnes*, p. 316.

47. Inverchapel to Foreign Office, 23 August and 2 September 1946, FO records, AN2653/1/45 and AN2759/1/45, respectively. On the latter date, the ambassador reported that now Britain "is recognized as the first and foremost partner in the new alliance, whose strength had been favourably reappraised and whose reliability is in no doubt."

Notes to Chapter 6
Shifting the Burden

1. William H. McNeil, *The Greek Dilemma: War and Aftermath* (Philadelphia, 1947), pp. 152, 204–6, 296. Reginald S. Leeper, *When Greek Meets Greek* (London, 1950), pp. 87, 188, 206. *Newsweek* (31 March 1947): 24–25.

2. Stephen G. Xydis, *Greece and the Great Powers, 1944–1947*

(Thessaloniki, 1963), pp. 135–40; and Llewellyn Woodward, *British Foreign Policy in the Second World War* (London, 1976), 3:435–39.

3. C. M. Woodhouse, *The Struggle for Greece, 1941–1949* (London, 1976), p. 149; and Xydis, *Greece and the Great Powers*, pp. 144ff.

4. Memorandum of conversation, 28 July and 5 August 1944, *FR*, 1944, 5:216–21. Xydis, *Greece and the Great Powers*, pp. 97–98. Xydis had access to Greek Foreign Office documents. Memorandum by the Joint Chiefs of Staff, 18 April 1945, Military records, JCS File List No. 400, Greece (11-2-44), "Equipment for the Greek Army." For an analysis of American policy in 1944–1945, see John O. Iatrides, *Revolt in Athens: The Greek Communist "Second Round," 1944–1945* (Princeton, 1972), pp. 286–87.

5. Harry S. Truman, *Years of Trial and Hope* (Garden City, N.Y., 1956), p. 99. Cabinet records, 14 August 1945, Cab (128/1) 21(45)4. The embassy's hope for American technical advisers and Makins's letter of 13 December 1945 are reported in "Greek Economic-Financial Situation: Chronology," November 1945 to January 1946, compiled on 10 January 1946, SD records, 868.51/1-1046. British Embassy to State Department, 4 December 1945, *FR*, 1945, 8:276–77. Concerning British hopes to involve the United States in economic discussions in London, consult ibid., pp. 296–97, and FO records, R485/2/19. Halifax to Foreign Office, 8 January 1946, FO records, R430/2/19. Leeper to Foreign Office, 11 January 1946, FO records, R595/2/19.

6. On 14 April 1944 MacVeagh thought that "Russia now aspires to supplant Britain as the dominating foreign power in connection with Greek affairs"; *FR*, 1944, 5:95–96. But Washington officials ignored the ambassador; see Iatrides, *Revolt in Athens*, pp. 120–21. MacVeagh to Secretary of State, 15 December 1945, *FR*, 1945, 8:284–88. MacVeagh to Secretary of State, 1 January 1946, ibid., p. 298. MacVeagh to Secretary of State, 11 January 1946, *FR*, 1946, 7:91–92.

7. The Grady mission and the visit of the U.S.S. *Providence* are discussed in Xydis, *Greece and the Great Powers*, p. 143, and see pp. 97–98 for the background to the $25 million loan. Also consult *FR*, 1945, 8:130–31, 138–39, 144. The United States financed about 70 percent of the U.N. Relief and Recovery Administration, and from October 1944 to the end of 1945 the UNRRA gave Greece approximately $300 million.

8. The visit of the U.S.S. *Missouri* is described in Xydis, *Greece and the Great Powers*, pp. 180–91; and MacVeagh to Secretary of State, 26 April 1946, SD records, 811.3368/4-2646.

9. Secretary of State to Truman, 10 November 1945, *FR*, 1945, 8:266–67. State Department feeling on aid to Greece appears in "Greek Economic-Financial Situation: Chronology," 6 December 1945 meeting, SD records, 868.51/1-1046. Concerning currency

talks, see Acheson to Winant, 10 January 1946, *FR*, 1946, 7:90; and Halifax to Foreign Office, 11 January 1946, FO records, R594/2/19 and R639/2/19. Byrnes's misgivings are recorded in a message to the Greek deputy prime minister, 15 January 1946, *FR*, 1946, 7:95–96; and see memorandum of conversation, 13 July 1946, ibid., pp. 180–82. Grady's instructions are in Herman B. Wells Papers, Folder "Mission to Greece," University Archives, Indiana University, Bloomington, Ind. Joint Chiefs of Staff paper, "Foreign Policy of the United States," 10 February 1946, Military records, JCS File List No. 92, United States (12-21-45).

10. Dimirios Delivanis and William C. Cleveland, *Greek Monetary Developments, 1939–1948: A Case Study of the Consequences of World War II for the Monetary System of a Small Nation* (Bloomington, Ind., 1949), pp. 143–45; and Xydis, *Greece and the Great Powers,* pp. 150–51.

11. Treasury reported its views to the American embassy in London which informed the State Department, 4 January 1946, SD records, 868.51/1-446. Harriman informed the department of the $6 billion request on 18 July 1946, *FR*, 1946, 7:183–85. Dalton's comment appears in Xydis, *Greece and the Great Powers,* p. 243. Tsaldaris, oral-history interview, HST Library, p. 1.

12. Xydis, *Greece and the Great Powers,* pp. 232, 258–265, 378.

13. Memorandum by the Joint Chiefs of Staff, 23 August 1946, *FR*, 1946, 7:857–58. Byrnes to Acheson, 20 August and 24 September 1946, ibid., pp. 192–93 and 223–24, respectively. Also see Clayton to Byrnes, 12 September 1946, ibid., pp. 209–13; and Acheson to MacVeagh, 15 October 1946, ibid., pp. 235–37. The Byrnes–Bevin understanding was revealed in a memorandum by the British embassy in Greece to the American embassy in Greece, 5 November 1946, ibid., pp. 913–15; and British embassy to State Department, 21 February 1947, *FR*, 1947, 5:32–37.

14. MacVeagh to Secretary of State, 19 October 1946, *FR*, 1946, 7:238–39. American credits are reported in Acheson to Greek chargé, 8 October 1946, ibid., pp. 232, 913–15. Inverchapel to Foreign Office, 21 October 1946, FO records, AN3234/1/45; and see minutes by F. B. A. Rundall, FO records, AN2657/1/45 and AN2724/1/45.

15. Alton R. Lee, "The Army 'Mutiny' of 1946," *Journal of American History* 53 (December 1966): 555–71.

16. Marshall's comments appear in Halifax to Foreign Office, 3 November 1945, FO records, AN3373/4/45. The ambassador reported after an earlier discussion: "Both Stimson and Marshall were fully alive to the risks of creating an impression on Russian mind that the Americans would soon be out of Europe." Halifax to Foreign Office, 14 May 1945, FO records, N5504/165/G. Whitehall opinion of American demobilization was stated in a minute of 11 January 1946 by B. E. F. Gage: it was a "lack of a sense of realism"; FO

records, AN95/1/45. Acheson's comment is in Matthew J. Connelly Files, cabinet meeting minutes, 11 January 1946, HST Library. Byrnes's and Patterson's feelings appear in a record of a meeting of the secretaries of state, war, and navy, 6 March 1946, SD records, 811.002/1-2446; and see Harry S. Truman, *Year of Decisions* (Garden City, N.Y., 1955), p. 509.

17. U.S. Bureau of the Census, *Historical Statistics of the United States, Colonial Times to 1970* (Washington, D.C., 1975), p. 1141. Forrest C. Pogue, *The Supreme Command, U.S. Army in World War II: European Theater of Operations* (Washington, D.C., 1954), p. 542. War Department staff study, undated, *FR,* 1947, 2:177–81. Richard F. Haynes, *The Awesome Power: Harry S. Truman as Commander in Chief* (Baton Rouge, 1973), p. 119.

18. *New York Times,* 13 September 1946. For an analysis of the speech, see J. Samuel Walker, *Henry A. Wallace and American Foreign Policy* (Westport, Conn., 1976), chap. 11. Wallace wrote in his diary on 17 October 1945: "British policy clearly is to provoke distrust between the United States and Russia and thus prepare the groundwork for World War III"; ibid., p. 129; and consult John Morton Blum, ed., *The Price of Vision: The Diary of Henry A. Wallace, 1942–1946* (Boston, 1973).

19. Statements from Vandenberg and Taft are reported in Margaret Truman, *Harry S. Truman* (New York, 1973), p. 316; and see Robert J. Donovan, *Conflict and Crisis: The Presidency of Harry S. Truman, 1945–1948* (New York, 1977), chap. 23. *Daily Herald* and *News Chronicle,* 14 September 1946, and *Manchester Guardian,* 16 September 1946. Minutes by Rundall and Butler, 14 September 1946, FO records, AN2803/4/45. Inverchapel to Foreign Office, 23 September 1946, FO records, AN2960/1/65.

20. M. Truman, *Harry S. Truman,* p. 317. Hadley Cantril and Mildred Strunks, eds., *Public Opinion, 1935–1946* (Princeton, 1951), p. 311. At Whitehall, Rundall wrote in a minute, 17 September 1946, that the embassy in Washington shared "our view that the anti-British strictures in Mr. Wallace's speech will have no deep effect"; FO records, AN2816/1/45.

21. George H. Gallup, ed., *The Gallup Poll: Public Opinion, 1935–1971* (New York, 1972), 1:604.

22. For the 1946 election and resulting budget, see Susan M. Hartmann, *Truman and the 80th Congress* (Columbia, Mo., 1971), chap. 1; Donovan, *Conflict and Crisis,* chap. 24; and Joseph M. Jones, *The Fifteen Weeks* (New York, 1955), pp. 89–99. Lodge's quip is in ibid., p. 91.

23. Jones, *Fifteen Weeks,* pp. 96–97.

24. Dalton's complaint appears in Robert H. Ferrell, *George C. Marshall* (New York, 1966), p. 115. Dreary living conditions are in Robert G. Kaiser, *Cold Winter, Cold War* (New York, 1974), pp.

16-17. Memorandum of Byrnes–Bevin conversation, 27 April 1946, SD records, 740.00119 Council/4-2746, Box c-228.

25. Economic problems are revealed in William L. Mallalieu, *British Reconstruction and American Policy, 1945–1955* (New York, 1956), pp. 33–43; House of Commons, *Accounts and Papers,* Command Papers 7046 (February 1947) and 9430 (April 1955). For Labour "optimism," see Command Paper 67-7 (December 1945).

26. Bevin's quip appears in Trevor Evans, *Bevin of Britain* (New York, 1946), p. 271. Armed-forces figures are in House of Commons, *Accounts and Papers,* Command Papers 6743 (February 1946) and 7046 (February 1947). Also consult C. M. Woodhouse, *British Foreign Policy since the Second World War* (London, 1961), pp. 77–79. H. G. Nicholas points out that in relation to population, Britain in December 1946 had twice as many men under arms as the United States did; *The United States and Britain* (Chicago, 1975), p. 116.

27. Comments and proposals by Laski and other leftists appear in M. A. Fitzsimons, *The Foreign Policy of the British Labour Government, 1945–1951* (Notre Dame, 1953), pp. 53–54; Elaine Windrich, *British Labour's Foreign Policy* (Stanford, 1952), chap. 11. Raymond Blackburn, "Bevin and His Critics," *Foreign Affairs* 25 (January 1947): 239–49.

28. "Protest by Labour M.P.'s against Government's Foreign Policy," 29 October 1946, FO records, N14755/97/38. *Hansard's Parliamentary Debates,* Commons, vol. 430 (18 November 1946), clm. 526ff. *Daily Telegraph,* 11 December 1946. For anti-Americanism in Labour party ranks, see Leon D. Epstein, *Britain—Uneasy Ally* (Chicago, 1954), and Michael R. Gordon, *Conflict and Consensus in Labour's Foreign Policy, 1914–1965* (Stanford, 1969).

29. Gallman to State Department, 18 November 1946, SD records, 741.00/11-1846, Box 3974.

30. Bevin's foreign-affairs address of 27 February 1947 demonstrates how little his policy had changed; *Hansard's Parliamentary Debates,* Commons, vol. 433 (27 February 1947), clms. 2296ff. State Department memorandum, 31 October 1946, SD records, 741.00/10-3146, Box 3974.

31. Many Britons felt that American policy toward the Kremlin had so hardened that London should become the mediator between Washington and Moscow! Whitehall officials saw no chance for the adoption of such a policy; minutes by Wilson Young, 20 October 1946, FO records, AN3148/1/45. American diplomats in London agreed with their counterparts but admitted that relations during autumn 1946 had become "somewhat strained" because of the Wallace speech, the Palestine issue, and the administration's retreat on price controls which had decreased the value of the British loan. Nevertheless, embassy officials still felt confident that Anglo-American ties were unshakable. Consult the series of "British foreign

policy reviews" first sent by the embassy to the State Department in autumn 1946, especially 25 October 1946 and 10 December 1946, SD records, 741.00/10-2546 and 741.00/12-1046, respectively.

32. Economic facts appear in Delivanis and Cleveland, *Greek Monetary Developments,* pp. 160, 188–95, and C. A. Munkman, *American Aid to Greece: A Report on the First Ten Years* (New York, 1958), pp. 46–50. For the civil war, see Woodhouse, *Struggle for Greece,* chap. 7; D. George Kousoulas, *Revolution and Defeat: The Story of the Greek Communist Party* (London, 1965), pp. 230–32; and Edgar O'Ballance, *The Greek Civil War, 1944–1949* (New York, 1966), pp. 131, 133, 142.

33. Pleas for military aid and Montgomery's visit appear in Xydis, *Greece and the Great Powers,* pp. 361, 432–36. British diplomats and military officials in Athens supported Greek requests for more aid from London; Norton to Foreign Office, 31 December 1946, FO records, R53/34/19; and Haddon to Williams, 28 January 1947, FO records, R1819/50/G. MacVeagh reported Montgomery's statements to the State Department, 3 December 1946, SD records, 868.00/12-346, a message partly reprinted in *FR,* 1946, 7:283, n. 73.

34. Xydis, *Greece and the Great Powers,* pp. 432–33. Whitehall informed the embassy in Athens, 15 November 1946, FO records, R16478: "We are sorry if we have given the impression that we wish to discourage the United States from extending immediate financial help to Greece. Nothing could be further from the truth, as we are anxious to interest the Americans in Greece in every way possible." McNeil was discouraged with the Greeks, tired of crisis after crisis, and ready to abandon some if not all of the commitment; McNeil to Sargent, 29 November 1946, FO records, R17463/1/G19; and see minute by M. S. Williams, 26 November 1946, FO records, R17544/1/19. Minutes of meeting between Treasury and Foreign Office officials, 29 November 1946, FO records, R17551/1/19. James F. Byrnes reports his meeting with Bevin in *Speaking Frankly* (New York, 1947), p. 300. Also consult Gallman to State Department, 31 January 1947, *FR,* 1947, 5:13–14.

35. Xydis, *Greece and the Great Powers,* pp. 432–38, 443–53, 661, n. 51; and see Secretary of State to MacVeagh, 3 January 1947, *FR,* 1946, 7:286–87.

36. Byrnes, *Speaking Frankly,* p. 300. Clayton made the comment during a meeting of the secretaries of state, war, and navy, 11 September 1946, SD records, 811.002/1-2446. For Byrnes's thoughts of Tsaldaris, see Byrnes to MacVeagh, 3 January 1947, *FR,* 1946, 7:286–87. Many Whitehall officials agreed with Americans who thought the Greeks exaggerated the crisis; Foreign Office to Athens embassy, 15 November 1946, FO records, R16478; and see the minutes in the file. Mark F. Ethridge labeled the Greek prime minister "a stupid fool" and, along with Paul A. Porter, organized a "Tsaldaris must go" clique after arriving in Greece; Ethridge oral-history inter-

view, HST Library, pp. 31–32. Porter evaluated Greek politicans in a message to Clayton, 17 February 1947, *FR*, 1947, 5:20–21.

37. Acheson to MacVeagh, 8 November 1946, *FR*, 1946, 7:262–63. Acheson to Wilson, 8 November 1946, ibid., pp. 916–17; Wilson's thoughts appear in his message to the secretary of state, 17 January 1947, *FR*, 1947, 5:7–8. Acheson to MacVeagh, 20 November 1946, *FR*, 1946, 7:265–66. For the action of the Export–Import Bank, see memorandum of conversation, 22 January 1947, *FR*, 1947, 5:11–12. Memorandum of Byrnes–Inverchapel conversation, 4 January 1947, ibid., pp. 1–2.

38. Gallman to Sargent, 20 December 1946, FO records, R1609/50/19. Ethridge to State Department, 17 February 1947, *FR*, 1947, 5:23–25. For other alarming messages urging American involvement, see ibid., pp. 16–17, 25. For Henderson's memorandum, see Acheson to Marshall, 21 February 1947, ibid., pp. 29–31; Henderson, oral-history interview, 14 June 1973, HST Library, pp. 75–88. Dean Acheson, *Present at the Creation: My Years in the State Department* (New York, 1969), pp. 290–91.

39. Porter said this to Kaiser, *Cold Winter, Cold War*, p. 161. For Porter's statements to the Greeks, see Xydis, *Greece and the Great Powers*, p. 463. Porter to State Department, 17 February 1947, *FR*, 1947, 5:17–22. Report of conversation between Thomas C. Rapp, deputy head of British economic mission to Greece, and Porter, 6 March 1947, FO records, R3055/50/19. Norton reported to Foreign Office on 25 February 1947: "My American colleague [MacVeagh] is not at present prepared to shoulder any responsibility of Greek internal problem"; FO records, R2619/4/19. Acheson to MacVeagh, 28 December 1946, *FR*, 1946, 7:285–86. MacVeagh to Secretary of State, 15 December 1945, *FR*, 1945, 8:284–88.

40. Halifax to Foreign Office, 23 April 1945, FO records, R7396/7396/19.

41. For other descriptions of the winter of 1947, see Jones, *Fifteen Weeks*, pp. 78–85; Donovan, *Conflict and Crisis*, chap. 29; and Kaiser, *Cold Winter, Cold War*, pp. 175–76.

42. Concerning opposition to Greek aid, see cabinet meeting minute, 15 January 1946, Cab (128/5) 5(46)2; on Germany, consult memorandum to the cabinet from Dalton, 18 October 1946, Cab (129/13) c.p. (46)385. Report of the ministerial committee on economic planning, 16 January 1947, Cab (128/9) c.m. (47). Hugh Dalton Papers, diary entry, 17 January 1947, London School of Economics and Political Science, London. Hugh Dalton, *Memoirs, 1945–1960: High Tide and After* (London, 1962), pp. 194–98. Dalton Papers, diary entry, 5 February 1947.

43. Britain had also contributed $3 billion to international relief programs since July 1945; see the Labour party pamphlet "Cards on the Table" and the London *Times*, 22 May 1947. Aid to Palestine and

Greece appear in *Hansard's Parliamentary Debates,* Commons, vol. 434
(6 March 1947), clm. 651; and see Fitzsimons, *Foreign Policy of the
British Labour Government,* p. 85. Defense expenditures are in R. N.
Rosecrance, *Defense of the Realm: British Strategy in the Nuclear Epoch*
(New York, 1968), app., table 1. For the white paper, see House of
Commons, *Accounts and Papers,* Command Paper 7046 (22 February
1947), p. 16.

44. Dalton, *High Tide and After,* p. 198.

45. Memorandum by Secretary of State for Foreign Affairs to
Cabinet, 25 January 1947, Cab (129/16) c.p. (47)34, and 14th conclusions, 30 January 1947, Cab (128/9) c.m.(47). Draft message, Bevin
to Inverchapel, undated (probably 4 February 1947), and draft letter, Bevin to Dalton, 10 February 1947, both in FO records, R1900/
50/19G.

46. Dalton to Attlee, 11 February 1947, FO records, R2443/50/
G19. Minute by Warner, 14 February 1947, FO records, R1900/50/
19G. Ralph W. Selby's suggestion about the Dominions is in a minute
dated 14 February 1947, FO records, R2823/50/G. Minute by Bevin,
18 February 1947, FO records, R2442/50/19G.

47. Jones, *Fifteen Weeks,* pp. 3–8. For both notes, consult British
embassy to State Department, 21 February 1947, *FR,* 1947, 5:32–37.

48. Connelly Files, cabinet meeting minutes, 7 March 1947.

49. Jones memorandum to Benton, 26 February 1947, Joseph M.
Jones Papers, Box 1, HST Library. Jones, incidentally, thought the
statement should be made by Marshall, "who is the only one in the
Government with the prestige to make a deep impression." And
consult Jones, *Fifteen Weeks,* pp. 129–48. Acheson, *Present at the Creation,* pp. 290–93; and see the State Department's proposals, *FR,*
1947, 5:41–61.

50. *The Public Papers of the President of the United States: Harry S.
Truman* (Washington, D.C., 1947), pp. 178–79. Also consult "The
Drafting of the President's Message to Congress on the Greek Situa-
tion," 12 March 1947, Jones Papers, Box 1.

51. The statements and other testimony appear in *The Legislative
Origins of the Truman Doctrine, Hearings Held in Executive Session before
the Committee on Foreign Relations, United States Senate* (Washington,
D.C., 1973), pp. 32, 48.

52. Jones, *Fifteen Weeks,* pp. 177–79. Hartmann, *Truman and the
80th Congress,* pp. 60–63. Joan L. Bryniarski, "Against the Tide: Senate Opposition to the Internationalist Foreign Policy of Presidents
Franklin D. Roosevelt and Harry S. Truman, 1943–1949" (Ph.D.
diss., University of Maryland, 1972), chaps. 4 and 5. Pepper's suggestion appears in *Legislative Origins of the Truman Doctrine,* pp. 105–17.
The Foreign Relations Committee came to the conclusion about not
helping the British after hearings with State Department officials,
ibid., p. 221. The department's thoughts on underwriting the British

were revealed in a paper, "Information Program on United States Aid to Greece," written by Jones: "We are not helping the British. It is an affirmative American policy. We are not taking over for the British"; 4 March 1947, Jones Papers, Box 1.

53. To be sure, the Truman Doctrine—and its worldwide implications—was much more than the British asked for or expected (see Chap. 7). From 1948 when massive American aid began arriving to 1952, the United States gave Greece approximately $1.1 billion; consult Munkman, *American Aid to Greece*, p. 58.

54. Francis Williams, *Ernest Bevin: Portrait of a Great Englishman* (London, 1952), pp. 263–64. Attlee's comment appears in Francis Williams, ed., *Twilight of Empire: Memoirs of Prime Minister Clement Attlee* (New York, 1962), p. 172. Roy Jenkins, *Nine Men of Power* (London, 1974), pp. 77–78; and see his booklet "British Foreign Policy since 1945" (Oxford, 1972), p. 5. For Dalton's role in the "Birth of the Truman Doctrine," see *High Tide and After,* pp. 206–9. Walter Lippmann supported the British theme in *Isolation and Alliances* (Boston, 1952), pp. 31–32; and so did Xydis, *Greece and the Great Powers,* p. 550, who wrote: "To Bevin, as much as to Truman—or almost—the Greeks owe a debt of gratitude for the momentous decision that usually bears the American President's name." Some Britons disagree with this interpretation; see R. H. S. Crossman, *The Charm of Politics and Other Essays in Political Criticism* (New York, 1958), pp. 20–25.

55. Norman A. Graebner, *Cold War Diplomacy, 1945–1960* (New York, 1962), chap. 3. John W. Spanier, *American Foreign Policy since World War II,* rev. ed. (New York, 1968), pp. 38–42. Louis J. Halle, *The Cold War as History* (New York, 1967), chap. 12. Herbert Feis, *From Trust to Terror: The Onset of the Cold War, 1945–1950* (New York, 1970), p. 178. William A. Williams, *The Tragedy of American Diplomacy* (New York, 1962), p. 370. Ronald Steel, *Pax Americana* (New York, 1970), pp. 21–27. David Horowitz, *The Free World Colossus: A Critique of American Foreign Policy in the Cold War* (New York, 1971), chap. 5. John L. Gaddis, *The United States and the Origins of the Cold War, 1941–1947* (New York, 1972), chap. 10. David S. McLellan, *Dean Acheson: The State Department Years* (New York, 1976), pp. 112–13. British diplomacy is allotted more importance in Daniel Yergin, *Shattered Peace: The Origins of the Cold War and the National Security State* (Boston, 1977), pp. 280–81, and of course, Robert M. Hathaway, Jr., "The Paradoxes of Partnership: Britain and America, 1944–1947" (Ph.D. diss., University of North Carolina, 1976).

56. Minute by Williams, 20 February 1947, FO records, R2751/50/G. Minute by Sargent, 17 February 1947, FO records, R2523/34/19G. Norton to Foreign Office, 19 February 1947, FO records, R2329/34/19. Norton, incidentally, not only embarrassed by his orders to inform the Greeks that aid would terminate, was so angered and

dissappointed that he refused to tell the Greeks until the American response was known; Norton to Foreign Office, 21 February 1947, FO records, R2451/50/19G. Bevin's papers in the Foreign Office for this period will not be opened until 1982, but one wonders if they will be very revealing since he rarely recorded his thoughts in Foreign Office minutes.

57. Acheson's statement of 13 March 1947 appears in *Legislative Origins of the Truman Doctrine*, p. 3. Hartmann, *Truman and the 80th Congress*, pp. 24–25. Acheson, *Present at the Creation*, p. 291. Clifford's comment is on a copy of the speech by Jones, 7 March 1947, Jones Papers, Box 1.

58. Acheson's statement of 1 April 1947 is in *Legislative Origins of the Truman Doctrine*, p. 88. Sargent to E. Bridges, 21 March 1947, FO records, R3442/50/G; and see Sargent to Norton, 20 February 1947, FO records, R2524/34/G19.

Notes to Chapter 7
The United States, Great Britain, and the Cold War

1. *Hansard's Parliamentary Debates,* Commons (17 April 1945). All American and British diplomats interviewed mentioned the warm regard they had for their counterparts, and the evenings spent over dinner discussing personal backgrounds and thoughts.

2. *New York Times,* 12 March 1947; other such comments appear in Joseph M. Jones, *The Fifteen Weeks* (New York, 1955), pp. 172–73.

3. Connally's remark of 13 March 1947 is in *The Legislative Origins of the Truman Doctrine, Hearings Held in Executive Session before the Committee on Foreign Relations, United States Senate* (Washington, D.C., 1973), p. 16; and consult Tom Connally, *My Name Is Tom Connally* (New York, 1954), p. 319.

4. Eben Ayers Papers, diary entry, 12 March 1947, HST Library. Harry S. Truman, *Years of Trial and Hope* (Garden City, N.Y., 1956), p. 105.

5. For American policy in Greece after 1947, see Lawrence S. Wittner, "The Truman Doctrine and the Defense of Freedom," *Diplomatic History* 4 (Spring 1980).

6. Memorandum by Jones, "Drafting of the President's Message to Congress on the Greek Situation," 12 March 1947, Joseph M. Jones Papers, Box 1, HST Library.

7. The label "first cold warrior" is mentioned and discussed by Loewenheim, Langley, and Jonas in their analysis of the Churchill–Roosevelt correspondence; consult *Wartime Correspondence*, pp. 66, 69. Although he does not use the label, Gabriel Kolko best illustrates

the theme in *The Politics of War: The World and United States Foreign Policy, 1943–1945* (New York, 1968), chaps. 15 and 20. Reston's article appears in *New York Times*, 31 May 1946.

8. Interview with Sir Frank K. Roberts, 25 July 1978. Foreign Office to UK representative in UN, 13 March 1947, FO records, R3397/50/19. Minute by Rundall, 9 June 1947, FO records, AN2000/40/45. Hugh Dalton, *Memoirs, 1945–1960: High Tide and After* (London, 1962), p. 209. For interpretations of the effects of the speech, see Richard M. Freeland, *The Truman Doctrine and the Origins of McCarthyism* (New York, 1972); and Michael Leigh, *Mobilizing Consent: Public Opinion and American Foreign Policy, 1937–1947* (Westport, Conn., 1976).

9. Inverchapel to Foreign Office, 2 February 1947, FO records, AN510/40/45. Churchill letter to Truman, 24 September 1947, HST Library, PSF, Folder "Churchill, Winston, 1947–1950"; and in the same file, Bevin to Truman, 8 April 1949, Folder "Foreign–British."

10. Inverchapel to Foreign Office, 1 March 1947, FO records, R2820/50/19; and see Sargent memorandum to Bevin, 18 March 1947, and Inverchapel to Foreign Office, 14 April 1947, FO records, AN1762/1019/45 and R5046/50/16, respectively.

Essay on Sources

World War II and the postwar period are undoubtedly two of the most popular topics in American history. Thirty years after the Truman Doctrine, a complete bibliography of that critical era would result in a full-length book. Traditional, New Left, and postrevisionist historians have created a small library, not to mention filling numerous periodicals. Therefore, it seems sensible to limit this essay to a discussion only of the most significant sources concerning Anglo-American relations from 1944 to 1947 and to remind the reader to consult the notes for specific topics.

Unpublished Documents

Great Britain

The most important British documents are located at the Public Record Office, Kew Gardens, London. Access is granted thirty years after the event on the upcoming January; therefore, records for all of 1947 were opened on the first working day of January 1978. Foreign Office records series 371, "General Political Correspondence," the primary collection, includes the important messages between Whitehall and the embassies and relevant minutes made by Foreign Office officials. The messages and comments are indispensable, and no study of Anglo-American relations is complete without them. The cabinet memoranda, minutes, and conclusions are also of considerable value. Cabinet members often presented policy during their meetings, and in the numerous cabinet series one discovers papers dealing with strategy and the rising Anglo-American military collaboration (Cab 105 and 122). The cabinet papers are indexed and accessible. Churchill's wartime papers (PREM) contain many messages to Eden and some to various ambassadors that reveal the prime minister's thinking; responses are usually included. Unfortunately, Churchill's and Eden's propensity to record their thoughts was not continued by Attlee and Bevin; the latter seldom wrote comments in Foreign Office minutes. The papers of the Ministry of Defense describe the military aspects of the war, and the documents dealing with diplomatic debates over strategy often appear in Foreign Office and cabinet documents.

The records at the Public Record Office are indexed, and archivists and research aides such as the *Guide to the Contents of the Public Record Office* (Her Majesty's Stationery Office, 1963) are available in the reading room.

United States

War and postwar American documents are scattered across the nation. Located at the National Archives in Washington, D.C., are the records of the State Department and those of the military at the Modern Military Branch. Unfortunately the State Department records are much more difficult to use than those of the Foreign Office because of the filing system and because important messages are usually kept in the same box with trivial ones ("send the ambassador's tuxedo"). The two most important record groups for diplomatic correspondence are 45 and 59. Research is easier in the Modern Military Branch where lists and indexes facilitate the search process. The papers of the Joint Chiefs of Staff include memoranda and messages about military and diplomatic topics, and the files of Adm. William D. Leahy contain messages that the admiral gave to Roosevelt and Truman. Concerning Anglo-American military policy, the recently opened American-British correspondence (ABC File) in record group 165 reveals such topics as the standardization of arms and the rising Anglo-American military cooperation in 1946.

The two presidential libraries hold a large number of documents and personal papers while offering comfortable surroundings and courteous and helpful archivists. The papers of both presidents are divided into files that are described and indexed in booklets. At the Roosevelt Library in Hyde Park, New York, consult the relevant diplomatic folders in the President's Secretary's File. The Map Room File contains all the Roosevelt–Churchill and Roosevelt–Stalin correspondence. At the Truman Library in Independence, Missouri, inspect the President's Secretary's File and the President's Official File. The Truman Library also has a large number of oral histories and dissertations concerning the Truman era that can be checked out overnight.

Unpublished Papers and Diaries

Great Britain

Generally speaking, the private papers of British officials are not very revealing, perhaps because so many of them recorded their thoughts in Foreign Office minutes or published memoirs. The two best guides to private collections are Cris Cook, *Sources in British Political History, 1900–1950*, vol. 2, *A Guide to the Private Papers of Selected Public Servants* (London, 1975); and Cameron Hazlehurst and Christine Woodland, *A Guide to the Papers of British Cabinet Ministers, 1900–1951* (London, 1974). Two of the most helpful manuscripts are located at the student room of the British Museum —the diaries of Oliver Harvey and Andrew B. Cunningham. Harvey details his anti-Americanism during the war and his changing attitudes toward the Soviet Union at the end of the war in Europe. Cunningham deals mostly with military events and feels warmly toward the United States. Hugh Dalton wrote an important diary that is stored at the London School of Economics and Political Science. He describes the conflict within the Labour government over his attempts to cut defense spending and reveals the cabinet crisis during the snowstorms of early 1947. The papers of Lord Halifax at Churchill College, Cambridge University, and at the Foreign Office (FO 800) add to his messages from Washington to Whitehall and give his thoughts on dealing with America.

Many collections are more disappointing, including the papers of Clement Attlee located at University College, Oxford University. Attlee's papers are skimpy and without a diary. The papers of Orme Sargent and Clark Kerr at the Public Record Office (FO 800) are not fully accessible; in any case, they are of little value compared to their comments and messages in Foreign Office records. Most of the personal papers of Churchill and Eden are in private hands and have not been opened for inspection; Bevin's papers as foreign secretary will not be available until 1982.

United States

The private papers of American leaders are more revealing. At the Library of Congress, the diary of Adm. William D. Leahy is filled with opinions and events that were not included in his memoirs, and the journal and diary of Joseph E. Davies are excellent for his trip to London in May 1945 and for the early months of the Truman presidency. Of lesser importance at the Library of Congress are the papers of Robert Patterson, which contain a few significant memoranda, and those of Cordell Hull, which generally concern an earlier era.

At the Roosevelt Library, investigate the papers of Harry Hopkins which contain some wartime correspondence with Churchill. Also see the Sherwood collection of the Hopkins papers which are drafts of and letters concerning *Roosevelt and Hopkins: An Intimate History* (New York, 1948). The multivolume presidential diary of Henry Morgenthau, Jr., is detailed and discusses his almost daily contact with Roosevelt and Truman. The presidential secretary, William D. Hassett, wrote a diary that contains little on foreign affairs but describes a president who was old and tired by 1945 and includes about twenty pages on the day Roosevelt died, 12 April 1945. Of lesser importance for a diplomatic study are the papers of Stephen T. Early and Samuel I. Rosenman.

The Truman Library holds some of the most important collections of personal papers. The diary of presidential assistant Eben Ayers heads the list. Ayers met with the president about five days a week, and his diary, opened in 1976, supplies one of the most detailed records of the early Truman years, including entries with the president's comments on key issues. The files of Matthew J. Connelly contain the minutes of cabinet meetings and expose the administration's changing attitude toward the Allies. The papers of Clark M. Clifford include memoranda describing the tougher policy toward the Kremlin that was initiated in 1946. Joseph M. Jones saved a sizable quantity of documents dealing with the origins of the Truman Doctrine and the Marshall Plan, many of which did not appear in *The Fifteen Weeks* (New York, 1955). There are other collections of lesser importance, such as the papers of Henry F. Grady, which avoid discussion of his mission to Greece in 1945, and those of George V. Allen, which contain little on his ambassadorship to Greece. The Clayton-Thorp file is important for economic issues but not for Anglo-American relations toward Russia, and the papers of Dean Acheson are disappointing, being mostly transcripts of seminars held at Princeton in 1953.

Other American collections include the papers of James F. Byrnes located at Clemson University in South Carolina. These manuscripts contain the letters supporting his tough policy announced in 1946. Unfortunately Byrnes did not keep a diary, but his assistant, Walter Brown, did occasionally record Byrnes's comments. At Yale University the papers of Henry L. Stimson include an excellent diary that has become available on microfilm. The calendar notes and record of Edward R. Stettinius, Jr., located at the University of Virginia, are also useful. The papers of Arthur H. Vandenberg are at the University of Michigan. Most of the comments the senator made about the

British have been published by his son, Arthur H. Vandenberg, Jr., in *The Private Papers of Senator Arthur H. Vandenberg* (Boston, 1952).

Other Unpublished Sources

There are two other valuable unpublished sources for the study of Anglo-American relations—Ph.D. dissertations and oral histories. The finest dissertation is by Robert M. Hathaway, Jr., "The Paradoxes of Partnership: Britain and America, 1944-1947" (University of North Carolina, 1976), which has been accepted for publication. Also from the University of North Carolina (1974) is Keith M. Heim, "Hope without Power: Truman and the Russians, 1945," in which the author interviewed important American officials. Joan Lee Bryniarski has written an interesting study, "Against the Tide: Senate Opposition to the Internationalist Foreign Policy of Presidents Franklin D. Roosevelt and Harry S. Truman, 1943-1949" (University of Maryland, 1972), and also see Ronald Frank Lehman II, "Vandenberg, Taft, and Truman: Principle and Politics in the Announcement of the Truman Doctrine" (Claremont College, 1975). From the University of Alabama (1973) comes Bertrand Fox Jarvis, "The Role of the Small Powers in the Development of the Western Bloc at the 1946 Paris Peace Conference: A Study into the Origins of the Cold War"; a more philosophical study is James Frederick Green, "The Political Thought of George Kennan" (American University, 1972). An older study from Indiana University (1954) is Frederick Karl Schilling, Jr., "Germany and Her Future: British Opinion and Policy, 1939-1947."

Fortunately, many of the dissertations dealing with the Truman era are on file at the Truman Library, and so are numerous oral histories. I have consulted about twenty-five interviews at the library; the following are the most important: Theodore Achilles (13 November 1972); Mark F. Ethridge (4 June 1974); Loy W. Henderson (14 June and 15 July 1973); H. Freeman Matthews (7 June 1973); Leonard Miall (17 June 1964); James W. Riddleberger (6 and 26 April 1972); Samuel I. Rosenman (15 October 1968 and 23 April 1969); Harry H. Vaughan (14 and 16 January 1963); and Constantine Tsaldaris (4 May 1964), in which the former Greek premier takes most of the credit for the Truman Doctrine. In addition I have recorded interviews with the following diplomats: Waldemar J. Gallman (16 and 27 April 1978); Theodore Achilles (17 April 1978); and Samuel Berger (18 April 1978). These interviews are available at the Indiana University Oral History Research Project, which also has the oral biography of Gallman (March 1975).

Published Documents

Great Britain

The *House of Commons Debates,* of course, is an indispensable source for the study of British foreign policy. Also important are the parliamentary *Accounts and Papers* that contain command or white papers stating government policy. These are especially revealing for Britain's postwar economic plight. For the debate and plans of the Labourites, consult *Labour Party: Report of the Annual Conference.* A multivolume compilation of Churchill's addresses is Robert Rhodes James, ed., *Winston S. Churchill: His Complete Speeches, 1897–1963* (London, 1974). Also of interest are the annual volumes of *British Speeches of the Day* published by the British Information Service. A good survey of important documents can be found in Joel H. Wiener, *Great Britain: Foreign Policy and the Span of Empire, 1689–1971* (New York, 1972). The annual *Survey* published by the Royal Institute of International Affairs is also worth looking at.

United States

Published American documents, especially diplomatic records, are more helpful than those of the British. The most impressive source for any book on American foreign affairs is the State Department's series entitled *Foreign Relations of the United States.* These volumes are filled with many of the most important messages and memoranda. Speeches of American officials and other documents appear in the State Department *Bulletin.* A convenient source of Roosevelt's cables is the volume edited by Francis L. Loewenheim, Harold D. Langley, and Manfred Jonas, *Roosevelt and Churchill: Their Secret Wartime Correspondence* (New York, 1975), which contains 548 messages between the two leaders, a chronology, and a detailed bibliography. For Truman's press conferences and speeches, consult *The Public Papers of the President of the United States: Harry S. Truman* (Washington, D.C., 1946 and 1947); for congressional comments and debates over foreign policy, see *Congressional Record.* An excellent record of the hearings held before the foreign-relations committee and concerning aid to Greece and Turkey is *The Legislative Origins of the Truman Doctrine* (Washington, D.C., 1973), and factual information for the era is found in the Council of Foreign Relations series entitled *The United States in World Affairs.*

Two sources of neither British nor American origin that should be consulted are *Correspondence between the Chairman of the Council of Ministers of the U.S.S.R. and the Presidents of the U.S.A. and the Prime Ministers of Great Britain during the Great Patriotic War of 1941–1945* which was published in 1957 in Moscow and in the next year by E. P. Dutton in New York as *Stalin's Correspondence with Churchill, Attlee, Roosevelt and Truman, 1941–1945.* Concerning the world organization and Bevin's arguments with the Soviet delegation at the London conference in early 1946, see *United Nations Security Council Official Records* 1, 1st ser., 1 (17 January–16 February 1946).

Biographies, Memoirs, and Published Papers

Excellent and accessible sources for the war and postwar eras are numerous British and American biographies, memoirs, and published papers. As there is virtually a library of information on the war leaders, only the most pertinent titles will be mentioned.

Great Britain

No book concerning Churchill's policy toward the Allies surpasses his own six-volume study, *The Second World War,* and especially important are the messages and memoranda in the final volume, *Triumph and Tragedy* (Boston, 1953). Lord Moran (Sir Charles Wilson) has recorded the prime minister's fears of Soviet power in the diary entitled *Winston Churchill: The Struggle for Survival, 1940–1965* (London, 1968). Some of Churchill's former subordinates have described their boss in *Action This Day: Working with Churchill* (London, 1968), edited by John W. Wheeler-Bennett, and an interesting analysis is A. J. P. Taylor et al., *Churchill Revised: A Critical Assessment* (New York, 1969). Also consult Kay Halle, ed., *Winston Churchill on America and Britain: A Selection of His Thoughts on Anglo-American Relations* (New York, 1970). Other Conservatives have written accounts, including Anthony Eden, *Days for Decision* (Boston, 1950), and more important, *The Reckoning* (Boston, 1965), which contain his views on the United States. Harold Macmillan's books, *The Blast of War, 1939–1945* (London, 1967), and the *Tides of Fortune, 1945–1955*

(London, 1969), mention his duties in the Mediterranean and relations with the Americans.

Concerning Anglo-American military relations, examine the *Memoirs* of Montgomery of Alamein (Cleveland, 1958). The field marshal discusses the differences in strategy and the rising cooperation between the British and American armed forces after the war. The diaries and notes of Field Marshal Alan Brooke have been compiled and written into *The Turn of the Tide* and *Triumph in the West, 1943–1946* (Garden City, N.Y., 1957 and 1959) by Arthur Bryant. These books condemn American shortsighted military policy. Andrew B. Cunningham, *A Sailor's Odyssey* (New York, 1951), mentions relations between the American and British navies, and Sholto Douglas, *Years of Command* (London, 1966), compares the U.S. Air Force and the RAF. Also concerning the RAF, see Lord Tedder, *With Prejudice: The War Memoirs of Marshal of the Royal Air Force* (London, 1966). Churchill's chief of staff, Hastings Ismay, has written *The Memoirs of General Lord Ismay* (New York, 1960), and the wartime director of the British military mission in Washington, Henry Maitland Wilson, records his American experiences in *Eight Years Overseas, 1939–1947* (London, n.d. [1949?]).

There are a number of studies by and about members of the Labour government. Clement Attlee, *As It Happened* (London, 1954), is not as revealing as the later series of interviews that were written into *Twilight of Empire: Memoirs of Prime Minister Clement Attlee* (New York, 1962), by Francis Williams. Williams also wrote a sympathetic biography of *Ernest Bevin: Portrait of a Great Englishman* (London, 1952) which gives the foreign secretary sole responsibility for getting the United States involved in Europe. For Bevin's background and career up to 1945, the finest book is the two-volume study by Alan Bullock, *The Life and Times of Ernest Bevin* (London, 1967). A number of Bevin's colleagues wrote about him, but seldom are these more than personality sketches. Although Lord (William) Strang, *Home and Abroad* (London, 1956), wrote an interesting chapter on the foreign secretary, Roderick Barclay, *Ernest Bevin and the Foreign Office, 1932–1969* (London, 1975), and Piers Dixon, *Double Diploma: The Life of Sir Pierson Dixon, Don and Diplomat* (London, 1968), are slim books that leave analysis to historians. Of more interest is Dean Acheson, *Sketches from Life* (New York, 1959), in which the author reveals his warm regard for Bevin. *The Life of John Maynard Keynes* (London, 1963) is examined by R. F. Harrod, who also discusses the negotiations for the British loan. Economic and diplomatic matters in 1946 and 1947 are investigated by Hugh Dalton, *Memoirs 1945–1960: High Tide and After* (London, 1962), and for a man that hates Dalton, consult *I've Lived through It All* (London, 1973) by the minister of fuel and power, Emanuel Shinwell. Both Dalton and Shinwell testify to a cabinet crisis in early 1947.

A few British diplomats left papers or wrote books that mention the United States. One of the most detailed accounts is David Dilks, ed., *The Diaries of Sir Alexander Cadogan, 1938–1945* (New York, 1971). Cadogan attended most of the war conferences and has some negative comments about inconsistent American foreign policy. Concerning Anglo-American-French relations, see A. Duff Cooper, *Old Men Forget: The Autobiography of Duff Cooper* (New York, 1954), and for the memoir of a diplomat who was stationed in Washington, see Lord (Paul) Gore-Booth, *With Great Truth and Respect* (London, 1974). Unfortunately *Fullness of Days* (London, 1957), by Lord Halifax is disappointing, and his biography by the Earl of Birkenhead, *Halifax: The Life of Lord Halifax* (Boston, 1966), avoids issues between the two democracies.

United States

President Roosevelt's views toward the British are revealed in a few books; perhaps the best account is Robert E. Sherwood, *Roosevelt and Hopkins: An Intimate History* (New York, 1948). A close look is also given by the president's chief of staff, William D. Leahy, *I Was There* (New York, 1950), and by Edward R. Stettinius, Jr., *Roosevelt and the Russians* (Garden City, N.Y., 1949). More important for domestic affairs than foreign policy are the following: *F.D.R.: His Personal Letters, 1928–1945* (New York, 1950), edited by his son Elliott and Joseph Lash; William D. Hassett, *Off the Record with F.D.R.* (New Brunswick, N.J., 1958); and Samuel I. Rosenman, *Working with Roosevelt* (New York, 1952). Anti-British sentiment is revealed in the two-volume *Memoirs of Cordell Hull* (New York, 1948) and in the biography by Julius W. Pratt, *Cordell Hull* (New York, 1964). Concerning Stettinius, the most informative work is Thomas M. Campbell and George C. Herring, *The Diaries of Edward R. Stettinius, Jr., 1943–1946* (New York, 1975), and also see the short monograph by Richard L. Walker, *E. R. Stettinius, Jr.* (New York, 1965). With the aid of McGeorge Bundy, Henry L. Stimson recorded his views in *On Active Service in Peace and War* (New York, 1947), and a fine biography is Elting E. Morison, *Turmoil and Tradition: A Study of the Life and Times of Henry L. Stimson* (Boston, 1960).

After the war American commanders recorded their opinions of British and Allied strategy in Europe. Forrest C. Pogue has written a superb biography of *George C. Marshall: Organizer of Victory* (New York, 1973) that describes American views of Churchill's military plans and contains an extensive bibliography. Also consult Pogue's *The Supreme Command* (Washington, D.C., 1954), one volume in the excellent series, *U.S. Army in World War II*. Eisenhower's ideas are revealed in the multivolume *Papers of Dwight David Eisenhower,* edited by Alfred D. Chandler (Baltimore, 1970), and also see two books by Stephen E. Ambrose, *Eisenhower and Berlin, 1945: The Decision to Halt at the Elbe* (Garden City, N.Y., 1967), and *The Supreme Commander: The War Years of General Dwight D. Eisenhower* (New York, 1970). An older work that shows friction between Eisenhower and Montgomery is Harry C. Butcher, *My Three Years with Eisenhower* (New York, 1946). Other American commanders had some thoughts about their British allies, and Martin Blumenson has nicely edited *The Patton Papers, 1940–1945* (Boston, 1974), and see Omar N. Bradley, *A Soldier's Story* (New York, 1951).

American diplomats have written some excellent autobiographies, and although most of them deal primarily with the Soviet Union, the following discuss relations with the British. The two best accounts are by the Russian experts George F. Kennan, *Memoirs, 1925–1950* (Boston, 1967), and Charles E. Bohlen, *Witness to History, 1929–1969* (New York, 1973). The memoir of W. Averell Harriman (with Elie Abel), *Special Envoy to Churchill and Stalin, 1941–1946* (New York, 1975) relies heavily on previously published State Department documents. Harriman also neglects his ambassadorship to London in 1946. Two older works are John R. Deane, *The Strange Alliance: The Story of Our Efforts at Wartime Co-operation with Russia* (New York, 1946), and Walter Bedell Smith, *My Three Years in Moscow* (Philadelphia, 1950). Robert D. Murphy, *Diplomat among Warriors* (Garden City, N.Y., 1964), occasionally reports conversations with British officials. A disappointing study of the wartime American ambassador's relations with the British is Bernard Bellush, *He Walks Alone: A Biography of John Gilbert Winant* (The Hague, 1968).

Historians of the Truman era are fortunate in that the president wrote a two-volume memoir of his years in office, and much of it is devoted to foreign policy. *Year of Decisions* and *Years of Trial and Hope* (Garden City, N.Y., 1955 and 1956) are usually concerned with Soviet-American relations and supply less information on the president's thoughts toward the British. More enlightening are the diary entries, memoranda, and letters in Robert H. Ferrell, ed., *Off the*

Record: The Private Papers of Harry S. Truman (New York, 1980). Some of her father's letters appear in Margaret Truman, *Harry S. Truman* (New York, 1973), and an older work from an insider is Jonathan Daniels, *Man of Independence* (Philadelphia, 1950). There are many biographies and autobiographies for the Truman years. James F. Byrnes tells his story in two volumes, *Speaking Frankly* and *All in One Lifetime* (New York, 1947 and 1958). Unfortunately he is vague on some issues, such as the origins of American involvement in Greece. Also consult the best examination of Byrnes as secretary of state, George Curry's *James F. Byrnes* (New York, 1965). Marshall's secretaryship is discussed in Robert H. Ferrell, *George C. Marshall* (New York, 1966). One of the most extensive memoirs of the era is Dean Acheson, *Present at the Creation: My Years in the State Department* (New York, 1969). Also consult the sympathetic study by David S. McLellan, *Dean Acheson: The State Department Years* (New York, 1976). A very useful diary for American policy in 1945 and 1946 is Walter Millis, ed., *The Forrestal Diaries* (New York, 1951); a more recent monograph is Robert G. Albion and Robert Howe Connery, *Forrestal and the Navy* (New York, 1962). *The Private Papers of Senator Vandenberg* (Boston, 1952), edited by Arthur H. Vandenberg, Jr., reveals his anti-Communist and pro-British sentiments. Vandenberg was a delegate to some of the Council of Foreign Ministers meetings with the Soviets, and so was Tom Connally, *My Name Is Tom Connally* (New York, 1954). There has been much written on Truman's controversial secretary of commerce, Henry A. Wallace. His intense distrust of Britain is evident in *The Price of Vision: The Diary of Henry A. Wallace, 1942–1946* (Boston, 1973), which has been edited by John Morton Blum. The best monograph is J. Samuel Walker, *Henry A. Wallace and American Foreign Policy* (Westport, Conn., 1976), and a weaker account is Richard J. Walton, *Henry Wallace, Harry Truman and the Cold War* (New York, 1976).

General Studies on Anglo-American Relations, 1944–1947

Concerning wartime relations between Britain and the United States, consult the official multivolume study by Llewellyn Woodward, *British Foreign Policy in the Second World War* published by Her Majesty's Stationery Office (London, 1976). William Roger Louis has written a detailed account, *Imperialism at Bay, 1941–1945: The United States and the Decolonization of the British Empire* (Oxford, 1977), and also see David Goldsworthy, *Colonial Issues in British Politics, 1945–1961: From "Colonial Development" to "Wind of Change"* (London,

1971). There are many other surveys of British-American relations, and some of the best include H. C. Allen, *Great Britain and the United States: A History of Anglo-American Relations, 1783–1952* (London, 1954); Leon D. Epstein, *Britain—Uneasy Ally* (Chicago, 1954); and, more detailed, William H. McNeil, *America, Britain, and Russia, 1941–1946* (London, 1953). Less useful for Anglo-American relations toward the Soviet Union are Edgar McInnis, *The Atlantic Triangle and the Cold War* (Toronto, 1959); C. M. Woodhouse, *British Foreign Policy since the Second World War* (London, 1961); R. B. Manderson-Jones, *The Special Relationship: Anglo-American Relations and Western European Unity, 1947–1956* (London, 1972); H. G. Nicholas, *The United States and Britain* (Chicago, 1975); and Joseph Frankel, *British Foreign Policy, 1945–1973* (Oxford, 1975). *The Foreign Policy of the British Labour Government, 1945–1951* (Notre Dame, 1953) is examined by M. A. Fitzsimons, and see Eugene J. Meehan, *The British Left Wing and Foreign Policy: A Study of the Influence of Ideology* (New Brunswick, N.J., 1960). Meehan wrote a fine chapter on the so-called foreign policy revolt of November 1946. Michael R. Gordon is more analytical in *Conflict and Consensus in Labour's Foreign Policy, 1914–1965* (Stanford, 1969). British defense policy is investigated in R. N. Rosecrance, *Defense of the Realm: British Strategy in the Nuclear Epoch* (New York, 1968), and concerning the atomic era consult two volumes by Margaret Gowing, *Britain and Atomic Power, 1939–1945* (London, 1964), and *Independence and Deterrence: Britain and Atomic Energy, 1945–1952* (London, 1974).

For the Truman era start with Richard S. Kirkendall, *The Truman Period as a Research Field: A Reappraisal, 1972* (Columbia, Mo., 1974), which includes an extensive bibliography up to 1973 and lists the holdings of the Truman Library. Since 1973 there have been some fine monographs published, such as Lynn E. Davis, *The Cold War Begins: Soviet-American Conflict over Eastern Europe* (Princeton, 1974). The winner of the Bancroft prize, John L. Gaddis, *The United States and the Origins of the Cold War, 1941–1947* (New York, 1972), is a balanced account. Other worthy studies include Richard F. Haynes, *The Awesome Power: Harry S. Truman as Commander in Chief* (Baton Rouge, 1973), and Lisle A. Rose, *Dubious Victory: The United States and the End of World War II* (Kent, Ohio, 1973). On the diplomacy of the secretary of state, see Patricia Dawson Ward, *The Threat of Peace: James F. Byrnes and the Council of Foreign Ministers, 1945–1946* (Kent, Ohio, 1979), and for a recent account of the conflict on the "northern tier," consult Bruce R. Kuniholm, *The Origins of the Cold War in the Near East: Great Power Conflict and Diplomacy in Iran, Turkey, and*

Greece (Princeton, 1980). A provocative account is Daniel Yergin, *Shattered Peace: The Origins of the Cold War and the National Security State* (Boston, 1977).

The most comprehensive surveys of the two presidential eras are Robert Dallek, *Franklin D. Roosevelt and American Foreign Policy, 1932–1945* (New York, 1979); Robert J. Donovan, *Conflict and Crisis: The Presidency of Harry S. Truman, 1945–1948* (New York, 1977), which also discusses domestic affairs; and Harold F. Gosnell, *Truman's Crisis: A Political Biography of Harry S. Truman* (Westport, Conn., 1980).

There are four studies on Canadian-American relations that also concern Britain. R. D. Cuff and J. L. Granatstein have written a survey entitled *Canadian-American Relations in Wartime, from the Great War to the Cold War* (Toronto, 1975). The best account of *Military Relations between the United States and Canada, 1939–1945* is by Stanley Dziuban (Washington, D.C., 1959). A heavily documented three-volume study is James Eayrs, *In Defense of Canada,* and especially see the last volume, *Peacemaking and Deterrence* (Toronto, 1972). Concerning "The Canadian-American Permanent Joint Board on Defense, 1940–1945," consult C. P. Stacey, *International Journal* 9 (1954): 107–24.

Anglo-American-Greek relations are examined by Stephen G. Xydis, *Greece and the Great Powers, 1944–1947* (Thessaloniki, 1963). Xydis was admitted into the archives of the Greek Foreign Office. An older description of British-Greek relations after the liberation in 1944 is Reginald S. Leeper, *When Greek Meets Greek* (London, 1950), and a better examination of that period is John O. Iatrides, *Revolt in Athens: The Greek Communist "Second Round," 1944–1945* (Princeton, 1972). A pro-British account of *The Greek Civil War, 1944–1949* (New York, 1966) is by Edgar O'Ballance, and the most complete account of internal affairs is C. M. Woodhouse, *The Struggle for Greece, 1941–1949* (London, 1976). The announcement of American aid to Greece has stimulated differing interpretations of the Truman Doctrine, which can be found in Athan G. Theoharis, *Seeds of Repression: Harry S. Truman and the Origins of McCarthyism* (Chicago, 1971); Richard M. Freeland, *The Truman Doctrine and the Origins of McCarthyism* (New York, 1972); and Michael Leigh, *Mobilizing Consent: Public Opinion and American Foreign Policy, 1937–1947* (Westport, Conn., 1976).

Index

249